OFF THE BEATEN PATH®
COLORADO →

Help Us Keep This Guide Up to Date

We would love to hear from you concerning your experiences with this guide and how you feel it could be improved and kept up to date. Please send your comments and suggestions to:

editorial@GlobePequot.com

Thanks for your input, and happy travels!

OFF THE BEATEN PATH® SERIES

ELEVENTH EDITION

OFF THE BEATEN PATH® COLORADO →

A GUIDE TO UNIQUE PLACES

ERIC LINDBERG

gpp®
travel

Guilford, Connecticut

Editor: Ashley Smith
Project Editor: Lauren Brancato
Layout: Joanna Beyer
Text Design: Linda R. Loiewski
Maps by Equator Graphics © Morris Book Publishing, LLC

ISSN 1539-6614
ISBN 978-0-7627-8103-4

Printed in the United States of America
10 9 8 7 6 5 4 3 2 1

Contents

About the Author

Eric Lindberg is a Denver-based travel writer and photographer specializing in adventure travel, culture, the outdoors, and offbeat, far-flung destinations. A member of the Society of American Travel Writers (SATW), he has won numerous photography and writing awards for work published nationally and abroad. Eric is the 2011 and 2013 Photographer of the Year, SATW. For more information, visit ericlindberg.com.

Acknowledgments

This book was written with the assistance of many people. The author thanks Gaylene Ore, Ore Communications; Rich Grant, Deborah Park, and Katie Converse of the Denver Metro Convention and Visitors Bureau; Mike Lane, Steamboat Ski & Resort Corporation; Anne Klein Barney, Durango Area Tourism Office; Beth Buehler, Gunnison-Crested Butte Tourism Association; Kim Farin, Boulder Convention and Visitors Bureau; and Diane Ehlert, Winter Park-Fraser Valley Chamber of Commerce.

Introduction

Colorado is a four-season destination offering unparalleled adventure and recreational pursuits, a thriving arts scene, a rich cultural heritage, flavorful cuisine, and 26 renowned ski areas and resorts. The state's breathtaking scenic landscape boasts natural hot springs, the headwaters of seven major rivers, many peaceful lakes and reservoirs, 12 national parks and monuments, and 54 mountain peaks that top 14,000 feet.

It's no wonder that Colorado's cities and small towns frequently appear on those "Best Places to Live in America" lists. The state has so much to offer that many people come and never leave. Even longtime residents constantly find new things to love about the state.

The mountains are perhaps the biggest draw. Every spring wildflowers fill the meadows, streams and rivers flow, and life returns to the high country. Summer means long, warm days, afternoon thundershowers, and exploring the forests and alpine reaches. In the fall, aspen shimmer golden against electric blue skies, and bull elk gather in the meadows to bugle and herd their cows. Winter is the time for thrilling downhill runs through fresh powder, quiet snowshoeing or cross-country ski tours deep into the woods, or sitting by a crackling fire in a cabin as snow swirls outside.

But there's more to the state than mountains. Colorado is the true West, and just outside any town or city another world begins, where ranches, farms, and scattered rural communities represent the western rural lifestyle. Much of the state's early pioneering history comes from agricultural beginnings on the plains and the valleys.

Colorado's Great Sand Dunes are the tallest in North America. The Pawnee Grasslands Buttes protect a Great Plains geography largely gone from the American landscape. Dinosaur bones can be inspected at Dinosaur National Monument. Rivers run through canyons, awaiting exploration by raft. Historic ghost towns and ancient Native American ruins remain to remind visitors of the first people to call this place home.

Along with the open spaces and natural beauty, Colorado is also a renowned cultural destination. Front Range cities are blessed with world-class performing arts, cuisine to satisfy any palate, a thriving music scene, a high concentration of microbreweries, extensive bike paths and parks, seven major league sports teams, and top-notch universities. And perhaps best of all, within easy access of each of these cities await the Rocky Mountains.

Colorado Off the Beaten Path travels to the far corners of the state and covers most points in between. It offers a mixture of unique, less-known

Author's Note

After attending a Colorado university for two years in the mid '70s, I left the state to see the world. Twenty years and 48 countries later, I returned, wondering whether I could call the place home once again. It was an easy decision. Even now after almost 20 years of wandering Colorado's roads and trails, I constantly discover more reasons to stay. Colorado is not a place where people often boast of having seen and done it all. Exploring the endless miles of mountains, canyons, rivers, and plains alone would take years if not a lifetime. And culture junkies have no shortage of activities; restaurants, theaters, museums, nightclubs, sports events, gallery openings, concerts, brewpubs, bookstores, and coffeehouses keep even the most jaded cultural sophisticate busy.

But the reason many choose to call Colorado home is the ease with which one can slip between the worlds of urban and wilderness. Swapping out my car for boots or bike tires or raft, I can climb a mountain, meander through a forest, or float a river, and be reminded once again of why I choose to live here.

destinations and more well-known locales. Both visitors and residents will find new places to explore and keep them busy for years to come.

This book is divided into five regions, with each chapter covering a region of the state.

Chapter 1 deals with the Front Range foothills area west of the Denver/Boulder corridor, where much of the state's population lives. Chapter 2 explores the state's northwestern mountains, including Rocky Mountain National Park, Trail Ridge Road, and Steamboat Springs. In Chapter 3 you follow one of Colorado's main arteries—I-70—through historic Georgetown and Glenwood Springs to the Western Slope city of Grand Junction, with side trips along the way. Chapter 4 goes into the state's vast southern region, including the spectacular San Juan Mountains, the ruins of Mesa Verde, and the unique towns of Telluride, Cortez, and Durango. Finally, Chapter 5 covers cosmopolitan Denver and the sprawling Plains. Throughout the book you will discover unique, hidden places overlooked by the casual traveler.

Happy trails!

Fast Facts about Colorado

COLORADO'S MAJOR NEWSPAPERS

The Denver Post (daily), denverpost.com
Westword Newspaper (weekly), westword.com

TRANSPORTATION: REGIONAL TRANSPORTATION DISTRICT (RTD)

RTD has an extensive bus system in addition to light-rail.
1600 Blake St.
Denver, CO 80202
(800) 366-7433
rtd-denver.com

WEATHER OVERVIEW

Residents claim that old cliché about the weather—if you don't like it, wait an hour—started in Colorado. The state is known for its ability to go from clear skies to thunderstorms, tornadoes, flash floods, and back before you've had time to complain about any of it. Temperatures can drop 30 degrees in a matter of hours, and just when you thought it was Indian summer in October, a blizzard can dump 3 feet of snow in two days' time. It never hurts to keep an eye on the sky, especially when traveling in the mountains.

The following best sums up the climate in Colorado:

- Semiarid

- Short springs

- Dry, often hot summers with brief periods of rain with thunder and lightning

- Warm, clear fall days with cool nights

- Mild winters, except in mountains

Average highs and lows in Denver (degrees Fahrenheit)

Jan 43/16	Apr 61/34	July 88/58	Oct 66/36
Feb 46/20	May 70/43	Aug 85/56	Nov 52/25
Mar 52/25	June 81/52	Sept 76/47	Dec 44/17

For more information about Colorado, contact the tourism office at:

Colorado Tourism Office
1625 Broadway, Ste. 1700
Denver, CO 80202
(800) 265-6723 or (303) 446-2422
colorado.com

Where to Stay & Where to Eat Price Codes

Listed at the end of each chapter are area accommodations and restaurants you'll want to check out.

The rating scale for hotels is based on double occupancy and is as follows:
Inexpensive: Less than $100 per night
Moderate: $100 to $200 per night
Expensive: More than $200 per night

The rating scale for restaurants is as follows:
Inexpensive: Most entrees less than $10
Moderate: Most entrees $10 to $20
Expensive: Most entrees more than $20

Front Range

When you first come upon the 70-million-year-old amphitheater at **Red Rocks Park,** west of Denver, the primeval scene takes your breath away. Huge reddish sandstone formations jut upward and outward. Each is higher than Niagara Falls. The view conjures up dinosaurs, sea serpents, and flying reptiles; indeed, tracks of those long-extinct creatures remain embedded in nearby rock, along with valuable fossil fragments. The saturated colors rival those of the Grand Canyon, and the tortured geology is evidence of earth-shattering, monolith-building cataclysms, retreating ancestral oceans, violent upwelling, and centuries of water erosion. Geographers once considered this site one of the Seven Wonders of the World.

Long before the first settlers arrived, the Ute tribe favored the area for camping. The US Geographical Survey showed up and began the first surveys in 1868. By 1906 financier **John Brisben Walker** had acquired the land, claiming the acoustics of these rocks would be perfect for an amphitheater. Walker eventually donated the land to the community, and in 1927 it was incorporated into the **Denver Mountain Parks System.**

N

| 0 | | 10 mi |
| 0 | | 10 km |

Construction started a few years later, followed in 1941 with the dedication of the tiered outdoor area. The local symphony came, producing perfect sound and aesthetic inspiration against a magnificent backdrop panorama of Denver and the plains far below. Triumphant ballet performances and celebrated orchestras wowed audiences. Over the years improvements were made to the stage and seating.

trivia

Long ago, a vast inland sea, which contained sediments that gradually built up on its floor, covered the Colorado area. After the sea receded, the sediments hardened and the forces of geology and erosion went to work over the next few million years to sculpt the formations you see at Red Rocks today.

However, the cost of bringing in large groups of classical musicians and opera companies proved to be financially draining. What's more, performers sometimes fought with winds that would tear away the orchestra's notes or with summer downpours that would drench the singers.

Since 1961 classical music has rarely been heard at the amphitheater. In 1964 the Beatles showed up, and along with an admission price of $6.60, rock and roll arrived at Red Rocks. From the 1970s forward to today, the summer season is packed with an assortment of rock, pop, blues, folk, jazz, and country-western stars—often with sellouts of the 9,450 seats. The stage is now covered, and tickets can be expensive, but the magical setting brings fans regardless of price.

Red Rocks is truly one of the world's great open-air stages. Many famous groups return year after year, claiming this venue among their favorite places to perform. For music lovers, sitting down to a summer show at Red Rocks as the sun sets and stars sparkle overhead is one of life's perfect moments.

At all other times, admission is free to Red Rocks. Many locals come here during the day for a vigorous workout of running or walking up and down the amphitheater stairs. An *Easter Sunrise Service* has been a strong Denver tradition for several decades. A 30,000-square-foot underground *Red Rocks Visitor Center,* entered from the top of the amphitheater, features an excellent exhibit on the venue, with its geological history and a chronological list of every performance over the last 50 years. Featuring sweeping views from terraces, elevator access for people with disabilities, and new restrooms, the visitor center is open to the public free of charge year-round. Also included are a meeting center (call 303-697-6047 for details) and a restaurant.

Hiking trails in the park surrounding the amphitheater offer hours of exercise or just quiet contemplation among the birdlife, browsing deer, and ancient geology. Mere minutes from the Denver suburbs, the splendor of Red Rocks can feel like another world.

Red Rocks, located at 16352 CR 93 in Morrison, is easy to reach via numerous routes. From Denver you can take West Alameda Avenue west, drive US 285 west to CR 470 to Morrison Road, or follow I-70 west and watch for the marked exit. The total distance varies between 14 and 17 miles, depending on your route. Hours are 5 a.m. to 11 p.m. daily; admission is free. For more information go to redrocksonline.com.

You can see the amphitheater from the hiking trails of *Mount Falcon Park,* a protected sanctuary in the foothills just above Red Rocks. In the early 1900s, John Brisben Walker, financier, entrepreneur, and visionary, built a mansion on a promontory high above the surrounding hills. His next project was to be a Summer White House for US presidents, but Walker's fortunes ultimately waned. The Summer White House was never built, and the financier's own

AUTHOR'S FAVORITES IN THE COLORADO FOOTHILLS

Beaver Brook Trail
(303) 697-4545
jeffco.us/openspace

Buffalo Bill Grave and Museum
(303) 526-0744
buffalobill.org

Central City Opera House
(303) 292-6700
centralcityopera.org

Chautauqua Park
(303) 442-3282
chautauqua.com

Eldorado Canyon
(303) 494-3943
parks.state.co.us

***eTown* Live Radio Show**
(303) 443-8696
etown.org

Glacier Homemade Ice Cream
(303) 499-4760
glaciericecream.com

Lookout Mountain Nature Center & Preserve
(720) 497-7600
jeffco.us/openspace

Matthews/Winters Park
(303) 271-5925
jeffco.us/openspace

Mount Falcon Park
(303) 271-5925
jeffco.us/openspace

Pearl Street Mall in Boulder
(303) 449-3774
boulderdowntown.com

Red Rocks Park and Amphitheatre
redrocksonline.com

Waterton Canyon
(303) 628-6189
denverwater.org/recreation/watertoncanyon

castle-like home was struck by lightning and burned down in 1918. The stone walls, fireplaces, and chimneys remain—an interesting destination for hikers.

The Mount Falcon area is surrounded by mountains, and in the distance you can spot Mount Evans (elevation 14,264 feet) and the Continental Divide. Other vistas of the 2,130-acre park include the Colorado plains and, with a little imagination and a clear day, Kansas.

The park is surprisingly serene; it is so vast that walkers, mountain bikers, and the occasional horseback rider easily spread out. No motorcycles are permitted, and cars are restricted to two parking lots. The well-marked foot trails are often shaded by conifer forests. In the winter, cross-country skiers, snowshoe enthusiasts, and anyone looking for a quick escape from the city come here to enjoy the views and explore the quiet trails.

Picnic tables entice families to the park, and the meadows are popular with kite-fliers and butterfly fans. Hikers find solitude among the daisies, scrub oak, and spruce. Here, at 7,750 feet above sea level, summers are cooler here than down below in Denver. Far from traffic, you hear only the light Colorado wind in the pines.

Mount Falcon Park is accessible via Highway 8 to Morrison (turn west on Forest Avenue and north on Vine Avenue) or via US 285 and the Indian Hills exit (stay on Parmalee Gulch Road for 5 miles to Picutis Road, and then follow signs to the parking area). Be prepared for a brief dusty road to the park entrance. For more information contact Jefferson County Open Space at (303) 271-5925; jeffco.us/openspace.

Mount Falcon Park and Red Rocks feel far from the city, but they are only 20 minutes west of Denver. Just south of Red Rocks, **Morrison Road** winds through the foothills toward higher country. It's a popular route into the mountains, but along the way there are little gems to be discovered.

One such place is the town of **Morrison.** On any given weekday, neighbors meet on the street corners to catch up on local news. Bicyclists ride the paths along Bear Creek and stop at a cafe for lunch. Visitors browse eclectic boutiques and people-watch the steady stream of locals, tourists, and on weekends, bikers. Indeed, at times, Morrison is very Norman Rockwellesque.

But along with a pleasant atmosphere, this community offers a treasure trove of antiques that will please collectors and browsers alike. Old western memorabilia, crafts, and unusual one-of-a-kind items pack tiny stores. Drop by any of several antiques shops along Bear Creek Avenue or on side streets. Whatever your pleasure—buying, selling, or window shopping—Morrison is a pleasant place to spend an hour or two and enjoy lunch or an ice-cream cone. For more information call the town of Morrison at (303) 697-8749 or write PO Box 95, Morrison 80465.

Tracks in Time

A visit to the Morrison area would not be complete without a stop at the outdoor museum known as **Dinosaur Ridge.** View more than 300 dinosaur footprints, all preserved in the sandstone of the Dakota Formation on the east side of the hogback. This National Natural Landmark is open for free viewing year-round, with interpretive signs providing information about the tracks and other fossils found in the area. Visitors can also arrange for a guided tour with the visitor center ($3 per person) or call ahead or check the website to find out about the next Dinosaur Discovery Day, held monthly on Saturdays from Apr through Oct. During these days guests enjoy free guided tours and activities at the center. For more information, call (303) 697-3466 or visit their website at dinoridge.org.

A 5-minute uphill drive from Morrison will take you to the much photographed locale of **The Fort,** which is a replica of Bent's Fort, an 1834 early Colorado fur-trading post. The thick, picturesque adobe building contains a small shop that sells authentic Native American jewelry and other items. But The Fort is best known as an award-winning restaurant, popular among locals for impressing out-of-town guests. The walls are covered with western oil paintings and original etchings celebrating the West. The cuisine features foods of the American West, both old and contemporary, with appetizers such as roast bison marrow bones, braised bison tongue, buffalo empanadas, and Rocky Mountain "oysters" (bull testicles). Entree selections include Elk Chop St. Vrain, prime rib of buffalo, tequila citrus-glazed salmon, and grilled quail, accompanied by an extensive wine list and original desserts. The Fort is located at US 285 and Highway 8. The restaurant is open for dinner Mon through Fri from 5:30 to 9:30 p.m., Sat from 5 to 10 p.m., and Sun from 5 to 9 p.m. For reservations call (303) 697-4771 or visit thefort.com.

Close to Denver, **Matthews/Winters Park** and the adjacent **Hogback** are popular for wildlife viewing, hiking, and **mountain biking.** The trails range from easy to moderately difficult. The park is a mixture of undulating grasslands, trails, and fields of silver-green sage, purple thistles, wild roses, and wild plums. Trails run through rabbitbrush and tall dill, and a short walk away from the parking lot the highway noise fades, replaced by birdsong and serenity.

The Hogback with its twisted geography running north-south dramatically separates the mountains and the plains. Red Rocks Park is nearby. Serious bikers can cross the road from the park and find a variety of paths. On the eastern face at 16831 W. Alameda Parkway is the Dinosaur Ridge Visitors Center. The Dinosaur Ridge Trail is a 1.5-mile path leading past hundreds of dinosaur tracks, a quarry of dinosaur bones, and unusual geologic formations. Call (303) 697-3466 or visit dinoridge.org for more information.

The park lies astride the entrance to **Mount Vernon Canyon,** which is one of the early routes to the goldfields of Central City and South Park. The big year here was 1859. Stagecoaches and wagons rolled through, and the nearby town of **Mount Vernon** had a 150-horse corral. For a while Mount Vernon became a stage stop. An inn, a saloon, and a schoolhouse were built, used, and abandoned. Once boasting 44 registered voters, the town of Mount Vernon lost its place in history after the railroads arrived.

Sunflowers, chokecherries, and willows now lean over the gravestones and crosses of long-gone pioneers: One marker reads I.I. DEAN, DIED AUGUST 12, 1860, AGED 31 YEARS, I AM AT REST. Not far from the few square gravestones that remain, picnic tables sit under leafy trees near Mount Vernon Creek.

trivia

Colorado's Front Range has an average of 300 days of sunshine per year—second only to Miami, Florida.

Weekends and summer evenings at the park are the busiest times, and the small parking lot fills quickly. The parking area is located off Highway 26, just south of I-70, and lies within the Mount Vernon town site. All Jefferson County Open Space parks are closed from 1 hour after sunset until 1 hour before sunrise unless otherwise noted by signage at individual parks. For more information contact Jefferson County Open Space at (303) 271-5925; jeffco.us/openspace.

Southwest of Denver, close to Chatfield Reservoir, is **Waterton Canyon** (denverwater.org/recreation/watertoncanyon). The canyon is popular with hikers and bikers who walk or ride the gravel road that follows the South Platte River. It can get crowded on summer weekends but Waterton Canyon is a delightful place anytime for a peaceful hour or two along the river.

To the west of Morrison, approximately 30 miles west of Denver on US 285, is the sign for **Meyer Ranch Park.** Here are 397 quiet acres with miles of well-maintained hiking trails winding through aspen groves and pine forests. Through the spring and summer, the meadows are home to Colorado's state flower, the columbine, shooting stars, lady slippers, and the purple Indian paintbrush. The trail names fit the surrounding scenery: Owl's Perch, Lodge Pole, and Sunny Aspen.

In the winter the hill near the park parking lot becomes a popular sledding and tubing destination. Motorized vehicles are not permitted here at any time, and dogs belong on a leash. The Meyer Ranch Park area has a history of homesteading, haying, and grazing. According to local legend, during the late

1880s the animals of the P. T. Barnum circus wintered here. The handsome Victorian-style Meyer home—still occupied by the Meyers—stands proudly across the highway. For more information about the park, contact Jefferson County Open Space at (303) 271-5925; jeffco.us/openspace.

The same US 285 will take you to a truly offbeat family destination that even many Denverites don't know about. Around 25 minutes from the city is *Tiny Town,* a Lilliputian village and miniature railway.

Tiny Town appeals to children and anyone interested in miniature re-creations. Imagine about a hundred toy-size, handcrafted buildings to peek into, and sometimes even crawl into, and you get the picture. This town has old miniature log cabins, a fire station, a post office, a water tower, a flour mill, a bank, stables, a schoolhouse, a rooming house, farms, ranches, barns, wind-mills, mines, and miners' shacks. There's even a miniature train ride around the entire Tiny Town village loop.

The attraction is run on a not-for-profit basis by the Tiny Town Foundation, which donates a portion of its annual proceeds to local charities. The distance from Denver is about 12 miles via US 285, turning south at South Turkey Creek Road. Bring a picnic and be prepared to pay $5 for adults and $3 for children ages 2 to 12. Children younger than 2 get in free. There is a $2 train fare per person. Open every day from Memorial Day weekend through Labor Day 10 a.m. to 5 p.m. Open weekends in May and Sept 10 a.m. to 5 p.m. For more information contact Tiny Town at (303) 697-6829; tinytownrailroad.com.

Continuing on US 285 heading southwest away from Denver, the road is sometimes narrow and curvy, so it's easy to miss the entrance to *Glen-Isle* resort, a cozy, unusual retreat for vacationers. These humble log cabins and a well-worn lodge are largely hidden from view by bushes and trees off the highway between Grant and Bailey. This unpretentious holiday settlement dates back to 1900 and is a popular retreat for families, couples, and singles who want to cook and who appreciate the silence of a 160-acre forest. The property is honeycombed with footpaths for hikers; horse trails are nearby, too. A National Historic Site, Glen-Isle is nicely old-fashioned; don't be surprised if you don't find a television set. For folks who don't want to cook, a dining room offers homey food. Prices are reasonable for these basic but comfortable accommodations. The lodge is open June through mid-Sept, cabins open all year. For more information call (303) 838-5461 or visit coloradodirectory.com/glenisleresort.

Just west of Denver, the plains of eastern Colorado end and the foothills of the Rockies begin. Nestled in a long valley with the jagged foothills rising on both sides, *Golden* is a historic town and home to the Colorado School of Mines.

Golden greets its visitors with a sign arched across Main Street that reads: HOWDY FOLKS! WELCOME TO GOLDEN, WHERE THE WEST LIVES. The concept of the West is among the most basic cornerstones of American folklore and legend. Its connotations extend well into the realms of history, geography, morality, and philosophy. To the traveler visiting the western states, it's an almost mythical sense of place blending with the past. Golden, with its 10 museums—a record for a town of its size—does not disappoint in either category.

The Golden story began back in 1859, when a man named Tom Golden set up a hunting camp with a few men. Soon some representatives of the Boston Company passed by on a wagon train, looking for a suitable place to establish a trading and supply base for the prospectors who were flooding the mining areas to the west. They liked the site and stayed.

trivia

Golden's Armory Building, built in 1913, is the largest cobblestone building in the country. Workers hauled 3,300 wagonloads of stream-worn boulders from nearby Clear Creek and quartz from Golden Gate Canyon to construct the building, which is located at 13th and Arapahoe.

Golden grew rapidly. Within a year it had a population of 700. By 1862 it became the territorial capital but lost this honor five years later to Denver. There was sporadic gold excitement in the immediate area but no big finds. Even today people still occasionally pan *Clear Creek* just west of town, and with the high price of gold, some of them even manage to pull a profit out of the fast-moving stream. Golden's early economy was built on trading. It was the major supply center for mining operations at Black Hawk, Central City, Idaho Springs, and other communities.

With the decline of mining, new economic bases emerged. Golden's present economy is based in part on two institutions, both of which have brought it international recognition: the Colorado School of Mines, for a century the leading school in the world devoted to mining and minerals, and Coors Brewery, one of the largest in the country.

To the west of Golden you'll find range after range of mountains, each higher than the last. These mountains serve the practical purpose of limiting the size to which Golden can grow—it currently has about 19,000 inhabitants. Unlike with other Front Range cities, the Rockies have protected Golden from becoming part of a growing urban sprawl.

A good first stop is the *Golden Visitors Center,* adjacent to the historic downtown at 1010 Washington Ave., for an overview of what to do while you're in town. Grab a cup of coffee there and browse through the informational touch-screen kiosk. The center, run by the Golden Chamber of Commerce, is open Mon through Fri from 8:30 a.m. to 5 p.m.; Sat from 10 a.m. to 4 p.m.; closed Sun. For more information call (303) 279-3113 or visit their website at goldenvisitorsbureau.com.

Consider a trip to nearby *Heritage Square* to get a sense of Golden's history. This rustic artisan and entertainment village was built on the 1860 town site of Apex, another mining boomtown. It has metalsmiths, jewelers, candy makers, tree-lined, lamp-lighted streets, and more, including horseback rides, an alpine slide and waterslide, a narrow-gauge train trip, a large family dinner theater, and plenty of free parking. Take exit 259 off I-70 and go north 1 mile. Open daily 10 a.m. to 9 p.m. (summer); 10 a.m. to 9 p.m. Mon through Sat and noon to 9 p.m. Sun (fall, winter, and spring). For more information call (303) 279-2789 or visit heritagesquare.info.

The *Colorado School of Mines* has an interesting, kid-friendly museum that fits the theme of the college. *The Geology Museum,* on the corner of 16th and Maple on campus, is almost an art gallery. Murals by Irwin Hoffman depict many periods in the development and history of mining. See minerals from around the world, a rock from the moon, Colorado's mining history, fossils, Colorado gem trails, and more. Regular hours are 9 a.m. to 4 p.m. Mon through Sat and 1 to 4 p.m. Sun; closed all CSM holidays and Sun during summer. Admission is free. Contact Colorado School of Mines, Department of Geology and Geological Engineering; (303) 273-3815; mines.edu/Geology_Museum.

Train buffs and anyone interested in old transportation and machinery will want to drop by the *Colorado Railroad Museum,* which displays many ancient, narrow-gauge locomotives and even a small depot. The narrow-gauge railroads of Colorado made it possible for miners and other fortune seekers to access the mineral riches of the Rocky Mountains. These tracks also allowed the wealth to be carried out and sent across the country. The history of railroads in Colorado is preserved in the 15-acre Colorado Railroad Museum. Here you will see the original rolling stock, including locomotives. A rail spur allows the facility to "steam up" different engines throughout the year.

The building itself, a masonry replica of an 1880 depot, houses some 50,000 photographs and artifacts. The basement contains one of the state's largest HO-scale model railroad exhibits, open to the public on the first Thursday of each month. It recreates some of Colorado's old rail lines, such as the one in Cripple Creek. Famous relics of the museum include the Rio

Grande Southern 1931 Galloping Goose No. 2 and the steel observation car used on the Santa Fe Super Chief, the Navajo. A bookstore sells more than 1,000 railroad-themed gifts, books and magazines, tapes, and mementos, while the **Robert W. Richardson Library** holds more than 10,000 railroad-specific publications.

Open every day except Thanksgiving, Christmas, and New Year's Day. Hours are 9 a.m. to 5 p.m. Admission is $10 for adults, $8 for seniors, and $5 for children ages 2 to 16 (children under 2 free); family admission (2 adults and children under 16) is $18. Contact the Colorado Railroad Museum at 17155 W. 44th Ave., Golden 80403; (800) 365-6263 or (303) 279-4591; coloradorailroad museum.org.

Golden in its early days was the true West, home to pioneers who left the civilized East in search of a new life. They were risk-taking, self-reliant doers on the path toward something better. These days Golden folks embody this spirit of the West with their love of the outdoors, and the town has an abundance of campers, backpackers, cyclists, and off-road enthusiasts. For many here, life is more about "doing" than sitting back and watching.

trivia

Golden is where Jolly Rancher candy was first produced, back in 1949.

Given the town's outdoorsy reputation, it should come as no surprise that Golden is home to the 37,000-square-foot **American Mountaineering Center,** located at 710 10th St. This center is the headquarters for the century-old American Alpine Club, the Colorado Mountain Club, the Outward Bound Wilderness, the Colorado Fourteeners Initiative, and the nonprofit organization Climbing for Life, which uses rock climbing to have a positive impact on at-risk youth in the Denver metro area. Stop by the center for a visit to the **Henry S. Hall Jr. American Alpine Club Library.** The library, with more than 25,000 volumes specific to rock climbing and mountaineering, is open to the public for research (only club members can check out books). Hours are Tues and Thurs, 10 a.m. to 7 p.m., and Wed and Fri, 10 a.m. to 6 p.m. For more information call (303) 384-0112 or visit americanalpineclub.org.

The center's museum, the **Bradford Washburn American Mountaineering Museum,** is the only one in the country devoted to the culture and spirit of mountaineering, and it houses numerous climbing exhibits and artifacts from the US and around the world. Admission is $5 for adults, $1 for children under 12. It's open Mon through Thurs 9 a.m. to 6 p.m., Fri from 9 a.m. to 4 p.m., and Sat from noon to 5 p.m. Closed on Sun. For more information, contact them at (303) 996-2755 or mountaineeringmuseum.org.

Golden Adventures

Thrill seekers will want to check out Heritage Square's *Alpine Slide.* After riding a chairlift nearly 500 vertical feet up the mountainside, visitors can cruise downhill for half a mile on one of two tracks, aboard a toboggan that fits on the tracks of the alpine slide. Those who can't get enough of heights can leap from a 70-foot tower— attached to a bungee cord, of course! Or they can try the go-karts, bumper boats, the maze, and a variety of amusement rides appropriate for smaller children. Contact Heritage Square at (303) 285-2990; heritagesquare.info.

Nearby *Golden Gate Canyon State Park* will give you an idea of how the foothills looked to the first miners who walked up here well over a century ago. Just 30 miles west of Denver, and with 168 campsites, 5 cabins, 2 yurts, and 35 miles of trails, the park is a serene mountain escape for hiking, bicycling, relaxing, and enjoying more than 12,000 acres of hills, canyons, meadows, and woods. From Golden take Golden Gate Canyon Road for 13 miles to the park. For more information call (303) 582-3707 or visit parks.state.co.us/parks/goldengatecanyon.

After a day of touring the museums and riding the alpine slide, or biking and hiking the nearby trails, how about a cold one? The famous *Coors Brewery,* the world's largest single-site brewery, offers free, self-guided tours on a first-come, first-served basis. No reservations are taken. Plan to spend around 30 minutes on the tour, which includes a close-up look at the malting, brewing, and packaging process. Afterward, visitors gather for a short tasting session in the hospitality room to sip limited servings of Coors products. You must be 21 or over to sample beer; minors can enjoy nonalcoholic drinks.

The brewery is located at 12th Street and Ford Street in Golden. Summer tour hours are Mon through Sat 10 a.m. to 4 p.m., Sun noon to 4 p.m. Winter hours are Thurs through Mon, 10 a.m. to 4 p.m., Sun noon to 4 p.m. Closed holidays. For more information contact (800) 642-6116 or (303) 277-2337; millercoors.com.

Before you leave Golden, ask yourself what could possibly epitomize the West more than the place where *Buffalo Bill* is buried? Buffalo Bill was a unique character of the frontier. And the museum that bears his name, 12 miles west of Denver on Golden's Lookout Mountain, has a uniquely western quality. Here are the mementos that bring a fascinating man to life: the paintings and posters that show him in full regalia on his white horse, with flowing white hair and beard, and a cowboy hat jaunty on his head. You can see his clothes, saddles, old weapons, a mounted buffalo, and numerous other artifacts at the ***Buffalo Bill Grave and Museum.*** More than half a million visitors come annually to see the exhibits and photographs that retrace his careers as a buffalo hunter, Indian fighter, army scout, and entertainer.

Born as ***William F. Cody,*** Buffalo Bill led an extraordinary life. As a long-time Pony Express rider, he was pursued by Indians, escaping (as he wrote), "by laying flat on the back of my fast steed. I made a 24-mile straight run on one horse." On another occasion he rode 320 miles in some 21 hours to deliver the mail. (En route he exhausted 20 horses for the journey.) He had few rivals as a hunter and was said to have shot 4,280 bison in a period of one and a half years. His slogan: "Never missed and never will / always aims and shoots to kill."

The buffalo shooting had a purpose, though; the meat was needed to feed some 1,200 men who were laying track for the railroad. And though William Cody had his battles with the Indians, he later learned the Sioux language and befriended the Cheyenne, among other tribes.

William Cody may have had his best years as a circus rider, actor, and showman, gaining fame all over the world. The first "Buffalo Bill's Wild West" show opened in 1883. The extravaganza toured for nearly three decades, spreading myths and legends of the American West around the globe. Almost a hundred mounted ***Sioux Indians*** chased wagon trains and a stagecoach; Annie Oakley and ***Johnny Baker*** amazed audiences with their marksmanship; 83 cowboys rode bucking broncos, thereby formalizing a cowboy sport into rodeo; and the entire Battle of Little Big Horn was re-created. Spectators could see live elk and deer from Colorado. There were horse races and even a bison hunt complete with a charging herd.

At its height, Buffalo Bill's show employed more than 600 performers. In one year he traveled 10,000 miles, performing in 132 cities in 190 days. (He was particularly popular in Europe.) Cody's flamboyant style and rifle-holding figure symbolized the Wild West in many European capitals. Buffalo Bill gave a command performance for Queen Victoria at Windsor Castle and amused Kaiser Wilhelm II in Berlin.

No fewer than 557 dime novels were written about Cody during his lifetime. His face beamed out from hundreds of thousands of posters. At his peak he was one of the most famous men in the world. Even today the distinctive goatee and silver hair continue to make him as recognizable as the kings, generals, and presidents who may have honored him.

Cody made one of the first movie westerns ever produced. Although near the end of his career, he also lived to see the start of the tourist industry as he opened the first hotel near Yellowstone National Park. Toward the end of his life, he turned into an entrepreneur and author. He gave most of his life's savings away to various good causes. His money ran out; his fame did not.

When Buffalo Bill died, President Woodrow Wilson wired his condolences. Former president **Teddy Roosevelt** called Cody "an American of Americans." The Colorado legislature passed a special resolution ordering that his body lie in state under the gold-plated rotunda of the State Capitol in Denver. Nearly 25,000 people turned out to pay their last respects and walk in his funeral on Memorial Day, June 3, 1917.

Buffalo Bill's grave is a few steps from the museum atop Lookout Mountain, with a good view of Denver and the plains. Anyone can come and see the burial place. It is marked by white pebbles. The simple legend reads: WILLIAM F. CODY 1846–1917.

The museum stands in a quiet conifer forest. First opened in 1919, it has been restored and improved over the years. The Pahaska Tepee Gift Shop sells original western artwork and western-themed toys, and serves food—including buffalo—in its large coffee shop.

Museum hours are 9 a.m. to 4 p.m. Tues through Sun, November 1 through April 30; open daily 9 a.m. to 5 p.m., May 1 through October 31; closed Christmas. Call (303) 526-0744 or write to 987½ Lookout Mountain Rd., Golden 80401; buffalobill.org for more information. Admission is $5 for adults, $4 for seniors, and $1 for children ages 6 to 15 (children under 6 free). For the most scenic drive, take US 6 west of Denver to Golden, turn left on 19th Street, and proceed uphill via **Lookout Mountain Road,** also called Lariat Trail due to its winding loops, all the way up Lookout Mountain.

Whether or not the museum is your final destination, no visit to Golden would be complete without a trip up Lookout Mountain. The Lariat Trail drive twists and turns up hairpin curves and narrow roads, rewarding travelers with spectacular views of Golden and Denver. At night the city below sparkles bright beneath the radiance of hundreds of stars.

As you continue south on Lookout Mountain Road after leaving Buffalo Bill's grave, a sign on Colorow Road will direct you to turn right toward the **Lookout Mountain Nature Center and Preserve.** Situated on 110 acres of a

Home on the Range

The city of Denver has continuously maintained a herd of bison since 1914 at **Genesee Park,** just down the hill from the Buffalo Bill Grave and Museum. The buffalo roam free in their natural habitat and are best seen in fall, winter, and early spring when park officials feed them daily. Take I-70 west to exit 254 (Genesee Park). The bulls and cows can be seen on either side of the highway—a tunnel under the road allows the animals safe passage.

Flying over Golden & Lookout Mountain

On warm weekday afternoons and during the weekends, the sky just southwest of Golden is the playground for daredevil hang gliders. The steep slopes of Lookout Mountain combine with steady updrafts to create the perfect location for launching hang gliders and riding the thermals for minutes, and sometimes an hour or more. Whenever cars fill the small roadside parking lot just before the Lookout Mountain Road, there's a good chance hang gliders will be soaring overhead.

fenced nature preserve, the center has a Discovery Corner, Observation Room, plant and animal displays, and a self-guiding nature trail (all wheelchair accessible). Admission is free. Nature Center hours are 10 a.m. to 4 p.m. Tues through Sun, and Sat and Sun from 10 a.m. until 5 p.m. from Memorial Day weekend through Labor Day weekend; the facility is closed on Mon and holidays. The preserve is open 8 a.m. to sunset daily. Also offered is a wide variety of hikes, activities, and nature classes ranging from "Tales of the Trail" to "Foxes in the City!" to night tours where you'll discover constellations and nocturnal animal activity. Most sessions require preregistration. The Nature Center is located at 910 Colorow Rd., just off Lookout Mountain Road, Golden. Call (720) 497-7600 or contact jeffco.us/openspace.

Of the many trails that explore the foothills outside Denver, one has been traveled for centuries. **Beaver Brook Trail,** curving around Lookout Mountain, was first used by the **Cheyenne** and **Arapaho Indians** as a lookout. It is among the state's more interesting paths, yielding views of the gorges below as it dips and climbs through a varied landscape of deciduous trees and dramatic Douglas fir. Hillsides of yucca, aster, and wild rose bloom in summer. Although you're close to Denver, the trail quickly leads you away from civilization.

The Beaver Brook Trail includes scrambling across several small boulder fields, making it a challenging hike. The trail, a little more than 14 miles out and back, remains blissfully quiet during the week. Weekends are busy, but those starting early will find solitude. If you hike up here in June and July, you'll be surrounded by lots of blossoming color. On the trail you may also spot the state flower, the blue Rocky Mountain columbine, as well as deer and abundant birdlife.

Wildflowers bloom later at the higher elevations, so by the time plants have already wilted around Golden (elevation 5,675 feet), flowers on the Beaver Brook Trail are just beginning to unfold. The higher you climb, the later the growth, the smaller the flower, and the cooler the air.

Small Colorado plants appear and disappear with the seasons, go underground, or take many years to mature. Certain wildflowers can sleep peacefully under the thickest snow cover, biding their time until spring. In summer the mountain flowers on the Beaver Brook Trail are as profuse as any in the region. They are all fragile, so take care not to trample or disturb them so those coming after you can also enjoy them.

The Beaver Brook Trail is an easy drive from Denver. Follow US 6 into Golden, turn left at the first traffic light (19th Street), then drive up Lookout Road for 3 miles. Before you get to Buffalo Bill's grave, look for a sign on your right. Admission is free, and the trail is open 1 hour before sunrise until 1 hour after sunset year-round. For more information contact Jefferson County Open Space at (303) 697-4545; jeffco.us/openspace.

Around 30 miles west of Denver up I-70 is a remnant of the Ice Age. *St. Mary's Glacier* is actually an ice field, covering a steep year-round snow bowl about 10 acres. In summer, when Denver swelters in a 95°F heat wave, it's about 45°F on the glacier, and people come to ski and snowboard here in July and August. Other visitors to the famous snowfield bring platters or tire tubes or even race downhill on shovels. Hikers, campers, and backpackers can be spotted at the 11,000-foot level as they scramble uphill past the last scrub pines. Less-energetic visitors come to sit on rocks and soak up the Colorado sun.

The ever-present snow and ice make St. Mary's Glacier a refreshing warm-weather trip, luring city dwellers as soon as the hiking trail opens each spring. After exiting I-70, the road follows a creek flanked by stands of conifers and aspen. After about 8 miles the road steepens and leads into a series of challenging curves and serpentines. Then the valley widens and the forest thickens. During snowmelt you see several rushing waterfalls, and at around 10,400 feet the parking lot appears. Hike up the rocky jeep trail or follow the uphill footpaths through kinnikinnik (evergreen groundcover), past the many fallen trees that are returning nutrients to the soil as they decompose. On weekends you'll share the trail with plenty of hikers.

Mother Cabrini Shrine

On a 900-acre hilltop on Lookout Mountain sits the Mother Cabrini Shrine. There is no charge to enter the famous little chapel, which was built in 1954 and devoted to Saint Frances Xavier Cabrini. The setting includes lovely fields, surrounding forests, and enough steps to make hikers happy. For more information call (303) 526-0758 or visit mothercabrinishrine.org.

TOP ANNUAL EVENTS IN BOULDER

MAY

Bolder Boulder 10K Race
(303) 444-7223
bolderboulder.com

Boulder Creek Festival
Memorial Day weekend
(303) 449-3137
bceproductions.com/
boulder-creek-festival

Chautauqua Summer Concerts and Events
May to Sept
(303) 442-3282
chautauqua.com

JUNE

Colorado Music Festival
Boulder Chautauqua Park
June through early Aug
(303) 449-1397
comusic.org

Noon Tunes
Front of Boulder County Courthouse
Fridays mid-June through mid-August
boulderdowntown.com/events/
noon-tunes

JULY

Boulder Outdoor Cinema and live music
Saturday nights, July and Aug
(855) 262-9324
boulderoutdoorcinema.com

Shakespeare Festival
CU–Boulder
July through Aug
(303) 492-0554
coloradoshakes.org

AUGUST

Boulder Kinetics
boulderkinetics.com

After half an hour of hiking you reach a cold lake, topped by the glacier. Don't be fooled by the harmless appearance. Mountain dwellers know the glacier's record; almost every year someone who skis too fast or careens downhill on a shovel gets bruised, bloodied, or even killed. On rare occasions cross-country skiers are buried by an avalanche. In winter, the ill-prepared and under-clothed can get frostbitten at higher elevations. Prudent visitors know that the mountains are unforgiving and come prepared.

From I-70 just past Idaho Springs, take exit 238, known as Fall River Road. A 12-mile drive brings you to the parking lot and the trailhead to St. Mary's Glacier.

Richest Square Mile on Earth

At one point in history, *Central City* vied with Leadville for Colorado's mining bonanzas. They called Central City the Richest Square Mile on Earth. In all, some $75 million in gold was found there. Although the rich veins are long gone, tourists can still do a bit of gold panning in nearby creeks. Surrounding the town are the bleached mountainsides, old abandoned mounds of earth, and mines from another era. Both Central City and neighboring Black Hawk are now reaping profits of a different sort since legalized gambling started up. Black Hawk has three times as many casinos as Central City, and as a result, Central City has retained more of its original historical appearance, at least for now.

With an abundance of buildings well over a century old, Central City and the adjacent Black Hawk together form the Central City/Black Hawk National Historic District. In Central City, sloping, winding *Eureka Street* has been beautifully restored. The redbrick buildings look as well preserved as those of Denver's Larimer Square. Central City's pharmacy and several other stores display relics in the windows.

For an overview of the area's history, visit the *Gilpin History Museum,* located at 228 High St. Housed in a brick building built in 1870 and used as a school until the 1960s, this 2-story museum includes a replica of a classic Main Street of the past. The Gilpin History Museum is open 11 a.m. to 4 p.m. daily, Memorial Day through Labor Day. For another window back into days gone by, visit the *Thomas House Museum* at 209 Eureka St. This Greek Revival frame house was built in 1874 around the entrance to a mine. The Thomas House Museum is open 11 a.m. to 4 p.m. Fri through Sun from Memorial Day through Labor Day. Entrance to each museum costs $5, or you can pay $8 for entrance to both. For more information contact (303) 582-5283; gilpinhistory.org.

The Gilpin History Museum, the Thomas House Museum, and the well-appointed Central City Opera House contrast dramatically with the miners' dwellings. The latter are small, modest cubes scattered across the pale gold, ocher, and russet slopes.

All Aboard!

The first train from Denver to Black Hawk rolled through on December 15, 1872. It took another six years for the line to extend to Central City. Regardless of the railroad's success, writer-explorer Isabella Bird once complained that she had never seen such "churlishness and incivility as in the officials of that railroad." She wrote of her disapproval in her excellent 1875 book about her adventures, *A Lady's Life in the Rocky Mountains.* Back then, the train traveled a 200-foot-per-mile grade through Clear Creek Canyon. Black rock walls rose more than a thousand feet on either side. You can still see those ominous walls if you travel Highway 6 through the area; it follows the same route as the railroad did.

The first frame houses sprang up during the 1860s, along with the mine dumps. Gold was being discovered not just in the river but in the mountain too. In 1859 a man named **John Gregory** had walked from Denver to 8,500-foot-high Central City, a trip of some 35 miles with an elevation gain of more than 3,000 feet. Gregory soon dug up a fortune. The word raced as fast as the spring waters of Clear Creek. Horace Greeley, a New York editor, heard about **Gregory Gulch** and traveled west to take a personal look. Greeley reported: "As yet the entire population of the valley, which cannot number less than four thousand, sleep in tents or under pine boughs, cooking and eating in the open air."

A mass of prospectors swarmed into the hillsides. Most never struck it rich and many left poorer than when they arrived, but some had a grand time. A theater was built. Sarah Bernhardt and Edwin Booth came to perform. The **Teller House Hotel** rose in 1872, built with care by fine craftsmen and artisans.

Large, carved bedsteads, marble-topped commodes, and tall rosewood and walnut highboys were ferried across the prairies and up the rough roads by teams of oxen and mules and on wood-burning trains. The fine hotel hosted famous people; President Ulysses S. Grant, Walt Whitman, Oscar Wilde, Baron de Rothschild, and assorted European noblemen and their wives all slept in Central City.

In 1874 most of the community burned down, but gold rebuilt it. Fewer than four years later there was a new opera house, which still stands. Built in 1878 by Welsh and Cornish miners, the **Central City Opera House,** located on Eureka Street, is home to the fifth-oldest opera company in the nation. This restored Victorian opera house holds an annual summer festival that draws patrons from nearly every state. Performances range from its popular one-act opera *The Face on the Barroom Floor,* which recounts the local lore behind the painting on the Teller House Bar floor, to classic operas such as Giuseppe Verdi's *La Traviata* and Puccini's *La Bohème*, as well as popular musicals

trivia

Sherill Milne and Beverly Sills both got their operatic starts in Central City.

such as *Oklahoma!* Central City Opera House invites opera buffs to sit back and relax in one of its 550 comfortable seats while taking in performances by known stars and future divas.

For show dates (performances are in summer), prices, and times, write to Central City Opera at 400 S. Colorado Blvd., Ste. 530, Denver 80246; visit central cityopera.org; or call (303) 292-6700. Opening night remains a prominent Colorado social event. Cars and busloads of opera-goers from nearby cities climb the road along *Clear Creek Canyon,* the same route taken by John Gregory more than 100 years ago.

These days gamblers also swarm to the area, since gaming was approved in the early 1990s for Central City and Black Hawk. New casinos have replaced many historic buildings and shops, and most visitors these days are more interested in games of chance than in the history of these former mining towns. Where parking was once hard to find, it is now almost impossible, but shuttle services run from Golden and other areas in Denver on a regular basis.

If you want to try your luck, stop at some of these Central City establishments: Doc Holliday, Famous Bonanza, Crystal Palace Casino, Dostal Alley, and The Reserve Casino. Down the road in Black Hawk, try Bullwackers, Black Hawk Station, Fitzgerald's, Bull Durham, Gilpin Hotel, Golden Mardi Gras, Isle of Capri, and Canyon Casino.

Central City and Black Hawk are less than an hour's drive from Denver via US 6 and CO 119. For more information, contact the Central City Marketing Office at PO Box 249, Central City 80427; (303) 582-5251; centralcitycolorado .com.

If you're heading north from Central City to Estes Park, your route will take you along one of Colorado's oldest and most picturesque drives. The *Peak to Peak Highway* was established in 1918. Following CO 72 and CO 7, it runs parallel to the Continental Divide, passing close to Golden Gate Canyon State Park, Arapaho and Roosevelt National Forests, and Indian Peaks Wilderness Area before reaching Estes Park and the entrance to Rocky Mountain National Park. Small towns along the way such as Nederland, Ward, and Allenspark have cafes, art galleries, and small shops. The Peak to Peak Highway is easily accessible from both Denver and Boulder.

Rock Canyons & Boulders

As you drive toward *Boulder,* the towering *Flatirons,* huge slabs of metamorphic sandstone thrust up by the same geologic forces that gave birth to the Rocky Mountains, dominate your view to the west. Now the city's trademark, the Flatirons—some of which reach heights of more than 1,000 feet—offer ample opportunities for rock climbers of all abilities. These monoliths also appeal to hikers and trail runners due to the abundance of trails through the meadows and hills surrounding the Flatirons. Forming the abrupt border between the plains and the Rocky Mountains, this stunning rock formation is a perfect destination for walking, wildflower watching, or sitting with friends and enjoying a warm Colorado afternoon. Located 22 miles northwest of Denver, Boulder is easily reached in about half an hour via the Boulder Turnpike, US 36.

Arguably in possession of the highest population of rock climbers per capita of any city or town in the US, Boulder enjoys its status as one of the centers of US *rock climbing.* This reputation becomes even clearer when you drive up nearby Boulder Canyon or Eldorado Canyon to watch the climbers clinging to the steep rock faces. Dozens of world-class climbing areas within several hours' drive, combined with two of the best indoor climbing facilities in the country right in Boulder, only add to the city's appeal. Rock climbing's popularity has grown tremendously since the early 1990s. Boulder's reputation as a climbing mecca spread quickly, attracting both experienced climbers and those eager to try for their first ascent.

Eldorado Canyon is one of the birthplaces of rock climbing in the US. Gorgeous sandstone cliffs soar above the canyon floor in shades of red speckled with greenish and golden-hued lichen that appears to take on its own luminescence when viewed in the right light. Formed of the same type of hardened sandstone that makes up the Flatirons—known as the Fountain Formation—the world-class walls of Eldorado Canyon enjoy international prestige within the rock-climbing community.

Hundreds of established routes await rock climbers of all abilities on the canyon walls, but none should be taken lightly. "Eldo," as climbers affectionately refer to the place, is known for its stiff grades, polished rock (especially on popular climbs), and sometimes scant protection. All of these factors mean that climbers should exercise caution when they first start out climbing in the canyon, perhaps choosing an easier route to allow themselves time to grow accustomed to the area.

Once a bastion for some of the state's hardest routes, Eldorado Canyon's heyday as far as pure difficulty for

trivia

President Dwight Eisenhower and his wife, Mamie, spent their honeymoon in Eldorado Canyon.

climbing moves has passed, but that doesn't relegate its challenges to second-tier status by any means. Exposure—that sensation you get when you can truly feel just how high above the canyon floor you are—is the name of the game on classic routes like the Naked Edge, the Yellow Spur, and even Bastille Crack. Easily identified as the crack that divides the Bastille formation (the crag that sits on the left of the road as soon as you start to drive up the canyon), it is an ever-popular classic; more likely than not you will see someone climbing it any given day, at any given time.

If scaling the walls isn't your idea of fun, Eldorado Canyon has plenty of other options. Tourists flock to the canyon in at least as many numbers as rock climbers, often clogging the narrow road up the canyon as they stop to gawk at tiny figures dangling from the walls high above. At the end of the canyon's road lies a lovely streamside picnic area with tables and barbecue grills, perfect for a family outing. Numerous hiking trails allow non-climbers to keep their feet on the ground while exploring the canyon's deeper realms. Kayakers and anglers delight in South Boulder Creek, which burbles its way down the canyon for most of the year, freezing over during winter months.

trivia

Tightrope walker and all-around daredevil Ivy Baldwin made 86 journeys across Eldorado Canyon on a tightrope suspended 582 feet above the ground. He made his last walk (and survived!) in 1948, at the ripe young age of 82.

Mountain bikers get a solid workout as they slog their way up the unrelenting ***Rattlesnake Gulch Trail,*** a short but strenuous trail that challenges the rider with 1,200 feet of elevation gain in 2 miles along some tight, technical single track. To find the trail, turn left on the Fowler Trail after passing through the first parking area in Eldorado Canyon State Park.

As with most Colorado destinations, weekdays here are almost always less crowded than weekends. To reach Eldorado Canyon State Park, 25 miles northwest of Denver, take the Boulder Turnpike to the Superior exit; turn south at the light and then turn right onto Highway 170 which will take you to Eldorado Springs. From Boulder, head south on Highway 93 and then take a right (west) on Highway 170 (Eldorado Springs Drive). The visitor center is located 1 mile up the canyon.

Eldorado Canyon State Park is open from dawn to dusk year-round. An $8-per-vehicle charge is required for entry. For more information call (303) 494-3943 or go to parks.state.co.us.

Another popular canyon destination is ***Eldorado Springs*** at the entrance to the canyon. This tiny, eclectic town not only serves as a gateway to the

Valmont Bike Park

Boulder is home to the largest free urban bike park in America. Opened in 2011, Valmont Bike Park is a 40-acre off-road bike park with competition-grade racing trails, big dirt jumps, a network of single-track trails, dual-slalom tracks, and more. Equivalent to the size of 30 football fields, the park offers off-road riding for all levels of riders. A trike track, kid's play area, learning loop, and restrooms make this a family-friendly park. Located at the corner of Valmont and Airport Roads. For more information go to valmontbikepark.org.

park but also is home to the **Eldorado Springs Pool** at the historic Eldorado Springs Resort, which makes for a great place to cool off during hot summer months.

Once a major tourist destination known as the "Coney Island of the West," Eldorado Springs Resort attracted more than 60,000 guests every summer during the early 1900s. The pool, built in 1906 and then advertised as the largest pool in the country, is filled to the brim with artesian water from the springs. Open from 10 a.m. to 6 p.m. daily from the Saturday before Memorial Day through Labor Day. Admission is $9 for adults, $5 for children and seniors. Call (303) 499-1316 for more information or go to eldoradosprings.com.

trivia

The pure, 76° water of Eldorado Springs flows at a constant rate of 200 gallons per minute. Bottled at the source, Eldorado Springs drinking water is available for purchase at grocery stores around the state.

To find out more about the history of rock climbing, as well as mountaineering and skiing, stop by **Neptune Mountaineering** on your way into Boulder. There you can explore owner Gary Neptune's impressive collection of climbing and skiing artifacts while you stock up on hydration packs, hiking boots, and energy bars. Make sure you grab an event schedule—Neptune Mountaineering hosts frequent audiovisual presentations on adventure sports, mountaineering, and travel. Usually held on Thursday nights, the slide shows are generally low in cost and high in fun.

The store (633 S. Broadway, Ste. A) is located on the upper level of the Table Mesa Shopping Center at the corner of Broadway and Table Mesa in Boulder. From Eldorado Springs, take Highway 93 north (it turns into Broadway). Open Mon through Fri, 10 a.m. to 8 p.m.; and Sat and Sun, 10 a.m. to 6 p.m. For more information call (303) 499-8866 or check the website at neptunemountaineering.com.

trivia

Boulder is the only US community that uses its own city-owned glacier, Arapahoe Glacier, for its water supply.

After stopping at Neptune's, continue along Broadway to Baseline Road, turning west to head up **Flagstaff Mountain,** the perfect place to mingle with rock climbers while taking in some beautiful scenery. Bouldering—a type of rock climbing that involves short, intense movements up the sides of the boulders, with the climber normally staying low to the ground—is a popular pastime on Flagstaff, and for good reason. Plenty of high-quality boulders dapple the flanks of Flagstaff, serving up myriad challenges that both delight and frustrate the numerous rock climbers who flock to the sharp, rough sandstone. Pull out at any of a number of locations along the road and follow the paths back to the boulders where you'll likely find some climbers who have come to test their skills for an afternoon. Continue strolling along one of the mountain's marked trails, or just grab a seat on one of the surrounding smaller boulders and relax in the shade of ponderosa pines while you watch the fun. The jagged ridge of the First Flatiron pokes out above the trees to the south, and obstructed views of the city of Boulder can be seen to the east.

trivia

Boulder has no shortage of trails to explore: The city's Open Space and Mountain Parks Department maintains 130 miles of trails in its open space program, used by walkers, hikers, bicyclists, horseback riders, dog walkers, birders, and photographers.

For more information on Flagstaff Mountain contact the City of Boulder Open Space and Mountain Parks Department, PO Box 791, Boulder 80306; (303) 441-3440; bouldercolorado.gov. Open year-round, parking lots open from 5 a.m. to 11 p.m. (midnight for Panorama Point parking lot). Daily permits can be purchased for $3 from any of the six well-marked, self-service stations located along Flagstaff Road.

For a treat, make dinner reservations at the **_Flagstaff House,_** one of Boulder's finer dining establishments. Nestled on the side of Flagstaff Mountain, this lovely restaurant is sure to delight even the most discriminating food lover. It's one of the pricier area eateries, (think $35 to $65 per person before wine), but in return you get gourmet New American cuisine complete with impeccable service, occasional complimentary appetizers from the chef, and a terrific wine list, not to mention sweeping views of Boulder. The Flagstaff House (1138 Flagstaff Rd.; 303-442-4640) is on the right as you drive up the mountain. Visit them at flagstaffhouse.com.

After dinner, walk off your meal with your date by taking a romantic moonlit stroll at **_Panorama Point_** (1 mile up Flagstaff Road from the base of

Celestial Seasonings

Take a free tour of the world-famous Celestial Seasonings tea company factory. The 45-minute stroll takes visitors through the plant to see how the various blends are processed and packaged. A few moments in the mint room are guaranteed to clear your sinuses. Tours run every day except major holidays and include tea tastings. For more information call (303) 581-1202 or visit celestialseasonings.com.

the mountain) or at one of the many other overlooks that line Flagstaff Road. If you're still feeling guilty about your marvelous dinner the next morning, you can always come back and bike up Flagstaff Road; it's one of the most popular workouts for local mountain and road bikers.

The tree-lined campus of the **University of Colorado at Boulder** (known to locals as simply "CU") warrants a visit, particularly in the summer when the university stages its annual **Colorado Shakespeare Festival**. During the season, you'll notice banners proclaiming the performances—and telling you to keep quiet—along Broadway as you head toward downtown Boulder. The festival performs several Shakespeare plays in July and August. National auditions attract actors from all over. Contact the festival organizers at (303) 492-0554 or coloradoshakes.org.

Macky Auditorium Concert Hall, also on the CU campus, hosts performances by the Boulder Philharmonic, the College of Music, visiting musicians participating in the Artists Series, and concerts by nationally known groups. For information call (303) 492-8423 or visit macky.colorado.edu.

Boulder also hosts the **Colorado Music Festival** from June through August. Visiting performers and composers lend their talents and energy to the festival. Reservations are required. Call (303) 449-1397 or write to 900 Baseline Rd., Cottage 100 (at Chautauqua), Boulder 80302 for details or visit colorado musicfest.org.

trivia

CU-Boulder's mascot is a live buffalo named "Ralphie." Six Ralphies—all females—have trotted around the football field since the original Ralphie made her debut in 1966.

Hopefully you haven't tired of rock formations yet—Boulder still has more to offer in this department. Turn west from town for a drive up **Boulder Canyon,** with a stop at beautiful **Boulder Falls.** Tall, granite outcroppings line Highway 119 as it wends its way up toward the rustic town of Nederland and the **Peak to Peak Highway.** Find the canyon via Broadway (Highway 93) in Boulder. Head west on Canyon Boulevard (Highway 119)—you can't miss it. Stop at the pullout 11 miles up the canyon on your left to park, and then cross the street for a short walk back to the falls. Free; open from dawn to dusk May 1 through October 31. For more information contact City of Boulder, Open Space and Mountain Parks Department, PO Box 791, Boulder 80306; (303) 441-3440; bouldercolorado.gov.

You'll probably catch glimpses of rock climbers on the formations as you drive up the canyon, weather permitting. In winter you're more likely to see people with crampons (metal-toothed attachments) on their boots and ice axes

Traditional vs. Sport Climbing

Most of the rock climbing done in Eldorado Canyon falls under the definition of traditional climbing, meaning that climbers place and remove virtually all the pieces of protection that they utilize on any given climb. These days, "sport climbing" has taken off in a variety of locations, including Boulder Canyon. In sport climbing, climbers hook devices called quickdraws into preplaced expansion bolts that are relatively permanent fixtures to the rock face, meaning that the bolts remain in the rock for the use of future parties.

in their hands hacking their way up frozen waterfalls and sheets of ice—Boulder Canyon attracts ice climbers, too. But with its classic rock climbs, both traditional and sport, the canyon most likely sees far more climbing traffic from those who like to feel the rock instead of ice beneath their fingers and under their feet in warmer weather. After all, some claim that the canyon's famous Country Club Crack (5.11c) was the hardest rock climb in the country for a period of time!

Seeing all this rock climbing around Boulder might spark your interest in trying out rock climbing yourself—but don't head out there uninformed. Though rock climbing is a relatively safe sport, you should receive proper instruction and learn the safety basics before trying it out on your own. Rock climbing also requires specialized equipment that can take a big bite out of your wallet. To get a thorough understanding of ropes and gear, novices take lessons or get an experienced climber to show them the ropes, so to speak. Boulder has a number of local schools and workshops that teach safe climbing.

South Boulder Creek Trail

Rain or shine, summer and winter, one of the most popular walkways in Boulder is the South Boulder Creek Trail. Located east of the main part of town, the trail doesn't tackle any of Boulder's hilly terrain but rather offers a nice, flat, 3.5-mile dirt path alongside South Boulder Creek. This route winds through trees and grasslands, offering interpretive signs along the way as well as the opportunity to see wildlife, from coyotes to entire prairie dog towns. Each season brings a different mood to the trail. In fall the trees burst into glorious shades of orange and yellow, while winter finds them stark and bare and the trail covered with snow. With spring come budding greenery, songbirds, and the fragrant scent of new growth. In summer the walk bursts with life. From Broadway in Boulder, head east on Baseline, passing Foothills Parkway. The trailhead, with plenty of parking, is on the right side of the street. Located on City of Boulder Open Space.

A reputable, established place to learn rock climbing in Boulder is the **Colorado Mountain School.** Affiliated with **Boulder Rock Club,** the AMGA-accredited school offers a wide range of classes for all ages and ability levels. Pretty much anybody can take a beginning climbing class—rippling abs and bulging biceps are not prerequisites. Especially at the more moderate levels of the sport, technique, balance, and flexibility count just as much as, if not more than, sheer strength.

Beginner classes often start in their indoor climbing gym. More adventurous novices can also try an outdoor lesson. Most guiding services, Colorado Mountain School included, offer beginning climbing courses, with the option for private instruction (more expensive). As with indoor classes, the school provides all the necessary climbing equipment, allowing the student to sample rock climbing without making any monetary investment beyond the price of the class.

Contact the Boulder Rock Club/Colorado Mountain School for details by calling (303) 447-2804 or (800) 836-4008 or going to totalclimbing.com. The facility is located at 2829 Mapleton Ave. Take US 36 into Boulder, and then head east on Mapleton. The club is on the north side of the street. Call for class schedules and to reserve a space.

For a tamer introduction to Boulder's famous monoliths, head up to pretty **Chautauqua Park.** This popular park has large, grassy meadows perfect for picnics and views of town. Hiking trails meander into the woods and up to the Flatirons. It's the location for the Colorado Music Festival, weddings, and summer film and music events. Follow Baseline Drive west from Broadway to 900 W. Baseline Rd.

One of the best places to feel the eclectic, funky mood of Boulder is on a stroll along the pedestrian **Pearl Street Mall.** Take Broadway north from the Canyon Boulevard intersection; the mall crosses Broadway a few blocks

Boulder Creek Path

From **Eben G. Fine Park** at the base of Boulder Canyon to 55th Street on the east side of town, the 7-mile-long wooded Boulder Creek Path winds its way along the creek, passing through some of the prettiest scenery in town. You can walk it, run it, bike it, bird it, push a baby stroller, or just pause and enjoy the surroundings. You'll never have to stop at intersections, since underpasses provide escape from traffic. And there's plenty to see along the way: xeriscape gardens, fishing ponds for kids, wildflowers, and stately old trees. A network of other paths connects with this main artery, allowing for easy access to virtually all areas of Boulder. West of town, the path follows Boulder Creek up Boulder Canyon for a ways, turning to dirt before it ends.

up. Locals and visitors mingle among boutiques, bookstores, and restaurants, many of which feature outdoor patios. Sculptures, fountains, cozy seating, and children's play areas along this 4-block thoroughfare help to make it one of the nation's most successful open-air pedestrian malls. Find a bench and enjoy some of the most colorful people-watching in the state. Talented musicians, jugglers, magicians, and other street performers entertain, especially on weekends and during the summer. The mall has been closed to auto traffic since the 1970s.

Every Sunday evening at the historic Boulder Theater, the popular radio program *eTown* takes to the stage and to the airwaves. This weekly radio variety show is taped before a live studio audience and broadcast to more than 150 cities coast to coast on National Public Radio. The relaxed format includes national and local music acts, a speaker, and discussions on the environment. Among many hundreds of past performers and guests are James Taylor, Rosanne Cash, Lyle Lovett, Al Gore, Emmylou Harris, Joan Baez, Jimmy Carter, and Ralph Nader. To purchase tickets to a live taping of the show call the Boulder Theater box office at (303) 786-7030 or visit online at bouldertheater .com. For a calendar of upcoming *eTown* shows go to etown.org.

If you have a sudden, uncontrollable craving for ice cream, head straight to locally based *Glacier Homemade Ice Cream & Gelato.* They have three locations: 3133 28th St., 1 block north of Valmont, (303) 440-6542; 4760 Baseline Rd. Ste. C, (303) 499-4760; and 1350 College Ave. by the university, (303) 442-4400; glaciericecream.com. Each store serves up to 80 flavors, all of which are made fresh in the store using premium ingredients. Popular flavors include coffee caramel crunch, death by chocolate, pralines 'n' cream, and bing cherry. The menu includes sorbets, banana splits, creamy gelatos, smoothies, root beer floats, hot fudge sundaes, and more—proof that this is "not just an ice-cream store."

As a college town with one of the most stunning settings in the country, Boulder is filled with eclectic people, activities, entertainment, dining,

Boulder Hiking

The *Mesa Trail,* one of Colorado's most scenic introductions to year-round hiking and trail running, is easily accessible. From Denver, drive the Boulder Turnpike (US 36) until you get to the Superior exit; Highway 170 will take you toward Eldorado Springs. Slow down until you notice the picnic tables and a small parking area on the right. The Mesa Trail is well marked. Cross a little bridge and soon zigzag through a landscape of sumac bushes, ferns, and sedges. The uphills are gentle enough, leading into impressive pine forests, with views of the Flatirons. The Mesa Trail winds up in Boulder's Chautauqua Park. In winter the trail is popular with cross-country skiers.

shopping, and organizations. Between the university and the city, you'll find plenty to keep you busy in any season. Find out what's happening in town by picking up a copy of the *Boulder Weekly* newspaper, available for free at many businesses around town, or peruse it online at boulderweekly.com.

Places to Stay in the Colorado Foothills

BAILEY

Glen-Isle Resort
US 285 near milepost marker 221
(303) 838-5461
coloradodirectory.com/glenisleresort
Inexpensive to Moderate
Historic lodge and cabins along the Platte River surrounded by Pike National Forest, rustic but comfortable, well-furnished cabins have fully equipped kitchens, linens and bedding, and fireplaces.

BOULDER

Alps Boulder Canyon Inn
38619 Boulder Canyon Dr.
(303) 444-5445 or
(800) 414-2577
(outside Colorado)
alpsinn.com
Expensive
Luxury B&B located 5 minutes from downtown; rooms include fireplaces, premium linens, full breakfast, afternoon tea, and WiFi. Some rooms have private whirlpool tubs for two.

Boulder Mountain Lodge
91 Fourmile Canyon Dr.
(303) 444-0882
bouldermountainlodge.com
Inexpensive to Moderate
Family-owned with 30 units, comprised of kitchenettes, full kitchens, suites, and a cabin. Hot tubs by creek, seasonal swimming pool.

Boulder Twin Lake Inn
6485 Twin Lakes Rd.
(303) 530-2939 or
(800) 322-2939
twinlakesinnboulder.com
Inexpensive
Modern country inn in a quiet residential neighborhood with 33 units offering free wireless Internet, minikitchens, full central kitchen with complete cooking facilities, and adjacent community park and pond.

The Bradley Boulder Inn
2040 16th St.
(303) 545-5200 or
(800) 858-5811
thebradleyboulder.com
Moderate to Expensive
Located steps away from the Pearl Street Mall, this is a 12-room luxury inn with full gourmet breakfast, evening wine and cheese, snacks throughout the day, and free wireless Internet. Some rooms include fireplaces, Jacuzzis, balconies with mountain views. No children under 14.

Briar Rose Bed-and-Breakfast Inn
2151 Arapahoe Ave.
(303) 442-3007 or
(888) 786-8440
briarrosebb.com
Moderate
Beautifully furnished, highly rated inn with 10 guest rooms. Delicious organic breakfasts are offered in a green and sustainable-oriented lodging.

Courtyard Boulder
4710 Pearl East Circle
(303) 440-4700
marriott.com
Moderate to Expensive
Pool, free wireless Internet, 2 miles from Pearl Street Mall.

Hotel Boulderado
2115 13th St.
(303) 442-4344 or
(800) 433-4344
boulderado.com
Expensive
Historic luxury hotel with Victorian decor in the heart of downtown and 1 block from Pearl Street. Free wireless Internet.

**Rodeway Inn & Suites
Boulder Broker**
555 30th St.
(303) 444-3330
rodewayinn.com
Inexpensive
Within walking distance
of the university, with free
continental breakfast and
wireless Internet.

St. Julien Hotel & Spa
900 Walnut St.
(720) 406-9696 or
(877) 303-0900
stjulien.com
Expensive
Elegant accommodations
close to Pearl Street offer
an infinity pool, a whirlpool
and spa, and free Internet.

CENTRAL CITY

Century Hotel and Casino
102 Main St.
(303) 582-5050
central-city.cnty.com
Inexpensive to Moderate

Free hot breakfast, 26
rooms, inexpensive hotel
restaurant.

**Hooper Homestead
Guest Quarter**
210 Hooper St.
(303) 582-5828
hooperhomestead.com
Moderate
Small, relaxing, 3-room
B&B with hot tub, friendly
service, wireless Inter-
net, parklike setting, and
nice views. Spa services
available.

Reserve Casino Hotel
321 Gregory St.
(303) 582-0800 or
(800) 924-6646
reservecasinohotel.com
Inexpensive to Moderate
Recently renovated rooms,
2 hotel restaurants.

GOLDEN

The Golden Hotel
800 11th St.
(303) 279-0100 or
(800) 233-7214
thegoldenhotel.com
Moderate
Overlooking Clear Creek,
close to Coors Brewery
and downtown, live music
Thursday evenings, com-
plimentary local shuttle,
free wireless Internet, pet-
friendly. Bridgewater Grill
in hotel offers a daily full
menu.

La Quinta
3301 Youngfield Service
Rd.
(303) 279-5565
lq.com
Inexpensive to Moderate
Free breakfast and wireless
Internet, outdoor swimming
pool, pet-friendly, affordable rates.

OTHER ATTRACTIONS WORTH SEEING IN THE COLORADO FOOTHILLS

BOULDER

Boulder History Museum
(303) 449-3464
boulderhistory.org

University of Colorado at Boulder
(303) 492-1411
colorado.edu

CENTRAL CITY

Coeur d'Alene Mine Shaft House
(303) 582-5283
gilpinhistory.org

GOLDEN

Coors Brewery
(303) 277-2337 or (800) 642-6116
millercoors.com

Golden Gate Canyon State Park
(303) 582-3707
parks.state.co.us/parks/
goldengatecanyon

Table Mountain Inn

1310 Washington Ave.
(303) 277-9898 or
(800) 762-9898
tablemountaininn.com
Moderate
Southwestern decor and
74 guest rooms make
this a Golden favorite.
The award-winning Table
Mountain Grill & Cantina
is part of the inn. Hot tub,
sauna, free wireless Internet, and a large lap pool
are also available.

Places to Eat in the Colorado Foothills

BLACK HAWK/ CENTRAL CITY

The Face Bar Restaurant

120 Eureka St., Central
City; main level of Teller
House
(303) 582-0600
ktrg.net/ktrouge/index.html
Moderate
Casual American cuisine
and a nice departure from
casino dining. Open for
appetizers, lunch, dinner,
and dessert on days with
opera matinees or evening
performances.

Millie's Restaurant

120 Main St., Central City
(303) 582-5914
famousbonanza.com
Inexpensive
Appetizers, soups, salads,
burgers, sandwiches,
entrees.

Rouge

120 Eureka St., Central
City; upstairs in Teller
House
(303) 582-0600
ktrg.net/ktrouge/index.html
Expensive
Modern twist on tradi-
tional steak house fare
in a historic setting.
Open for dinner only on
dates with evening opera
performances.

BOULDER

Boulder Dushanbe Teahouse

1770 13th St.
(303) 442-4993
boulderteahouse.com
Moderate
Popular restaurant housed
in a teahouse, serves a
wide variety of international
entrees for lunch and dinner, extensive tea selection.

Flagstaff House

1138 Flagstaff Rd.
(303) 442-4640
flagstaffhouse.com
Expensive
Fine French-American din-
ing with breathtaking views
of Boulder, extensive wine
cellar.

The Gondolier on Pearl

1600 Pearl St., #1
(303) 443-5015
gondolieronpearl.com
Moderate
Italian cuisine, serving Boulder for over 50 years.

Illegal Pete's

1447 Pearl St.
(303) 440-3955 or
(303) 444-3055

1320 College Ave.
illegalpetes.com
Inexpensive
Friendly cafe serving an
extensive menu of Mexican
cuisine made from fresh,
all-natural ingredients.

The Kitchen

1039 Pearl St.
(303) 544-5973
thekitchencommunity.com
Expensive
Popular community eatery
serving innovative American
cuisine inspired by Euro-
pean bistro fare.

The Mediterranean Cafe

1002 Walnut St.
(303) 444-5335
themedboulder.com
Moderate
Popular spot serving Italian, Spanish, French, and
Greek cuisine, tapas, salads and seafood, paella,
pastas, grilled items, and
wood oven pizza. Over 40
wines by the glass.

Q's

2115 13th St.
(303) 442-4880
qsboulder.com
Moderate to Expensive
Creative American cuisine
using seasonal, local,
organic, and sustainably
produced ingredients.

Rio Grande

1101 Walnut St.
(303) 444-3690
riograndemexican.com/
boulder
Inexpensive to Moderate
Loud, fun Mexican res-
taurant with wicked-good
margaritas and freshly

FOR MORE INFORMATION

BOULDER

Boulder Convention and Visitors Bureau
2440 Pearl St., 80302
(303) 442-2911 or (800) 444-0447
bouldercoloradousa.com

CENTRAL CITY/BLACK HAWK

Central City–Black Hawk Visitor Center
121 Main St.
Central City, 80427
(303) 582-3345 or (888) 589-5919
centralcitycolorado.us

Gilpin County
203 Eureka St.
Central City, 80427
(303) 582-5214
co.gilpin.co.us

GOLDEN

Greater Golden Chamber of Commerce
1010 Washington Ave.
Golden, 80402
(303) 279-3113
goldencochamber.org

---

prepared entrees. Indoor dining and rooftop patio.

Tangier Moroccan Cuisine
3070 28th St.
(303) 443-3676
tangiermoroccancuisine
.com
Moderate
Authentic Moroccan cuisine in a friendly atmosphere. Dinner only. Belly dancing on Friday.

GOLDEN

Ali Baba Grill
109 Rubey Dr.
(303) 279-2228
alibabagrill.com
Moderate
Tasty Lebanese and Persian cuisine cooked fresh daily in a friendly setting.

Bridgewater Grill
800 11th St.
(303) 279-2010
bridgewatergrill.com

Moderate to Expensive
Salads, steaks, seafood, burgers, and American classic dishes at the Golden Hotel. Live music in the lounge on Thursday evenings.

Chart House
25908 Genessee Trail Rd.
(303) 526-9813
chart-house.com
Expensive
Seafood, steaks, extensive wine list, and decadent desserts in an elegant setting.

Sherpa House Restaurant
1518 Washington Ave.
(303) 278-7939
ussherpahouse.com
Moderate
Authentic Tibetan, Nepalese, and Indian cuisine with an interior restaurant decor based on a traditional sherpa home in Nepal.

Table Mountain Inn
1310 Washington Ave.
(303) 277-9898
tablemountaininn.com
Moderate
Fresh southwestern and American cuisine.

MORRISON

The Fort
19192 Hwy. 8
(303) 697-4771
thefort.com
Expensive
Historic, award-winning restaurant combines flavors of the early West with contemporary cuisine. Wide range of game, meats, southwestern flavors, and an extensive wine list.

Rocky Mountain National Park Territory

If you come to **Estes Park** during the high summer season—and want to be above the melee—you might consider the short uphill drive to the **Stanley Hotel and Conference Center.** It stands above the busy town like a white castle. The 100-room Stanley reminds you of those old Swiss Grand Hotels—aristocratic, flawlessly kept up, frequently restored, and a monument to good taste and good manners.

The hotel is all stately white columns, Victorian furniture, fireplaces crackling in the lobby, rooms with impeccable white linen, polished cherrywood furniture, and antique dressers. The handwrought leaded-glass windows, spotless tablecloths in the elegant dining room, and comfortable bar add to a feeling of being on vacation. Miles of walks surround the hostelry, which is at an elevation of 7,500 feet.

The historic hotel was built by the inventor of the Stanley Steamer automobile. Back in 1905, doctors gave **F. O. Stanley,** who had tuberculosis, only a few months to live. Stanley gathered his wife, her maid, and his controversial Steamer and

Estes Park: The Best Views

The *Estes Park Aerial Tramway,* west on US 34 to Moraine Park Road, carries passengers to the 8,896-foot summit of Prospect Mountain for an unmatched look at the community and surrounding mountains. Ride in one of two suspended cabins and view the Continental Divide, and then picnic at the summit. For more information call (970) 586-3675 or visit estestram.com.

left Massachusetts, heading for the Colorado Rockies. Stanley lived another 37 years, to the age of 91. His palatial hotel opened in 1909, and the "all-electric" hotel charged $8 a day, gourmet meals included. Celebrities such as Theodore Roosevelt, John Philip Sousa, and Molly Brown came, adding to the grandeur. More recently, novelist Stephen King found inspiration for his novel *The Shining* while staying at the hotel.

The hotel still hosts guests with deluxe accommodations. Nonguests can enjoy the Cascade restaurant and Steamer Cafe, admire the architecture and the views, and stroll the grounds. Contact Stanley Hotel at 333 Wonderview Ave., Estes Park 80517; or call (970) 586-3371 or (800) 976-1377 or visit stanley hotel.com.

The town of *Estes Park* (elev. 7,522 feet) is the eastern and most popular gateway to Rocky Mountain National Park. For those not camping in the park, the town offers a variety of hotels, motels, and cabins. The main thoroughfare through town is lined with shops catering to tourists. During July and August traffic slows to a crawl. Those passing through on the way to the park should look for the sign just inside the town limits for the bypass road that avoids the traffic.

Despite the touristy downtown scene, many thousands of visitors enjoy Estes Park each summer. Shoppers have fun browsing for Native American crafts and jewelry, outdoor gear, and western wear. Kids ride go-karts, play miniature golf, or speed down a giant slide. Fishing and golf are close by. And there's a full calendar of music, theater, and entertainment events throughout the summer. Just keep in mind that you will be sharing the town with plenty of others.

trivia

The Stanley Hotel earned some of its more recent notoriety as the setting that inspired Stephen King's novel, *The Shining.* King wrote roughly half of the manuscript for the novel while staying in room 217 at the hotel. He returned to the Stanley Hotel in 1997 to make the ABC miniseries version of *The Shining* (the motion picture was filmed elsewhere).

Break the Ice: Ice Climbing near Estes Park

The **Colorado Mountain School (CMS),** the sole concessionaire permitted to guide rock and ice climbs in Rocky Mountain National Park, offers classes out of their Estes Park location. Wintertime is the perfect season to test yourself on the park's frozen waterfalls under the watchful eyes of one of CMS's expert guides. They also offer instruction in mountaineering, backcountry skiing, and other outdoor activities. From introductory 1-day courses to an intensive, multiday advanced course, CMS has classes appropriate for all skill levels. Contact CMS at 341 Moraine Ave., Estes Park 80517; (303) 447-2804 or (800) 836-4008; totalclimbing.com.

To avoid the crowds, plan your visit for late spring or fall, or in summer arrive by mid-morning.

Estes Park is 65 miles northwest of Denver and easy to reach via the Boulder Turnpike (US 36) through **Lyons.** For more information contact the Estes Park Chamber Resort Association, 500 Big Thompson Ave., Estes Park 80517; (970) 586-4431 or (800) 443-7837; estesparkcvb.com or estes-park.com.

Most people who come to Estes Park do so with another destination in mind. The east entrance to **Rocky Mountain National Park** is just a few miles beyond the town. Leave behind the noise and congestion of Estes Park, step into the natural grandeur of the park with its high peaks, meadows, and rivers, and you will see the reason you came here. With almost no commercial activity inside the park, the landscape looks much as it did when Mr. Stanley first arrived more than 100 years ago.

trivia

Rocky Mountain National Park's annual budget is about $10 million—which may seem like a lot, until you consider that the park has nearly 3.4 million visitors each year!

With 415 square miles of park, there's no shortage of acreage to explore. The park has more than a hundred peaks over 11,000 feet. The highest is **Longs Peak** at 14,259 feet. Surrounding those mountains is a vast wonderland of lakes, waterfalls, streams and rivers, meadows, forests, and tundra.

The best way to explore the park is to leave your car and walk some of the 355 miles of hiking trails. Trails ranging in difficulty from easy to extreme lead to remote valleys, sprawling meadows, and granite peaks. Several popular ones are short, level paths to beautiful lakes and waterfalls. Some trails to consider: Nymph, Dream, and Emerald Lakes; Ouzel Falls; Adams Falls; Bear Lake; Lulu City; Deer Mountain.

Frequent nature presentations and guided walks sponsored by the park are a great way to get kids interested in their surroundings. Backpackers obtain permits and disappear into the mountains for days at a time. The streams and lakes offer trout fishing. For many, sitting next to a meadow or river and watching the afternoon go by is reward enough.

In the summer, wildlife watchers may spot deer, elk, sheep, beaver, coyotes, pikas, and many bird species. Afternoon lightning and thunderstorms are not uncommon, cooling the air with rain before they blow to the east. In the winter, bundle up and choose from dozens of cross-country skiing and snowshoeing destinations.

trivia

The 1,000-foot east face of Longs Peak, a vertical granite cliff known as the Diamond, attracts rock climbers from all over the world.

For many, autumn is the best time of all, with its seemingly endless string of clear, warm days. The evenings turn crisp and the nights are chilly, so bring an overcoat. After Labor Day you'll find less competition for campground spaces, lodging, restaurant tables, and traffic lanes.

Visitors in the fall get two additional bonuses: Aspen turn golden, and elk gather in the meadows to defend harems and bugle their high-pitched calls. Both events begin in September and last well into October, with exact dates varying slightly from year to year. For many Coloradans, coming to the park to hear the elk and watch the fall colors is an annual tradition. The Park Visitor Center can provide forecasts in early fall on foliage and elk activity.

One of the park highlights is the drive along spectacular **Trail Ridge Road** (US 34), the highest continuously paved highway in the US. Climbing 4,000 feet from Estes Park, the road winds along for 48 miles before dropping down to Grand Lake. Eleven miles of the road are above tree line in an arctic tundra environment, with the high point at 12,183 feet. Up here the air is thin and the ultraviolet rays are strong. It's a fragile world of tiny plants and flowers, alive in summer with birds and small mammals.

Like most important Colorado highways, Trail Ridge has a long history. The first human travelers along this route were Utes and other Native American tribes following the already marked trails of wild animals. Miners used it in the 1880s. In 1929 Congress approved the highway, and in 1935 the road was finally completed.

Multiple parking areas along the way are the starting points for exploring the area. To truly experience this unique ecosystem, leave the car and set out on one of the designated trails. Keep an eye on the weather to avoid lightning storms; the first half of the day is generally less prone to storms. Stay on trails to avoid damaging the fragile foliage underfoot.

The season is short for a drive on the road, though. Deep snows and snow-drifts cover Trail Ridge all winter and spring. The road is open from around Memorial Day until the first heavy snowfall, usually in mid-October.

More than three million people visit the park each year. As a result, sites in the five campgrounds fill up fast. If you're camping, make reservations in advance. Without reservations from July through Labor Day, arrive by midday for the best chances for a site. There are private campgrounds around Estes Park, but they also fill up quickly.

The best way to avoid crowds is to visit before Memorial Day or after Labor Day, when children are in school. Renting a room or cabin around Estes Park may also be easier than getting a drop-in campsite in the park during peak months.

trivia

Legend says the Utes shunned Grand Lake, believing its mists were the spirits of the women and children who drowned in the lake during an attack by the Cheyenne and Arapaho Indians.

The park entrance fee is $20 for a private vehicle, good for seven consecutive days. The Rocky Mountain Annual Pass at $40 is good for a year. Travelers age 62 and older can purchase the National Parks and Federal Recreation Lands Senior Pass—a lifetime pass to all national parks for a onetime $10 charge.

You have four options for getting to the park from Denver. One of two quickest routes is driving through Boulder and Lyons (use US 36); from Boulder it's about 34 miles to Estes Park and the east gate to the national park. The other is to travel some 70 miles north from Denver on I-25 north to Highway 66, then west on 66 until it joins US 36 to Estes Park.

You can also come on the spectacular Peak to Peak Highway (Highways 119, 72, and 7) from Black Hawk. The drive is especially enjoyable in late fall when aspen trees burst into gold. Plan on 2 to 3 hours, depending on sightseeing stops, to reach the national park via this route. For a more leisurely course, head west from Denver on I-70, cross Berthoud Pass via US 40, and then get to Rocky Mountain National Park via Grand Lake. You can do a loop by returning to Denver using one of the previous two routes. For more information contact Rocky Mountain National Park, 1000 Hwy. 36, Estes Park 80517; (970) 586-1206; nps.gov/romo.

After spending the day on Trail Ridge Road, you can continue west and drop into a wide river valley with meadows and thick stands of pine, spruce, and aspen. After exiting through the park's west entrance, you will come to the town of **Grand Lake,** which skirts the shores of Grand Lake itself. This unusually blue lake—the largest natural lake in the state—will be dotted with

Grand County Fishing

Grand County has some of the largest bodies of water in the state: natural Grand Lake and man-made reservoirs Lake Granby and Shadow Mountain Lake. They are home to rainbow, brook, mackinaw, brown, and cutthroat trout. The area is also popular for winter ice fishing. Local streams are also well-known for *fly fishing.* Try Willow Creek, the Fraser River, and the Colorado River in the area west of Granby for brook, rainbow, and brown trout.

sailboats in August, its marinas filled with yachts. At an elevation of almost 8,400 feet above sea level, Grand Lake boasts the "World's Highest Yacht Club." The high surrounding peaks stand over a stunning, Swiss-like scene.

The first people to visit here many centuries ago were Paleo-Indians, crossing the high mountain passes in search of game. In the 1800s, Arapaho, Sioux, and Cheyenne began venturing here, resulting in fierce conflicts with the Utes who lived throughout the area. Trappers, traders, and explorers trickled in, and in 1875 gold, silver, copper, and lead discoveries touched off a mining boom. Ten years later the boom went bust, and the population dropped from 600 to 80 year-round residents.

But the beauty of the area was not forgotten. Tourists, ranchers, and sportsmen began coming to the lake, and when Rocky Mountain National Park was designated in 1915, the future of Grand Lake as a tourist destination was firmly sealed.

Today Grand Lake can serve as an overnight getaway or the base for a week of exploring the area. The lake is a major landlocked sailing destination with frequent regattas. It's also a haven for dozens of classic wooden Chris-Craft boats and during the warm months they're often out on the water. During the summer marinas rent kayaks, canoes, rowboats, paddleboats, and motorboats. Lakes and nearby streams give anglers numerous places to wet a line. Stables offer horseback rides along mountain trails.

With mountains on all sides, there's no shortage of hiking trails. The East Inlet Trail leads to a spectacular set of cascading falls, continuing into a mountain valley with a river and large meadows. Just inside the west park entrance are a variety of hikes to choose from, including the trail to Lulu City, an abandoned mining town with only a few foundations remaining from a once-thriving settlement.

If you arrive in Grand Lake and realize you've forgotten an essential piece of outdoor equipment, there's a good chance that ***Never Summer Mountain Products*** on Grand Avenue will have what you need. They're open year-round, and the store is also a good resource for advice on local hiking, camping, and fishing.

But Grand Lake is about more than outdoor pursuits. The town is an idyllic setting to spend a lazy summer day just wandering. The last 6 blocks of Grand Avenue, the town's main street, are filled with boutiques, restaurants, and shops. The beach area has plenty of benches and grassy areas to sprawl with a good book. Stop by the ***Kauffman House Museum*** for a fascinating peek into the past. Exhibits, photos, books, and descriptions of the area over the last century help bring to life the history of a region that was anything but dull. Volunteer docents answer questions and share information about the collection of antiques and memorabilia. The museum is open from 11 a.m. to 5 p.m. daily from Memorial Day to Labor Day. It's located in a log house on the hill overlooking the lake, just above the beach. Admission is $5; children under 13 free. For more information go to kauffmanhouse.org.

After a day spent outdoors, you'll also be happy to return to Grand Lake to choose from a handful of restaurants. At Sagebrush Barbecue and Grill, a basket of peanuts arrives as soon as you're seated. Follow the crowd and toss your discarded shells on the floor. Several ice-cream parlors offer cool, creamy desserts, but locals claim the best is the homemade ice cream at little Myauchi's Snack Bar across the street from the beach. Blue Water Bakery has homemade baked goods and tasty coffee. For an incredible weekend breakfast buffet, visit Fat Cat Cafe, where British owner Sally wants you to feel "comfortable, cozy, and well fed." You will.

In winter the handsome, wooden summer homes along the lake are abandoned. The souvenir shops along the boardwalk close down; only a few saloons and a tiny grocery stay open. Trail Ridge Road is closed. At the same time, the cross-country skiing possibilities are plentiful. The Rocky Mountain National Park entrance is only a mile away, and you see Nordic skiers even on the golf course. Noisy snowmobile enthusiasts show up with their machines. Most winter tourists stay in nearby ***Granby;*** those not on a budget head to the C Lazy U Ranch.

Grand Lake in winter is popular for riding snowmobiles. But the roaring engines and blue exhaust fumes quickly shatter the deep stillness that winter brings to the Rockies. One place to escape the snowmobiles is the ***Grand Lake Touring Center*** (415 CR 48, Grand Lake 80447; 970-627-8008; grandlakeski.com). From the intersection of Highway 40 and Highway 34 go east on 34 for 16 miles to Country Road 48

trivia

Grand Lake is also known as the "Snowmobile Capital of Colorado," due to its more than 300 miles of trails.

AUTHOR'S FAVORITES IN THE NORTHWESTERN MOUNTAINS

C Lazy U Ranch
(970) 887-3344
clazyu.com

Devil's Thumb Ranch for cross-country skiing
3530 CR 83, Tabernash
(970) 726-5632
devilsthumbranch.com

Grand Lake
(970) 627-3402 or (800) 531-1019
grandlakechamber.com

Ice Cream at Myauchi's Snack Bar
Grand Lake by the beach

Rocky Mountain National Park
(970) 586-1206
nps.gov/romo

Stanley Hotel for lunch
(970) 586-3371 or (800) 976-1377
stanleyhotel.com

Strawberry Park Natural Hot Springs
Steamboat Springs
(970) 879-0342
strawberryhotsprings.com

Trail Ridge Road
(Rocky Mountain National Park between Grand Lake and Estes Park)
(970) 586-1206
nps.gov/romo

Vista Verde Guest & Ski Ranch
(800) 526-7433 or (970) 879-3858
vistaverde.com

Winter Park
(800) 903-7275 or (970) 726-4118
playwinterpark.com

and turn left at the sign marked Golf Course Road. Yes, under all that snow is a golf course! The Ski Touring Center is set in beautiful terrain, and the 35 kilometers of trails are immaculately kept up. Some of the runs are surprisingly steep—especially for a golf course!—but other trails are gentle enough for beginners. The center is open daily through the winter from 9 a.m. to 4 p.m. For more information contact Grand Lake Area Chamber of Commerce, PO Box 429, Grand Lake 80447; (970) 627-3402 or (800) 531-1019; grandlake chamber.com.

For a memorable retreat from the outside world, try the *C Lazy U Ranch* in the Willow Creek Valley. This is no ordinary dude ranch. Private, secluded, and open year-round, the 8,000-acre ranch offers endless outdoor activities and gourmet western cuisine. In summer and fall, choose from horseback riding (with a personal horse during your stay), fishing, hiking, mountain biking, yoga, tennis, swimming, and trap shooting. Winter means downhill skiing over at Winter Park, cross-country skiing, ice skating, sledding, horseback riding, and warming up in the heated outdoor pool or hot tub. Even though you can get cell phone reception here, this luxurious ranch is a perfect place to unwind, relax, and be pampered.

Rates are high and commensurate with the ranch's amenities and all-inclusive package. C Lazy U is open June 1 through March 1 for destination travel; March 1 through May 31 for group retreats. Take I-70 to exit 232, then along US 40 to Highway 125. You'll see the sign. For more information and to make reservations, contact C Lazy U Ranch, 3640 CO 125, Box 379, Granby 80446; (970) 887-3344; clazyu.com.

A 10-mile drive west from Granby along US 40 toward *Kremmling* will take you to *Hot Sulphur Springs Resort.* Once used by the *Ute Indians* as a place for bathing and healing, the resort has been in operation for 140 years. Facilities include 22 pools and private baths, and a summer swimming pool. Anyone staying at the resort gets free use of the outdoor pools. Massage, body treatments, and facials are available. For those not staying at the resort, guests 12 and older can soak in the outdoor pools for $17.50 a day; the price is $11.50 for kids age 3 to 11 (4 pools) and free for children under 3 (4 pools). Private, adults-only pools are $15 per hour per person. Open every day from 8 a.m. to 10 p.m. Reservations are recommended for all services; call for details. Hot Sulphur Springs Resort, 5609 CR 20, Hot Sulphur Springs 80451; (970) 725-3306 or (800) 510-6235; hotsulphursprings.com.

Another guest ranch offering a true Colorado experience is *Devil's Thumb Ranch.* Located about a 10-minute drive north of Winter Park, this upscale resort has a new lodge, cabins in the woods, and two restaurants. Guests enjoy horseback riding, mountain biking, trout fishing, and exploring 5,000 acres of meadows, forests, and streams. In winter the ranch opens their Nordic center with 100+ kilometers of groomed trails for some of the best cross-country skiing in the country. From Winter Park, take US 40 past Fraser. About 2 miles after Fraser, turn right on Highway 83. The road forks a short distance after this; turn onto the right-hand fork and follow it for 3 miles. For more information, contact Devil's Thumb Ranch Resort & Spa, 3530 CR 83, PO Box 750, Tabernash 80478; (970) 726-5632; devilsthumbranch.com.

Winter Park

Winter Park is one of Colorado's most beloved ski resorts, and for good reason: great runs for all skill levels, consistent snowfall, and close proximity to Denver. But just like elsewhere in the state, Winter Park is a year-round destination. In summer and fall the ski slopes and surrounding mountains transform into a playground for mountain bikers, with over 600 miles of marked and mapped trails, from single tracks to backcountry roads. Hikers, fishing enthusiasts, and lovers of the outdoors find plenty to do in the surrounding national forests. Festivals and special events fill the calendar during the warm months. Colorado's longest alpine slide is here. In town, a variety of unique restaurants keep locals and visitors well-fed. Kids are welcome everywhere, and there's easily enough to keep vacationers busy for several days.

Three of the Winter Park Resort lifts that move skiers up the mountain all winter haul a different load in summer: mountain bikers and their bikes. Miles of trails include jumps, obstacles, and fast downhill runs, along with more leisurely rides. For information and directions to other bike routes in the area, drop by one of several area bike shops or the Winter Park Visitor Center and get a free Winter Park/Fraser mountain biking trail guide.

trivia

Mary Jane, one of Winter Park Resort's three mountains, is ideal for more advanced skiers. Not only has it been voted the best mogul mountain in North America year after year, it's also home to the infamous run named Outhouse.

Yes, biking is big here. The area is becoming a mecca for riders, and several important competitions are held here each summer. One event in particular is especially fun for spectators. *Colorado Freeride Festival* freestyle mountain bike competition (970-726-1564; trestlebikepark.com) is a 4-day festival of jumps, big-air tricks, downhill races, and stunts. The Winter Park and the Fraser Valley Chamber of Commerce website at playwinterpark.com lists dates for this and other local events such as the Winter Park Jazz Festival and Alpine Art Affair. Both these events have been held here for more than 30 years.

The main drag through the towns of Winter Park and Fraser is a series of strip malls and shopping complexes that's not especially conducive to strolling. But it's worth browsing to find places like *Winter Park Trading Company,* a sporting goods consignment store, *B Jammin' in Cooper Creek Square,* for fun family souvenirs, *Ski Depot Sports* (78717 US 40) for outdoor gear, and several thrift stores with excellent merchandise in Fraser.

Ride the Divide

For an exhilarating winter adventure, take a snowmobile tour with *Grand Adventures* (grandadventures.com) from Winter Park to the Continental Divide. Topping out at almost 12,000 feet, the tour is perfect for beginner and intermediate riders, offering a thrilling ride and sweeping views of the Winter Park ski area and Fraser Valley.

A hearty, healthy breakfast is a wise prelude to an active day in the mountains. *Carvers Bakery Cafe* behind Cooper's Creek Square, *Rise and Shine Cafe* downtown next to the Conoco station, and *Mountain Rose Cafe* next to the post office are all local favorites. For friendly local coffeehouses, try *Rocky Mountain Roastery* along the main drag or *Mountain Grind* in Cooper's Creek Square, with outdoor seating by the fountain. Lunch and dinner in the area offer a range of choices including Mexican, German, Japanese, Italian, and Colorado cuisine.

Winter Park Resort, with 142 runs, has the fourth largest terrain area of any ski resort in Colorado. Neighboring *Mary Jane* ski area is famous for its ski moguls, and if you want to learn how to master moguls, there's no better place. There's no celebrity parade here, and not much in the way of wild nightlife. But the amount of snow and the varied terrain make this a Colorado favorite year after year.

For $48, nonskiers can take a 2-hour ride to the summit in a heated vehicle called a snowcat, stopping at the top for a hot chocolate and photos before heading back down the mountain. Cross-country skiing and snowshoeing are available at *Devil's Thumb Ranch* (970-726-5632; devilsthumbranch.com), *Snow Mountain Ranch/YMCA of the Rockies* (ymcarockies.org), or along many of the area's easily accessible trails. Nighttime sleigh rides through a quiet winter landscape are available through Devil's Thumb Ranch and *Dashing Through the Snow;* (970) 726-0900 or (888) 384-6773.

To avoid the hassle of renting a car, many visitors take advantage of *Home James Transportation Services,* with their frequent shuttle vans that run from *Denver International Airport* (DIA) directly to lodging properties in Winter Park. The cost is $65 for adults, with discounts for groups of 3 or more. Children ages 2 to 11 are $32.50. They also go to the YMCA, Devil's Thumb, and Grand Lake. Contact them at PO Box 279, Winter Park 80482; (800) 359-7503; homejamestransportation.com.

In decent weather the 67-mile drive from Denver to Winter Park will take less than 2 hours. Go west on I-70, then north on US 40 over Berthoud Pass.

Grand Adventure Balloon Tours

Passing through Winter Park in the summer and looking for a fun adventure? Try a hot air balloon flight. Launching in Fraser, the tour takes you and your companions soaring up above the treetops with aerial views of the surrounding mountainous terrain. For reservations and information, contact Grand Adventure Balloon Tours, PO Box 1124, Winter Park 80482; (970) 887-1340; grandadventureballoon.com.

Playground for Cross-Country Skiers

After a 10-minute drive north from Winter Park, near Tabernash you come to the turnoff for the year-round *Snow Mountain Ranch/YMCA of the Rockies.* Thanks to more than 100 kilometers of cross-country skiing, the ranch has become one of Colorado's most popular Nordic ski centers. The setting is quiet and remote: no shops, restaurants, or movie theaters in the vicinity, no television in the rooms; and for dinner you line up with other guests for simple, wholesome meals. Apart from cross-country skiing, you can try snowshoeing, tubing, ice skating, swimming in an indoor pool, and in summer, a wide variety of outdoor activities and family programs. For more information contact YMCA of the Rockies, PO Box 169, Winter Park 80482; (970) 887-2152 or (303) 443-4743; ymcarockies.org.

Located north of Kremmling, *Latigo Ranch* has 60 kilometers of groomed trails ranging from flat track to challenging advanced. Surrounding the ranch is over 200 square miles of national forest awaiting backcountry skiers. For more information call (970) 724-9008 or go to latigotrails.com.

Winter Park Resort opens in Nov and closes in Apr. Resort hours are 9 a.m. to 4 p.m. Mon through Fri and 8:30 a.m. to 4 p.m. Sat, Sun, and holidays. For more information on summer and winter activities contact Winter Park and the Fraser Valley Chamber of Commerce; (800) 903-7275; playwinterpark.com, or Winter Park Resort; (303) 316-1564; skiwinterpark.com.

Colorado's Winter Park Ski Resort offers the *National Sports Center for the Disabled* (NSCD), the world's largest teaching program for physically challenged skiers. More than a thousand volunteers and a staff of 54 participate in it. Each ski season, nearly 30,000 lessons are given here. The NSCD provides services for people with almost any disability. More information on the program can be obtained by writing or calling National Sports Center for the Disabled, PO Box 1290, Winter Park 80482; (970) 726-1540 or (303) 316-1540; nscd.org.

Yampa Valley & Routt National Forest

In 1875 *James Crawford,* the first white settler of *Steamboat Springs,* arrived here from Missouri with two wagons, his family, his horses, and a few head of cattle. He was attracted to the area by a newspaper article. The author of the piece described his view from the top of the Park Mountain Range as "a wilderness of mountain peaks and beautiful valleys, dark forests and silvery streams—a deserted land except for immense herds of elk and deer and buffalo which had not yet learned by experience to shun the presence of man."

The Yampa Valley's idyllic setting and mild climate made the eventual "presence of man" inevitable. Even before Crawford built his log cabin along the west bank of **Soda Creek,** the Yampa Valley had sheltered Ute Indians and, later, French and English fur trappers.

Cattle ranchers found Steamboat's emerald-green slopes ideal for fattening their herds en route to market. Hot and cold running water in the forms of three creeks, numerous hot springs, and the flow of the **Yampa River** lured more and more settlers to the valley.

trivia

One of North America's largest elk herds ranges is near Steamboat Springs.

Recreational skiing first came here in the early 1900s, when Norwegian Carl Howelsen introduced the sports of ski jumping and ski racing to the community.

Today Colorado's northernmost ski town is a delightful blend of western ranch culture and outdoor adventure where tourists come for a taste of mountain life. Along with fleece and skiwear, you will see plenty of jeans, Stetsons, cowboy boots, and saddles. Skiing is a strong tradition in Steamboat. The town has produced numerous world-class skiers, and many Olympians first cut their ski teeth here.

In summer, the fields outside town are ripe with hay. Horses graze in sprawling meadows. The Yampa River flows through the valley, and mountains rise on all sides. Tourists come to browse the shops along Lincoln Avenue, float down the Yampa on inner tubes, ride the gondola for some high altitude hiking, and fish area streams and lakes. Dude ranches offer guests horseback riding and the experience of a working ranch. Especially in summer, the town is a tranquil blend of rural Colorado and relaxing tourist destination.

Like other Colorado ski towns, Steamboat has no dearth of kitschy tourist stores. But tucked between the fast-food joints and T-shirt shops, or hidden down quiet backstreets, are little gems waiting to be discovered. Try **Off The Beaten Path** bookstore at 68 9th St. for a morning latte and a browse through

Yampa Street

Running parallel to the Yampa River, Yampa Street in downtown Steamboat is a compact, pleasant stretch of trendy restaurants, bars, shops, and stores. It's popular with bicyclists, walkers, and anyone who enjoys relaxing next to a mountain river. Take a stroll, bring lunch to a riverside overlook, and enjoy some of the town's best free entertainment.

local photo books. ***Sweet Pea Market,*** housed in an old pole barn along the river at 729 Yampa St., offers fresh produce, homemade pies, and a coffee bar with free wireless Internet. Historic ***F.M. Light and Sons*** has been at 830 Lincoln Ave. for more than 100 years, outfitting customers in authentic western wear.

But you didn't come to Steamboat just for shopping. Perhaps the most unique way to explore the valley is to rent an inner tube from one of several shops in town and float down the Yampa River. The trip takes 45–60 minutes depending on stops, allowing floaters to meander lazily downstream. Local guidelines require "tubers" to start below Fletcher Park, which has a parking lot and easy access to the river. Take-out is around the 13th Street Bridge. Several commercial outfits offer tubes and shuttle service back to your car. Although the water is tame, this is a natural river with an unpredictable flow. Life jackets or helmets are suggested, especially for weak swimmers and children. Local tubing rules include no littering, glass, or dogs, and respecting the marked quiet zones along three residential areas. Go early in the day to avoid the crowds and afternoon thunderstorms.

One of the area's more popular hikes begins close to town. ***Fish Creek Falls*** is a cascading 283-foot waterfall that crashes over a cliff and drops into the canyon creek below. A quarter-mile trail leads to the falls. From there, a 6-mile hike goes past the Upper Falls, up switchbacks, and around a meadow area to Long Lake. Along the way hikers will get stunning views of the Yampa River and town. The waterfall runs heaviest during the spring runoff. As the snowpack disappears from the high peaks in early to midsummer, the flow decreases. Reach the trailhead by heading east on Lincoln Avenue, then turning left on 3rd Street. At the next stop sign turn right onto Fish Creek Falls Road. Continue for 3 miles to the parking lot. The Forest Service charges $5 per vehicle per day.

Howelsen Hill ski jump is famous worldwide among the ski jumping community. Its long, steep jump has launched many world records. But you don't have to wait for winter to watch jumpers racing down the steep run. When the snow melts, a porcelain surface on the jump gives young skiers a

Winter in Steamboat Springs

With 165 trails over almost 3,000 acres of terrain, giant **Steamboat Ski Area** has something for everyone. Its northern location is blessed with some of the highest annual snowfall in the state. Plenty of lifts, short lines, a prestigious ski school, and a top-notch ski patrol all add to the resorts' quality. Free mountain tours are offered daily at 10:30 a.m. starting outside the upper gondola terminal at the top of Vagabond. Choose from runs like Tomahawk, Buddy's Run, Stampede, Giggle Gulch, Last Chance, High Noon, Calf Roper, and Chutes.

Four Nordic centers, Steamboat Touring Center, Howelsen Hill, Steamboat Lake, and Lake Catamount, cater to cross-country skiers. In addition, many public lands are open and free for use, such as the popular Rabbit Ears Pass area.

With national forests on all sides, Steamboat abounds with free snowshoeing opportunities. At the ski resort, Steamboat's Ambassadors offer guided snowshoe tours daily at 1 p.m. Tours depart from the Information Center in Gondola Square and wind along a 1-mile loop from the top of Steamboat Gondola, with sweeping views of Yampa Valley and the Flat Top Mountains. Call (970) 871-5444 to sign up in advance. Participants will need a gondola foot pass.

place to practice during the warm months. They lift off at the end of the jump and soar impossible distances before alighting in the grass below. They practice throughout the week and on weekends. The jump is located across the Yampa River next to the rodeo arena. Ask for directions around town.

During the warm months the **Howler Alpine Slide** at Howelsen Hill is open for business. A chairlift takes you up the hill and high above town. At the top, climb onto a plastic sled for an exhilarating ride curving and bending down a 2,400-foot track. Proceeds from the alpine slide benefit the young athletes of the Steamboat Springs Winter Sports Club.

For a combination sightseeing ride and hike/bike, take the gondola ride up **Mount Werner** at the ski resort. Within minutes the town and valley to the west shrink to a tiny panorama far below. Eliminate the cawing ravens, drop some cows on the hillsides and squint just a bit, and this could be the Swiss Alps. At the top, biking and hiking trails fan out in every direction, and you can explore the surrounding alpine landscape before returning on the gondola, or heading down the mountain on foot or bike. The gondola will take your bike along with you. Bring your own bike or rent one at any of several places around town or the ski resort.

Yes, Steamboat does have springs. A walking tour downtown will take you past 10 hot springs, easily identified by their pungent smell. In town you can visit **Old Town Hot Springs** (steamboathotsprings.org) with eight hot spring-fed pools, two waterslides, massages, and a fitness center. For a rustic hot springs experience, check out **Strawberry Park Natural Hot Springs** (970-879-0342; strawberryhotsprings.com), located about 7 miles outside of downtown Steamboat Springs. With three main pools varying in temperature and gorgeous stonework, this special place warrants a visit. The unpaved upper part of the road can be challenging if wet or snowy. Ask in town for directions. Hours are 10 a.m. to 10:30 p.m. (admission until 9:30 p.m.) Sun through Thurs, and 10 a.m. to midnight (admission until 10:30 p.m.) Fri and Sat. Admission to the pools is $10 for adults, $5 for teenagers, $3 for children 3 to 12. (Children younger than 3 are free.) After dark, only adults are admitted and clothing is optional.

trivia

Steamboat Springs received its name in the early 1800s from French trappers, who mistakenly thought that they heard the chugging steam engine of a steamboat. In fact, they were hearing a natural mineral spring.

When it comes to quirky mountain town festivals and events, Steamboat Springs doesn't disappoint. Several times each winter, spectacular torch-lit parades stream down the ski slopes at the Torchlight Parades & Fireworks. The **Cowboy Downhill** each January is the result of placing 70 professional rodeo cowboys and cowgirls, many with questionable skiing skills, on skis and snowboards instead of horses and bulls. Locals and visitors cheer on their favorites, who are dressed in chaps and cowboy hats during slalom races, roping and saddling in the snow, and a wacky cowboy stampede race at the end. The Annual Winter Carnival, enjoying its 100th year in 2013, celebrates the season with ski jumping, slaloms, a tubing party, the Diamond Hitch parade, madcap street events for kids on snow-covered Lincoln Avenue, and a brilliant fireworks display at Howelsen Hill with the famous Lighted Man.

One of the year's most anticipated celebrations is **Springalicious.** Each April as the winter ski season winds down, the mountain heats up with free concerts featuring national acts, a super-cheap 4-day ski pass, the splashdown pond skimming competition, and more. The highlight of the festival is the **Cardboard Classic,** Steamboat's traditional rite of spring every April for more than 30 years. Piloting homemade crafts constructed only from cardboard, glue, string, masking tape, and duct tape, contestants race down Stampede run at the base of the Steamboat Ski area to a hysterical and chaotic finish. Information for these and other events can be found at steamboat.com.

Steamboat's most colorful weekend is a festival of vibrant colors and art. The annual **Hot Air Balloon Rodeo** combines with the Annual Art in the Park as a staple of summertime in Steamboat. Early in the morning more than 40 hot

Downhill All the Way

No, it's not about skiing, but about the annual **Steamboat Springs Marathon,** which takes place in early June. Starting out at an elevation of 8,128 feet and finishing at 6,728 feet, the marathon really is mostly downhill, but don't let that fool you. Though *Runner's World* magazine cited this course as one of the "10 Most Scenic Marathons of the Year" and one of the "Top 10 Destination Marathons in North America," it's still quite a challenge. Spectators stand along Lincoln Avenue or at the finish line at the courthouse lawn. The marathon is limited to 500 runners, and it fills early. For more information call (970) 879-0880 or visit runningseries.com.

air balloons rise and drift across the valley. Later on, West Lincoln Park hosts Steamboat's biggest arts and crafts festival.

For a less wacky, more authentic western event, the **Steamboat Springs Pro Rodeo Series** (steamboatprorodeo.com) runs on Friday and Saturday evenings most weekends during the summer from June through Labor Day. Some of the best cowboys from Colorado and Wyoming compete in bull riding, team roping, steer roping, barrel racing, and bareback riding. Come early for the barbecue and live entertainment.

If you find yourself hankering for yet more cowboy culture, consider the **Annual Cowboy's Roundup Days,** going strong for more than 100 years. Held over several days leading up to and including the Fourth of July, this is small-town Independence Day celebrated in true western style. From all-you-can-eat pancake breakfasts, parades, and free concerts to evening rodeos, ranch rodeo competitions, and one of the biggest fireworks shows in the state, this is a mountain party unlike any other in Colorado.

The Saturday Farmers' Market on 6th Street between Lincoln and Oak brings locals in search of buffalo meat, organic peaches, gourmet bakery breads, sheep cheese, barbecue pork sandwiches, and other edible specialties and local handicrafts. The market is open from 8 a.m. to 2 p.m., beginning in June and running through Aug.

Steamboat Springs is also home to one of the country's best automobile driving schools. But don't expect to learn how to parallel park here. The

trivia

Steamboat boasts more than 100 natural hot springs.

Bridgestone Winter Driving School is patterned after similar facilities at European ski resorts. In operation since 1983, the school is open from mid-Dec through early March. The track is a snow- and ice-covered course with enough turns, loops, and straights to satisfy anyone who envisions being a race-car driver.

But this is not play. You often share your class with law enforcement officers and ambulance personnel. Although these people are professional drivers, they recognize the need for practice, and many return every year. But every skill level is welcome.

The school's three tracks are designed for safety and forgiving of mistakes. In case of a spinout—and there will be spinouts!—the snow walls catch the car and hold it safely with no injury to driver or machine.

After the 1-day class, you will feel confident in your ability to avoid collisions due to ice- and snow-covered roads. Six levels of instruction are available in half-day and full-day sessions to match your winter driving skills. Costs start at $270 for a half-day of instruction. For more information contact the Bridgestone Winter Driving School at (800) 949-7543; winterdrive.com.

Steamboat Springs is closer to Denver (around 156 miles) than Aspen (approximately 200 miles). From Denver, the 3-hour drive follows I-70 west to the Silverthorne exit (exit 205). Head north on Highway 9 to Kremmling, and then west on US 40, which takes you over Rabbit Ears Pass and into Steamboat. Arrival by air is also possible; daily direct flights land at *Yampa Valley Regional Airport,* near Hayden, which is 22 miles from the ski area.

Fishing Steamboat

The area around Steamboat Springs offers numerous fishing opportunities. Three local shops—Straightline, Steamboat Flyfishers, and Bucking Rainbow—offer guided trips, float trips, gear, and advice on where to wet your line.

Anglers will love *Steamboat Lake State Park,* which allows fly, lure, and bait fishing for its cutthroat and rainbow trout year-round. Camping, waterskiing, swimming, and boating are available. Take US 40 west through Steamboat Springs for 2 miles, and then turn north on CR 129 and go another 26 miles. Cost is $6 for a vehicle day pass; $14–18 per night for camping. For information contact (970) 879-3922; parks .state.co.us.

To the south of town, *Stagecoach Reservoir* offers fishing, boating, waterskiing, camping, biking, and in the winter, cross-country skiing and ice fishing. Go 4 miles east of Steamboat on US 40, then south on CO 131 for 5 miles to Routt CR 14. Drive 7 miles south on CR 14 to the park entrance. A daily pass is $6; camping is $8–18 per night. For information contact (970) 736-2436; parks.state.co.us.

Fishing licenses may be purchased from most sporting goods and convenience stores in Colorado. A 1-day license costs $9 and a 5-day license costs $21 for residents. An annual fishing license costs $26 for residents and $56 for nonresidents.

TOP ANNUAL EVENTS IN THE NORTHWESTERN MOUNTAINS

JANUARY

Winter Carnival
Grand Lake
Jan or Feb
(970) 627-3402 or (800) 531-1019
grandlakechamber.com

ALL SUMMER

Rocky Mountain Repertory Theatre
Grand Lake
(970) 627-5087
rockymountainrep.com

Steamboat Springs Pro Rodeo Series
(970) 879-1818
steamboatprorodeo.com

JULY

Colorado Freeride Festival
Winter Park
(970) 726-1564
trestlebikepark.com/colorado-freeride-festival.html

Cowboy Roundup Days
Steamboat Springs
July 4 weekend
(970) 879-0880
steamboat-chamber.com

Rocky Grass Bluegrass Festival
Lyons
late July
(303) 823-0848 or (800) 624-2422
bluegrass.com/rockygrass

Rooftop Rodeo
Estes Park
mid-July
(970) 586-6104
rooftoprodeo.com

Winter Park Jazz Festival
(970) 726-4118
playwinterpark.com

SEPTEMBER

Longs Peak Scottish Irish Festival
weekend after Labor Day
(800) 90-ESTES or (970) 586-6308
scotfest.com

For information on year-round Steamboat Springs, contact Steamboat Springs Chamber Resort Association, PO Box 774408, Steamboat Springs 80477; (970) 879-0880; steamboat-chamber.com. For ski resort information, contact Steamboat Ski & Resort Corporation, 2305 Mt. Werner Circle, Steamboat 80487; (970) 879-6111 or (800) 922-2722; steamboat.com.

The ***Vista Verde Guest & Ski Ranch*** sits at the end of a rugged road, 30 miles north of Steamboat Springs. Another standout among Colorado dude ranches, it's among the best choices in the state for a family or couples vacation. More than 500 acres of ranch to explore, and thousands more in the surrounding Routt National Forest, mean riders, cyclists, and hikers have an almost unlimited choice of trails. Apart from horseback riding, this dude ranch offers supervised hiking, cycling, fly fishing, whitewater rafting, and even rock-climbing instruction. In winter, you can cross-country ski, backcountry ski, sled, snowshoe, and ride horses. Enthusiastic staff make sure there's never an idle moment, unless of course you prefer to read a book, soak in your private hot tub, or just find a quiet meadow and enjoy the secluded surroundings. For more information contact Vista Verde Guest & Ski Ranch, Inc., PO Box 770465, Steamboat Springs 80477; (800) 526-7433 or (970) 879-3858; vistaverde.com.

Continuing west on US 40 past Craig and Maybell, you will eventually reach the out-of-the-way ***Dinosaur National Monument,*** which straddles the Utah border. You get to it via the small town of Blue Mountain, or via Dinosaur, another small town.

A new visitor center has exhibits and displays describing the Jurassic environment and its inhabitants, and the auditorium shows films about the monument. Built over the world-famous ***Carnegie Dinosaur Quarry,*** the nearby, newly rebuilt ***Quarry Exhibit Hall*** provides public access to the 1,500 fossilized dinosaur bones that were deposited here around 149 million years ago. But it's the surrounding area, once a real-life Jurassic Park (without the Hollywood actors, of course), that is true dinosaur fossil bone country. Even without the visitor center, it's hard to ignore this magnificent landscape of giant sandstone cliffs, gray-green sage, juniper, and piñon pine. And the spectacular Yampa River is never far away. A variety of hikes and two self-guided driving tours take visitors deeper into this unusual park.

To access the Quarry Exhibit Hall, visitors must first stop at the Quarry Visitor Center located approximately a quarter of a mile from the exhibit hall. For more information contact Dinosaur National Monument, 4545 E. Hwy. 40, Dinosaur 81610; (435) 781-7700; nps.gov/dino. Entry to the monument is $10 per vehicle.

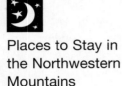

Places to Stay in the Northwestern Mountains

ESTES PARK

Ponderosa Lodge
1820 Fall River Rd.
(800) 628-0512
ponderosa-lodge.com
Inexpensive to Moderate
On the banks of the Fall River, quiet, individually decorated rooms, riverside picnic area with patio and grills.

Rocky Mountain Park Inn
101 S. Saint Vrain Ave.
(970) 586-2332 or
(800) 803-7837
rockymountainparkinn.com
Moderate
Located 3 blocks from downtown and the riverwalk with an indoor heated pool and whirlpool, free wireless Internet. Pet-friendly, 100 percent nonsmoking. Each room includes a $20 breakfast voucher.

The Stanley Hotel
333 E. Wonderview Ave.
(970) 586-3371 or
(800) 976-1377
stanleyhotel.com
Expensive
Elegant, historic, built and preserved in the tradition of the grand hotels from another era. Restaurant and cafe on-site, free wireless Internet, and a spectacular view across the valley.

GRANBY

Bar Lazy J Guest Ranch
447 CR 3, Parshall
(970) 725-3437
barlazyj.com
Expensive
All-inclusive dude ranch on the banks of the Colorado River offers meals, horseback riding, "Gold Medal" fly fishing, hayrides, mountain biking, campfires, kid's programs, and more.

C Lazy U Ranch
3640 CO 125
(970) 887-3344
clazyu.com
Expensive
All-inclusive dude ranch with gourmet meals, luxury lodging, horseback riding, fly fishing, hiking, whitewater river rafting and canoeing, in-house spa, and more.

Devil's Thumb Ranch
PO Box 750
3530 CR 83
Tabernash 80478
(970) 726-5632
devilsthumbranch.com
Expensive
Two good restaurants, a spa, some of America's best cross-country skiing in winter, and an abundance of mountain scenery make this an easy yet luxurious place to unwind.

Drowsy Water Ranch
PO Box 147
Granby, 80446-0147
(970) 725-3456
drowsywater.com
Expensive
All-inclusive dude ranch on 600 acres with horseback

riding, swimming, western dancing, campfires, children's programs, and more.

Inn at Silver Creek
62927 US 40
(970) 887-4080 or
(888) 878-3077
silvercreekgranby.com
Expensive
Hotel and condominium-style suites and rooms, indoor/outdoor heated swimming pool and hot tubs.

Snow Mountain Ranch at YMCA of the Rockies
1101 CR 53
(800) 777-9622
ymcarockies.org
Inexpensive to Moderate
Affordable lodging, many activities for families, excellent cross-country skiing in winter, hiking in summer. Pay-as-you-go buffet dining options.

Trail Riders Motel
215 E. Agate Ave.
(970) 887-3738
Moderate
Affordable lodging, clean and quiet, run by friendly management.

Vagabond Ranch Huts
(303) 242-5338 or josh@
vrhuts.com
vrhuts.com
Inexpensive
Drive into during summer, ski into during winter, comfortable, fully stocked log home and huts in the Never Summer Mountains north of Granby. Shuttles and snowmobile sleigh available. Quiet retreat deep in the mountains.

GRAND LAKE

Daven Haven Lodge Cabins

604 Marina Dr.
(970) 627-8144
davenhavenlodge.com
Moderate
Twelve comfortable, fully
equipped cabins with lodge
create a secluded feeling
even though located close
to Main Street.

Gateway Inn

200 W. Portal Rd.
(970) 627-2400
gatewayinn.com
Moderate
Spacious rooms, Internet
access.

The Inn at Grand Lake

1103 Grand Ave.
(800) 722-2585 or
(970) 627-9234
innatgrandlake.com
Inexpensive to Moderate
Historic inn on the main
boardwalk, convenient to
downtown dining, shop-
ping, and the lake.

The Rapids Lodge

209 Rapids Lane
(970) 627-3707
rapidslodge.com
Inexpensive to Moderate
Lodge rooms, suites, and
condominiums located just
off Main Street. The Rapids
Restaurant offers riverside
dining.

Western Riviera Motel and Cabins

419 Garfield St.
(970) 627-3580
westernriviera.com
Moderate
Lakeside accommodations,
free Internet.

Winding River Resort

Road 491 outside Grand
Lake
(970) 627-3215
windingriverresort.com
Moderate
Cozy, quiet lodge and
cabins on the North Fork of
the Colorado River. Camp-
ing and RV facilities also
available.

KREMMLING

Latigo Ranch

201 CR 1911
(970) 724-9008
latigotrails.com
Expensive
All-inclusive dude ranch
includes 3 meals, horse-
back riding and instruction,
overnight pack trip, rafting,
children's program, gratuity, and more.

Muddy Creek Cabins

3rd Street and Kinsey
(970) 724-9559
muddycreekcabins.com
Moderate
Ten cabins at the base of
the Kremmling Cliffs along
Muddy Creek. Kitchenettes
with minifridge, free wireless Internet; most cabins
have gas fireplace.

STEAMBOAT SPRINGS

Alpine Rose Bed & Breakfast

724 Grand St.
(970) 879-1528 or
(888) 879-1525
alpinerosesteamboat.com
Moderate
Outdoor hot tub, free wireless Internet, 5 blocks from
downtown.

Alpiner Lodge

420 Lincoln Ave.
(970) 879-1430 or
(800) 340-9169
alpinerlodgesteamboat.com
Inexpensive
Downtown location, pet
friendly, affordable, breakfast included.

Bear Claw Condominiums

2420 Ski Trail Lane
(970) 879-6100 or
(800) 232-7252
bear-claw.com
Moderate to Expensive
Located at the ski slope,
with heated swimming
pool, sauna, whirlpool, and
courtesy shuttle during ski
season.

Home Ranch

54880 CR 129, Clark
(970) 879-1780 or
(800) 688-2982
homeranch.com
Expensive
All-inclusive dude ranch
in an idyllic valley with
horseback riding, fly fishing, cross-country skiing,
multisport adventures, kid's
programs, and gourmet
cuisine. Summer vacations
require a 7-day stay.

Ptarmigan Inn

2304 Apres Ski Way
(970) 879-1730 or
(800) 538-7519
Inexpensive to Moderate
Formerly a Best Western,
good value, hot tub and
heated pool, ski slope
location.

Rabbit Ears Motel
210 Lincoln Ave.
(970) 879-1150 or
(800) 828-7702
rabbitearsmotel.com
Moderate
Family-owned since 1971,
affordable and pet-friendly
with free wireless Internet.

Scandinavian Lodge
2883 Burgess Creek Rd.
(800) 233-8102 or
(977) 475-6923
steamboatscandinavian
lodge.com
Moderate to Expensive
Lodge and condos, heated
pool, hot tub, walk or
short shuttle to ski slopes,
pet-friendly.

**Sheraton Steamboat
Resort**
2200 Village Inn Ct.
(970) 879-2220 or
(866) 716-8134
sheratonsteamboatresort
.com
Expensive
Steamboat's only ski-in/ski-
out resort.

Trailhead Lodge
1175 Bangtail Lane
(970) 879-9000
steamboatresorts.com
Expensive
Highly rated 86-suite lodge,
friendly and helpful staff,
hot tubs, free wireless
Internet, steps away from
the gondola to the ski area.

**Vista Verde Guest & Ski
Ranch**
3100 CR 64
PO Box 770465, 80477
(800) 526-7433 or
(970) 879-3858
vistaverde.com
Expensive
Luxury all-inclusive dude
ranch in a secluded setting
with gourmet meals, beer
and wine, horseback riding,
rock climbing, rafting, and
more all included.

WINTER PARK

Alpine Resort Properties
78884 US 40
(970) 726-5701 or
(877) 747-3029
alpineresortproperties.com
Moderate to Expensive
Choose from more than 40
different lodging options:
small condos, townhomes,
and ski-in/ski-out homes.

**Beaver Village
Condominiums**
PO Box 349, 80482
(800) 824-8438 or
(970) 726-8813
beavercondos.com
Moderate to Expensive
Affordable condos, cabins,
and townhomes in town
and next to the ski resort.

Destinations West
120 Zerex St., Fraser
(970) 726-8881 or
(800) 545-9378
mtnlodging.com
Moderate to Expensive
Wide variety of cabins,
homes, townhomes, and
duplexes, many with hot

tub, laundry facilities, and
garage. All guests have
access to clubhouse,
pool, hot tub, and laundry
facilities at Beaver Village
Condominiums.

**The Rocky Mountain
Chalet**
15 Country Road 72
(866) 467-8351
therockymountainchalet
.com
Moderate
Affordable boutique hotel
with a variety of room settings including suites and
open loft rooms, and a
large gourmet kitchen available to guests.

Viking Lodge
78966 US 40
(970) 281-2271 or
(800) 281-2271
skiwp.com
Inexpensive to Moderate
Cozy, eclectic, somewhat
dated but affordable ski
resort accommodations in
downtown Winter Park.

The Vintage Hotel
100 Winter Park Dr.
(800) 472-7017 or
(970) 726-8801
vintagehotel.com
Moderate to Expensive
Located at the entrance to
Winter Park Resort, pet-
friendly, with free wireless
Internet, an outdoor pool,
sauna, and hot tub.

Wild Horse Inn
1536 CR 83, Fraser
(970) 726-0456
wildhorseinncolorado.com
Moderate to Expensive
Handcrafted log lodge,
with free wireless Internet,
sauna, hot tub, breakfast
included, pet-friendly.

**Winter Park Central
Reservations**
(866) 239-3994
winterparkresort.com
Moderate to Expensive
Variety of condos, town-
homes, and hotel rooms at
Winter Park Resort.

Zephyr Mountain Lodge
201 Zephyr Way
(970) 726-8400 or
(877) 754-8400
zephyrmountainlodge.com
Moderate to Expensive
Luxury ski-in/ski-out condos at the base of Win-
ter Park ski slopes with
outdoor hot tubs, heated
underground parking, free
wireless Internet.

Places to Eat in the Northwestern Mountains

ESTES PARK

Mama Rose's
338 E. Elkhorn Ave.
(970) 586-3330
mamarosesrestaurant.com
Moderate to Expensive
Casually elegant Italian
cuisine with homemade
pastas and sauces, exten-
sive wine and regional beer
list.

**Nicky's Steakhouse on
the River**
1350 Fall River Rd. West
(970) 586-5376
nickysestespark.com
Moderate to Expensive
Prime rib, steaks, northern
Italian cuisine, seafood and
Colorado trout, located on
the Fall River.

**Twin Owls Steakhouse at
Black Canyon Inn**
800 MacGregor Ave.
(970) 586-9344
twinowls.net
Expensive
Casual fine dining in a
charming 1920s log cabin
serving organic, grass-fed
beef, game, seafood, poultry, pork.

FRASER

Elevation Pizza
551 Zerex Ave., Ste.
C-106, in the Fraser Valley
Center
(970) 726-0066
elevationpizzaco.com
Inexpensive
Freshly made dough,
homemade tomato sauce,
and a variety of familiar and
signature toppings.

Pearl Dragon II
45 Grand County Rd. 804
(970) 726-5252
Inexpensive to Moderate
Quality Chinese restaurant
popular with locals.

GRANBY

Grand River Coffee
100 E. Agate Ave.
(970) 887-0469
Inexpensive
Friendly walk-in or drive-
through coffee and
espresso place with affordable prices.

Ian's Mountain Bakery
358 E. Agate Ave.
(970) 887-1176
Inexpensive
Longtime local favorite
serving pizzas, sandwiches,
pastries, breakfast, and
lunch.

Java Lava
200 W. Agate Ave.
(970) 887-9810
Inexpensive
Good breakfast sand-
wiches and burritos, full
coffee and tea selection.

Longbranch Restaurant
185 E. Agate Ave.
(970) 887-2209
Inexpensive to Moderate
Authentic German cuisine
in a cozy alpine atmo-
sphere. Service can be
slow.

Maverick's Grille
15 E. Agate Ave.
(970) 887-9000
mavericksgrille.com
Moderate
Family dining with steaks,
chicken, burgers, and
game along with Colorado
microbrews and wine.

Seven Trails Grille at Granby Ranch
1000 Village Rd.
(970) 887-5200
granbyranch.com
Moderate
Seasonal menu of Italian-inspired fare with specialty salads, daily specials, and entertainment.

GRAND LAKE

Blue Water Bakery
928 Grand Ave.
(970) 627-5416
Inexpensive
Breakfast and lunch with good sandwiches, pastries, and coffee.

Fat Cat Cafe
916 Grand Ave.
(970) 627-0900
Inexpensive to Moderate
Friendly breakfast and lunch cafe run by an expat Brit. The weekend buffet brunch here is legendary, among the best in Colorado.

Grand Lake Brewery and Tap House
915 Grand Ave. and 9921 US 34
(970) 627-1711
Inexpensive to Moderate
Hearty pub fare and signature beers in a fun local setting.

Pancho and Lefty's
1120 Grand Ave.
(970) 627-8773
Moderate
Decent Mexican food and a lively atmosphere.

Rapids Lodge Restaurant
209 Rapids Lane
(970) 627-3707
rapidslodge.com
Moderate to Expensive
Sandwiches, small plate entrees, elk, prime rib, steak, trout, salmon, streamside dining for lunch and dinner.

Sagebrush Barbecue and Grill
1101 Grand Ave.
(970) 627-1404
sagebrushbbq.com
Moderate
Barbecue, salads and soups, steak, fish, and game. Occasional evening musical entertainment.

Terrace Inn
813 Grand Ave.
(970) 627-3000
grandlaketerraceinn.com
Expensive
Upscale bistro dining serving contemporary cuisine including salmon, steak, and roasted duck.

STEAMBOAT SPRINGS

Boathouse Pub
609 Yampa
(970) 879-4797
boathousepubsteamboat .com
Moderate
On the banks of the Yampa River with a deck overlooking the water. Diverse menu and live music some evenings.

Cafe Diva
1855 Ski Time Square Dr.
(970) 871-0508
cafediva.com
Expensive
Eclectic, creative kitchen with a seasonally changing menu offers a variety of nouveau cuisine and traditional entrees.

Cafe Sweet Pea
729 Yampa St.
(970) 879-1221
Inexpensive to Moderate
Healthy, creative menu including smoothies, sandwiches, subs, salads, and fish, meat, and poultry selections.

Creekside Cafe & Grill
131 11th St.
(970) 879-4925
creekside-cafe.com
Moderate
Hearty breakfast and lunch menu with popular entrees such as eggs Benedict and green chili.

La Montana
2500 Village Dr., #102
(970) 879-5800
lamontanasteamboat.com
Moderate to Expensive
Southwestern and Mexican cuisine, good margaritas.

Mazzola's Italian Restaurant
917 Lincoln Ave.
(970) 879-2405
mazzolas.com
Moderate
Casual Italian dining and a varied menu in a diner atmosphere.

Off The Beaten Path Book Store, Coffee House & Bakery Cafe
68 9th St.
(970) 879-6830 or
(800) 898-6830
steamboatbooks.com
Inexpensive
Great local bookstore and cafe serving salads, soups, smoothies, baked goods, and well-prepared coffees and teas. Wine served in the evenings.

Ore House at Pine Grove
1465 Pine Grove Rd.
(970) 879-1190 or
(800) 280-8310
orehouseatthepinegrove.com
Expensive
Steak, seafood, and game.

The Shack Cafe
740 Lincoln Ave.
(970) 879-9975
steamboat-dining.com
Inexpensive to Moderate
Popular with locals, breakfast and lunch at affordable prices.

Sweetwater Grill
811 Yampa St.
(970) 879-9500
thesweetwatergrill.com
Moderate
Affordable, family-friendly restaurant on the river serving healthy, natural, fresh food. Frequent live music in the lounge.

WINTER PARK

Carlos and Maria's
Cooper Creek Square
(970) 726-9674
Inexpensive to Moderate
Mexican and Tex-Mex cuisine.

Carvers Bakery Cafe
983 Vasquez Rd.
(970) 726-8202
carvers-wp.com
Inexpensive
Serving breakfast and lunch for over 30 years. Large menu and good food.

Deno's Mountain Bistro
78911 Hwy. 50
(970) 726-5332
denosmountainbistro.com
Moderate to Expensive
Fine dining with steaks, chops, seafood, chicken, pasta, pork, and an award-winning wine list.

Fontenots Fresh Seafood and Grill
78336 Hwy. 40
(970) 726-4021
fontenotswp.com
Moderate to Expensive
Seafood, steaks, and original dishes with a New Orleans Cajun accent.

Gasthaus Eichler
78786 US 40
(970) 726-5133
gasthauseichler.com/restaurant
Moderate to Expensive
Traditional European dining for lunch and dinner with an emphasis on German cuisine.

Hernando's Pizza and Pasta Pub
78199 Hwy. 40
(970) 726-5409
hernandospizzapub.com
Inexpensive to Moderate
Variety of pastas, pizzas, and Italian sub sandwiches.

Mountain Rose Cafe
78542 Hwy. 40
(970) 726-1374
mountainrosecafe.com
Inexpensive
Diverse breakfast and lunch menu of traditional and unique homemade entrees. Wine, beer, and full bar service.

Rise and Shine Cafe
78437 Hwy. 40
(970) 726-5530
Inexpensive to Moderate
Deservedly popular cafe for homemade baked goods, breakfast, and sandwiches.

Tabernash Tavern
72287 US 40
(970) 726-4430
tabernashtavern.com
Expensive
Creative, well-rounded international menu of appetizers, entrees, soups, salads, and desserts.

CENTRAL MOUNTAINS →

Beyond the Front Range

Most travelers in a hurry to cross Colorado take I-70, the wide, fairly straight thoroughfare that cuts east-west across the upper third of the state. Yes, it's the quick route between Grand Junction and Denver, and as far as highway scenery goes, it's probably one of the prettiest drives in the country. But those rushing through will miss out on the central mountains that contain some of the state's highlights.

Although the region deserves weeks of exploring to do it justice, many of the places of interest on the eastern side can be seen during a day trip from Denver. Each fall, when aspen begin changing and entire mountains turn shimmering gold, locals around the state hit the roads and trails to appreciate the fleeting magic of this brilliant display. Everyone has his or her favorite route, but one of the more popular ones is a loop trip: Denver, Idaho Springs, Silver Plume, Breckenridge, Fairplay, and back to Denver. The trip can be done in a day, or easily stretched into two or more days with stops along the way. But don't wait for September and October to take this drive; no matter when you go, it's

a diverse sampling of small mountain towns, western geography, and stunning scenery.

Beginning in Denver, head west on I-70 toward the mountain community of Idaho Springs (altitude 7,540 feet). Those wanting to explore the eastern side of the Mount Evans Wilderness can turn south here, climbing up into the high country above the tree line. Continue west past Georgetown, the historic mining town of beautifully preserved Victorian homes that's worth a visit on its own. This is also the access point to the western side of Mount Evans and dramatic Guanella Pass at over 10,000 feet.

As you continue along I-70, the mountains rise steeply and the valley turns narrow. Spruce, fir, and aspen blanket the mountains. Shortly before the Eisenhower Memorial Tunnel—weather permitting, of course—turn off on US 6 at the sign for *Loveland Pass* and head up to the *Continental Divide* (11,990 feet). The views are unbeatable from up here, so stop and take in the alpine panoramas, including meadows of wildflowers in the summer. Afterward, cruise down the mountain past Keystone ski resort to Dillon Reservoir.

The reservoir area is popular with boaters, anglers, cyclists, and the osprey that nest annually along the lake. Linger here and stretch your legs at the picnic and camping grounds on the south side of the lake beyond the marina

AUTHOR'S FAVORITES IN THE CENTRAL MOUNTAINS

Colorado National Monument
(970) 858-3617
nps.gov/colm

Georgetown
(303) 569-2840
historicgeorgetown.org

Glenwood Canyon
(970) 945-6589
glenwoodchamber.com

Gore Range/Pass
(970) 638-4516
fs.fed.us

Grand Valley Wineries
(970) 464-5867 or (303) 399-7586
grandvalleywine.com

Lake Dillon Recreational Area
(970) 468-5100
townofdillon.com

Mount Evans
(303) 567-3000
mtevans.com

Museum of Western Colorado
(970) 242-0971
museumofwesternco.com

Palisade Orchards Tours
(970) 464-7458
palisadecoc.com, palisadetourism.com

Rifle Falls State Park
(970) 625-1607
parks.state.co.us/parks/rifefalls

Safe Travel in Colorado

Colorado is renowned for its afternoon thunderstorms that proliferate during the summer months but are possible year-round. For this reason, outdoor activities — particularly those involving a long distance from safe shelter — should be done only with careful planning and attention to time. If you do find yourself caught up in a thunderstorm, take refuge in a car (with the windows up) or a substantial building — not a shallow cave or rock outcropping. If no safe shelter is available, seek a low-lying area or trench with shrubs or trees of similar stature. Avoid lone trees, open spaces, higher exposed ground, water, and contact with two different objects (such as rock and ground). Also maintain a 15-foot distance from others. Crouch low to the ground with both of your feet together and cover your ears. For more safety tips, visit the National Lightning Safety Institute's website at lightningsafety.com.

Flash flooding can pose a real danger in narrow canyons, even on days that begin with clear skies and sunny weather. Be sure to check weather reports for thunderstorm predictions and always have a backup plan.

Drinking water from lakes, rivers, and streams is not exactly the wilderness treat it once was. Unless you want to find out just how nasty a bout of giardiasis can be — think diarrhea, stomach cramps, and a visit to the doctor — avoid drinking water from lakes, streams, or rivers unless you purify it first. Bring adequate drinking water (minimum of 2 liters per person per day) and, for backcountry trips, a water purification filter, which can be purchased from most sporting goods stores. You can also purify water by boiling it for at least 20 minutes to kill all disease-causing organisms.

and away from I-70 or follow the signs to Frisco, staying on the road around the lake. After Frisco, swing left onto Highway 9 and head down the valley to Breckenridge.

This former mining community is in the middle of another bonanza. In 1859 it was gold. Now it's skiing, vacation homes, and mountain life. Stay the night to enjoy the restaurants and shops, or continue driving through thick forests past beaver ponds to ***Hoosier Pass.*** You're surrounded by 14,000-foot peaks— Quandary Peak, Mount Lincoln, Mount Sherman—as you drop down into Placer Valley, leaving the subalpine terrain and returning to forests and streams.

At the town of Fairplay, turn north on US 285 through South Park. Keep an eye out for antelope in the surrounding grasslands and approach the steep incline toward Kenosha Pass. Dropping into the valley along the South Platte River, the road twists through a valley of pastures and grazing horses before coming to the tiny settlement of ***Grant.*** From there you climb up Crow Hill, then pass communities whose names signify Colorado: Pine Junction, Deer Creek, Conifer, Indian Hills, Aspen Park. Then it's a quick drop out of the foothills back to Denver, where you began your circle tour 175 miles ago.

Idaho Springs is a short drive west on I-70 from Denver, and the area makes an interesting half-day trip. Stroll along the short main street and browse the shops, some of which are in historic buildings from the mining days. Take a walking tour with the Historical Society of Idaho Springs (303-567-4382) to learn more about the history and mining past of the area. Two museums, the *Heritage Museum* and Visitor Center (open daily; 2060 Miner St.; 303-567-4382; historicidahosprings.com) and the *Underhill Museum* (1416 Miner St.) offer interesting tidbits, artifacts, and memorabilia about the area's colorful past.

If you decide to spend the night, keep in mind that the local motels, while not fancy, are among the lowest-priced in Colorado. A quick drive down Colorado Boulevard will give you a dozen or so to choose from. If you reach the area around lunch- or dinnertime, Idaho Springs's *Beau Jo's Pizza* is well-known in Colorado for its varieties and its "pizza by the pound." You can build your own pizza here as well (1517 Miner St.; 303-567-4376; beaujos .com). Open Sun through Thurs from 11 a.m. to 9 p.m. and Fri and Sat from 11 a.m. to 9:30 p.m.

Another excellent dining choice is *Two Brothers Deli.* For fast, quality sandwiches, breakfast wraps and specials, soup, salad, smoothies, hot drinks, and free wireless, this is a smart stop before or after hiking, skiing, or exploring the town. Located at 1424 Miner St. (303-567-2439; twobrothersdeli.com). Open daily 6 a.m. to 8 p.m., Fri through Sun until 9 p.m.

The gold rush may be long over, but at the *Phoenix Gold Mine,* located at the west end of Idaho Springs, anyone can try a hand at what brought thousands of men to Colorado back in the 1800s . . . gold panning!

This is the only working gold mine in Colorado that is open to the public. Take a tour guided by actual miners. Better yet, dig your own samples—you

Little-Known Facts about Idaho Springs

- Some of Colorado's earliest gold strikes took place here in 1859.

- The Ute Indians were the first to discover and use its famous hot springs.

- When it was completed after 17 years in 1915, Argo Tunnel was the world's longest mining tunnel. The 5-mile-long tunnel once ran all the way to Central City, another gold rush town. Unfortunately, only a portion of the tunnel remains, and it is not open to the public.

- The highway that runs to the summit of Mount Evans from Idaho Springs is the highest paved driving road in North America.

even get to keep what you find. Gold panning costs $8 per person, which is included in the price if you take a tour. Walking tours with panning cost $5 for children under 12, $15 for adults. Tours cost only $10. Open from 10 a.m. to 5 p.m. daily May to Oct, 10 a.m. to 4 p.m. Nov to Apr. *NOTE:* The temperature in the mine is only 42–54°F, so dress accordingly.

To get to the Phoenix Gold Mine, take I-70 eastbound to exit 239, and then take Stanley Road southwest to Trail Creek Road. For more information call (303) 567-0422 or write PO Box 3236, Idaho Springs 80452; phoenixgold mine.com.

Most of Colorado's highest places can only be attained by a long, arduous hike. The rewards are worth the effort: sweeping views of the Rockies for miles in all directions, alpine wildflowers, and the shrill whistle of marmots and pikas. But there are several places around the state where you can enjoy these grand views with little more effort than steady pressure on the gas pedal and both hands on the steering wheel.

The road to 14,264-foot-high **Mount Evans** is the highest paved auto road in the US. Starting at 8,700 feet in Idaho Springs, it winds steadily upward, rising through spruce and pine forests. As you go higher, the views only get better. You will pass through several ecological zones, an ancient bristlecone pine forest, and alpine lakes before reaching the summit. Keep an eye out for mountain goats and bighorn sheep that are often seen near the summit. And be prepared for cold weather at the top. It can be 90°F in Denver and 40°F on top of the mountain. The vista from the viewing platform is one of Colorado's premier scenic overlooks.

The road to the top of Mount Evans usually opens in May and stays open until the first significant snowfall of the year—meaning that if you want to tackle the peak in winter, you'll need to plan accordingly by packing snowshoes or cross-country skis and having the necessary wilderness skills to do so safely.

Once the road has been opened for the season, it is accessible 24 hours a day. Cost is $10 for a 3-day vehicle pass, on sale at the entrance station. There is also a mechanical collection station that accepts cash ($1, $5, $10 bills) and credit cards; it will issue you a valid pass.

Any sunny summer day will do to make your drive up to the summit, but weekdays are preferable if you want to avoid the crowds. In addition, visiting very early or very late in the day increases your chances of seeing the many animals that call Mount Evans home.

If you're starting your journey in Denver, you can choose to approach the mountain via Bergen Park and return via Idaho Springs, or vice versa. Expect to see stunning Colorado scenery along the way, including large, fertile meadows,

TOP ANNUAL EVENTS IN THE CENTRAL MOUNTAINS

APRIL

Fruita Fat Tire Festival
late Apr
(970) 858-3894 or (970) 858-4881
fruitamountainbike.com

JUNE

Aspen Music Festival
June through Aug
(970) 925-3254
aspenmusicfestival.com

Breckenridge Music Festival
(970) 453-9142 or (800) 753-9142
breckenridgemusicfestival.com

Festival of Film
Breckenridge
(970) 453-6200
breckfilmfest.com

Grand Junction Farmers' Market Festival
Thurs June through Sept
(970) 245-9697
visitgrandjunction.com

Strawberry Days
Glenwood Springs
mid-June
(970) 945-6589
strawberrydaysfestival.com

AUGUST

Peach Festival
Palisade
mid-Aug
(970) 464-7458
palisadepeachfest.com

dense lodgepole pine forests, aspen trees, ponderosa pine, Douglas fir, and thick bushes of wild raspberries in season, as well as the occasional chipmunk or squirrel.

Placid *Echo Lake* makes for a nice stopping point en route to the summit. Park and stretch your legs, and perhaps enjoy a picnic lunch, do some fishing, or join hikers on one of several trails heading into the woods. If you're visiting after Thanksgiving, expect to see a vast frozen expanse—the lake often freezes completely, and you can glide across it on cross-country skis, reaching numerous trails that yield great views. But even in summer it gets cool up here, so dress warmly and bring extra layers. Theoretically, for every 1,000 feet of elevation gain in the Rockies, you can compare your journey to traveling 200 miles north. Of course, this means you get to experience the cooler air in each zone on the way up, not to mention the shifting vegetation.

Above Echo Lake, a beautiful and complex world lies at your feet. Follow trails through alpine tundra, stooping to study the small grasses, sedges, herbs, and the almost microscopic plants with their tiny flowers. These plants grow close to the ground in order to withstand the harsh conditions at this altitude.

At one point on the way up you will see posted signs for the bristlecone forest hunkered on both sides of the road. If you take a close look at the twisted forms of these ancient trees, you can read the story of their struggle for survival in this unforgiving setting. Each dwarfed bristlecone and leaning Douglas fir in this area shows the signs of withstanding blizzards and summer storms as well as coping with blazing sunlight followed by rains. This wild weather destroys most exposed buds and conifer seeds, limiting the trees' reproduction. Some trees are bent and twisted from the relentless wind, while others are bleached from the sun or blackened and split by lightning strikes. At timberline, the already small array of trees becomes even sparser, with only single, isolated soldiers standing to face the elements.

Above timberline, in Colorado's alpine life zone, the fauna changes, too. Marmots often show themselves sunning on warm boulders. Well-camouflaged ptarmigan can be spotted browsing among the grasses or leading their brood of chicks across the tundra. Tiny pikas scurry between rocks as they gather grasses for the long winter. Mountain goats are frequently seen up here, and once in a while you'll spot a bighorn sheep. Don't feed any animals; they stay much healthier with a natural diet.

Mount Evans's upper reaches are also dotted with lakes. At 11,700 feet, you'll spot Lincoln Lake; it's 800 feet below the highway. Then at 12,830 feet, Summit Lake awaits, complete with a short trail overlooking the picturesque Chicago Lakes, some 1,400 feet below. The Forest Service warns parents not to let their children run around in this area due to the sudden drop-offs—the highway has few guardrails.

Finally, complete the journey by pulling into the parking lot at 14,130 feet. Get out of your car and hike that last 134-foot gain in altitude to the summit via a quarter-mile hike along a trail. Catch your breath—the air is much thinner up here than it is on the plains, so visitors from the flatlands should walk slowly and take in the scenery. And if the thin air doesn't take away your breath, the views surely will.

Start your tour to Mount Evans on I-70. Take exit 240 in Idaho Springs onto the Mount Evans Highway (Highway 103). After Echo Lake, pay your fee and head onto Highway 5, which will take you to the summit. For a change of pace on the way back, continue west along Highway 103 to Bergen Park, and then take Highway 74 and I-70 to Denver. The distances are moderate—it's only 28 miles from Idaho Springs to the summit of Mount Evans. For more information call the Clear Creek Ranger Station at (303) 567-3000 or write to the CCRD Visitor Information Center, PO Box 3307, Idaho Springs 80452; mountevans.com.

Idaho Springs is home to the ***Edgar Experimental Mine,*** where students and faculty from the Golden-based Colorado School of Mines try their hands

Loveland in Wintertime—or All Year Long

Loveland Ski Area—which is nowhere near the city by the same name—has always been a favorite ski spot for Denverites. And for good reason. A big plus is Loveland's proximity—just 55 miles from Denver via I-70. There are no passes to cross and no Eisenhower Tunnels, either (which Loveland publicists call "a big bore").

Snowboarding is big here, and the ski area has excellent instructors. If you've been a skier your whole life, try snowboarding. It's definitely a different experience from ski-ing, and worth it to discover the distinction. Many Colorado skiers start snowboard-ing and never return to skiing.

The ski center shuts down in late spring when the snow melts, and since Loveland Ski Area does not have hotels or offer condominiums, that's it for winter sports. In summer the slopes fill up with mountain flowers and hikers out to enjoy the high country.

To arrange snowboarding lessons or for more information contact Loveland Ski Area, PO Box 899, Georgetown 80444; (303) 569-3203 or (800) 736-3754; skiloveland .com. Loveland Ski Area is open from Nov through Apr; lift ticket prices run from $22 to $59 depending on your age and the season.

at traditional mining methods and put to use the most recent technological advances. Open to the public for tours throughout the year from Mon through Fri, 8 a.m. to 4 p.m. Admission is $10 for adults, $6 for seniors, and $6 for children ages 6 to 16. To reserve a tour: call ahead at (303) 567-2911; contact rkcooper@mines.edu or mining.mines.edu/Mining-Edgar-Mine; or write to 365 8th Ave., PO Box 1184, Idaho Springs 80452.

In autumn the wind whistles through the well-kept streets of **Georgetown,** rattling the windows of its many Victorian houses. The winter snows pile up high here, and spring is slow to come at an elevation of 8,500 feet. The moun-tains rise so steeply on all four sides of Georgetown that even the summers are cool; the sun shines on the town for only a few hours a day.

Yet, this community 45 miles west of Denver has more ambience, more sightseeing, and more genuine concern for preserving its past than many other Colorado cities. The city officials have spent substantial sums to rebuild and preserve the pink-brick houses, the old-time saloons, and the museums that conjure up the 19th century of gold and silver riches. The antiques shops, silversmiths, and weavers are among the best in the state. The craft shops are unique and worth browsing, and often offer better deals than those of Vail, Aspen, and other ski resorts to the west.

Unlike Vail, which rose from a cow pasture, Georgetown is a historic community. And residents are proud of it. On a clear spring day in 1859, two prospecting brothers, George and David Griffith, struggled their way up Clear Creek searching for minerals. Unsuccessful at the other mining camps in Colorado, the two prospectors reached out for new, untried land, and this time they had luck—they found gold.

After their discovery the Griffith brothers did a highly unusual thing for gold or silver seekers of the time—instead of just digging up the mountain and leaving with their wealth, they brought their entire family out from Kentucky to live permanently in their valley. The tiny settlement they founded became known as George's Town, and although no more significant strikes were made, it grew steadily for five years.

Then in 1864 assays showed an extremely high silver content. The boom was on. Over the next 30 years, the mines in and around the town produced more than $200 million worth of silver. The town became known as the Silver Queen of the Mountains—and in 1868 it was renamed Georgetown.

By 1880 some 10,000 people made the city their home. Fortunes and reputations flourished. Elaborate mansions were built. Hotels served fine cuisine in gilt rooms with elegant furniture. An opera house brought Broadway productions and favorite classical operas to the wealthy.

All this came to an abrupt end when the silver panic of 1893 hit, with silver prices dropping to almost nothing. Almost overnight, mines, mills, and livelihoods vanished. The town became a ghost of its past glory.

Georgetown languished this way for more than six decades. As more people moved to the state, tourism followed, and interstate highways transported millions of travelers to the mountains. People discovered the beautiful old Victorian homes and set about restoring them to their former grace. Unlike other Colorado mining towns, Georgetown was never totally destroyed by fire, so today it has more than 200 carefully preserved historic buildings.

Luckily for Georgetown, forward-thinking residents and town officials passed a historic preservation ordinance many years ago. The local historical society actively watches over its Victorian treasures to ensure they will be around for many years. One of Georgetown's landmarks is the French-style **Hotel de Paris Museum,** full of Tiffany fixtures, lace curtains, and hand-carved furniture. Open from Memorial Day through Labor Day 10 a.m. to 4:30

trivia

Two historic Georgetown homes, the Bowman-White House and the Hamill House, exemplify the city's Victorian style. Learn more at historicgeorgetown.org.

p.m., and on weekends from Sept to Dec noon to 4 p.m. Adults are $5, seniors and students $3. Contact (303) 569-2311; hoteldeparismuseum.org.

Georgetown is a perfect town for parking and wandering. Walk in any direction and discover dozens of well-preserved homes well over a century old. The small business district has a mix of antiques shops, art galleries, a bookstore, and several restaurants. During the first two December weekends, a well-known Christmas market with small booths and outdoor stalls is a popular place for holiday shopping.

Georgetown is a good base for travelers who plan to explore the **Continental Divide** in summer or ski country in winter. It's also the best starting point for the spectacular drive to 11,669-foot **Guanella Pass.** Running through forests of aspen, fir, and spruce at lower elevations, the road climbs up a glaciated valley past meadows and cascading creeks. Camping, hiking, fishing, fall aspen foliage, and winter cross-country skiing and snowshoeing are some of the attractions. At the pass, tundra and willow thickets replace the forest, and in summer tiny wildflowers add color to the landscape. Look for ptarmigan in all seasons, white in winter and mottled brown in summer.

trivia

A mysterious Frenchman named Louis Dupuy originally ran the Hotel de Paris; some Georgetown people say he left a large family in France.

Mount Bierstadt, one of Colorado's "fourteeners," is the large mountain looming to the east. The trail to the summit starts from the parking lot. Other trails lead hikers across the tundra. Passenger cars can easily traverse the well-graded road, but it will be too narrow in places for RVs. Remember to bring warm clothes; the weather at the pass is often much colder than in Georgetown. For more information, visit georgetowncolorado.com/guanella.htm.

Georgetown is about an hour west of Denver via I-70. For information about Georgetown, contact the Downtown Georgetown Community Center, 613 6th St., PO Box 444, Georgetown 80444; (303) 569-2888 or (800) 472-8230; historicgeorgetown.org.

Want to experience a bit of the Colorado West? Then plan a vacation at one of Colorado's dude ranches. Imagine riding horseback with family and friends through an aspen grove to a sunny meadow full of wildflowers. Along the way you pass weathered settler's cabins with caved-in roofs and sagging door frames, the wood bleached and cracked by a century in the sun. The trail leads across brooks, through willow thickets, and then slowly down a steep, rocky slope. The riders move with care, savoring the moment as they hang on firmly. A light warm breeze blows through the pines. Alone with their

Georgetown Fishing

The lakes in this area are often crowded during the summer, with the exception of *Silver Dollar Lake.* A somewhat steep, 3-mile round-trip trail leads to the lake, which yields good catches and offers peace and quiet. From Georgetown, head 8.5 miles south on Guanella Pass Road. Turn right at the SILVER DOLLAR LAKE sign.

thoughts, far away from crowds and freeways, they find rhythm in the creak of the leather saddles and the clicking of the hooves. Arriving at a sunny forest clearing, everyone finds a log to sit on. Coffee steams. The cowboys fry up eggs and sausage. It's morning in the Rockies.

Ask dude ranch visitors what's so special about staying in one of these places and they'll mention the informality, the quiet seclusion, the good food, and the friendliness of the place. With an average of 20 to 80 guests, it's easy to become acquainted with the staff and guests. The mood is calm and relaxed. But there's also plenty to do: horseback riding, fishing, hiking, mountain biking, and just relaxing with a good book are a few of the many options. You can stay as busy as you like, or you can do nothing at all. Either way, you'll be well taken care of.

The names say a lot: C Lazy U Ranch, Tumbling River Ranch, Drowsy Water Ranch, Peaceful Valley Ranch. They are just a few of the many endearing places set in romantic, isolated Colorado locations. Some of them still breed cattle or horses. A Colorado dude-ranch vacation is one of the most satisfying, genuine holidays available today. The air is clean, days are warm, evenings cool, and the mountain scenery is absolutely spectacular. Most dude ranches are family-oriented, with separate programs especially for kids.

Accommodations range from rustic to deluxe. Colorado has some 40 dude ranches, generally located in the scenic mountain regions. These are small, self-contained worlds that feel far from city life. There are lots of horse trails for novices, guided breakfast rides, ghost-town trips, and even extended rides into the wilderness. Some dude ranches arrange river-rafting trips, or you can rent a jeep. Archery, boating, rock climbing, fishing, and even golf are possibilities. And there are usually hot tubs and plenty of soft lounge chairs.

How much does a dude-ranch vacation cost? Less than you'd expect. A week at an average guest ranch costs considerably less than a Caribbean cruise for the family. Everything is included: meals, activities, and accommodations.

The Peaceful Valley Ranch near Lyons is known for its summer evening entertainment including square-dancing. This ranch has a special teen program, trips to ghost towns, and even English riding instruction. Lyons is easy to reach from Denver via the Boulder Turnpike; then continue on Highway 7 and Highway 72. For more information contact the ranch at 475 Peaceful Valley Rd., Lyons 80540; (303) 747-2881 or (800) 955-6343; peacefulvalley.com. Open year-round.

The *Tumbling River Ranch* in Grant seems hewn out of native rock and local wood. At night you can hear the tumbling river outside your window. The ranch stands at 9,200 feet, and most evenings the stars shine brighter than in any city sky. The ranch features not only trail riding but also a handsome outdoor heated pool. The food is excellent, and there are enough activities to keep you busy all summer.

Grant is a short trip southwest from Denver via US 285. For more information contact Tumbling River Ranch, PO Box 30, Grant 80448; (303) 838-5981 or (800) 654-8770; tumblingriver.com. Open from June 1 through September 30.

To explore the many dude ranch choices across the state, contact the Colorado Dude and Guest Ranch Association, PO Box D, Shawnee, 80425; (866) 942-3472; coloradoranch.com.

Driving east on Highway 70, after you've climbed out of steep Glenwood Canyon and dropped down from Vail Pass into *Summit County,* you'll see a large lake on your right. If you're coming west from Denver, you'll cross the Continental Divide at 11,158 feet and after a quick drop into Summit County, the road straightens out, and there it is—*Lake Dillon.*

No matter which direction you're coming from, this lake is hard to miss. With its 26-mile shoreline, the water on a summer day is often a deep blue, dotted by white sails, and alive with small motorboats, canoes, and kayaks skimming the surface. Anglers fish from shore for rainbow trout. Osprey nest here each year. Bike paths run the length of the lake, continuing all the way to Breckenridge 10 miles away.

Mountains surrounding the lake are the domain of climbers, hikers, and horseback riders. Streams are everywhere: Blue River, Snake River, Ten Mile Creek. Almost all the water spills into the reservoir, flowing toward Denver, through the unseen Roberts Tunnel, not far from *Dillon.* Highway traffic along I-70 moves fast along the north side of the lake, and if you're in a hurry, you may miss the sign for Dillon and continue toward Denver, 78 miles to the east.

Once you pull off the highway and drive into town, you leave the road noise behind. Dillon is a convenient base for exploring Lake Dillon and the surrounding mountains, and the ski destinations of Breckenridge, Copper, and Keystone are a short drive away. But unlike other Colorado mountain towns, there are no old buildings here. No dilapidated miner's cabins, no Victorian houses. The hotels, condos, restaurants, sports stores, and boutiques are all newer structures. The lakeside setting seems perfect for an early settlement, but oddly, there is no trace of the historical past here.

Dillon did not always sit at the edge of the lake. In fact, until the 1960s, there was no Lake Dillon. The story of Dillon is one of development, water rights, and changing times.

The old town, originally situated to the east, was named after an early prospector. The area saw off-and-on gold mining, a little railroading, lumber trading, and much ranching. The first post office opened here in 1883. With the advent of the car came garages and service stations. Roads improved, and more tourists showed up "to breathe the exhilarating Rocky Mountain air," as one advertisement put it. A longtime resident remembers the Dillon of the 1930s: "Ranchers picked up their mail here," he says, "and it was a place for a beer on Saturday night."

trivia

In the early 1960s, the original town of Dillon—the whole town!— was moved in order to make way for the Lake Dillon reservoir.

But on the other side of the mountains, Denver was growing, and it desperately needed more water. All through the forties and early fifties, the Denver Water Department bought up lands and ranches with water rights. Then, in 1955, Dillon residents were told about the coming storage reservoir. It would flood their town.

After many meetings and complex legal work, the machinery ground into high gear. Dillon had to move. Some people left for warmer climates; others settled in nearby villages. But the citizens decided to create a new Dillon on a hill of pine and evergreen. Here was a chance for a model town.

Down in the valley the old community was dismantled stick by stick. Because the water supply had to be pure, all buildings had to go. Some were cut in half and hauled elsewhere by trucks. Others had to be burned down. The Water Board uprooted telephone lines, removed old pipes, buried the last rusty tin cans. Even the peaceful graveyard, with its rococo stones and metal crosses, had to be shifted to higher ground. The school was moved, and the church found a new home in the reborn Dillon.

Slowly the dam rose until it stood 231 feet high at some points and was capable of backing up 257,000 acre-feet of water. The Harold Roberts Tunnel, more than 23 miles long and costing $50 million, was completed to connect the reservoir with rivers flowing into Denver. Water from thawing snows and the mountain streams steadily accumulated in the reservoir behind the dam.

One August day, the waters rushed over the top and through the "glory hole" spillway into the outlet tunnel. By then nothing was left of the old Dillon town site. The roads that led to it now lay under about 150 feet of water. The old Dillon was no more.

Among the trees to the west stands the new Dillon. The town officials and the city planners conceived it well. Buildings can be no higher than 30 feet, providing unobstructed views of the lake. Dillon's signs are subdued, modest, and inviting. There is little neon. Only natural materials—the stone and wood of the Rockies, plus glass—are permitted for the houses. The wood may be stained but not painted. The lots and homes are spread out. And timber is cut sparingly, for conservation's sake.

Development continues in Dillon and around the 3,300-acre lake. New shopping areas and businesses appear regularly. The city is currently dealing with the pine beetle infestation that is affecting the entire western US, and many trees are being removed to control the spread of the beetles. Despite the uninvited guests in the surrounding forest, the town and the lakefront remain an enjoyable place to rent a canoe, ride a bike, or walk around and enjoy the local shops and eateries.

The **Dillon Marina** hosts a number of fun community events, including regattas throughout the summer. For details call (970) 468-5100; visit dillon marina.com; or write PO Box 1825, Dillon 80435; townofdillon.com. Free Friday night concerts take place throughout the summer at the Lake Dillon Amphitheatre; call (970) 262-3400 for details. Each Friday the Farmer's Market with free entertainment takes place on Buffalo Street downtown. For more information about events and attractions in Dillon during your stay, call (970) 468-2403; visit townofdillon.com; or write Town Office, 275 Lake Dillon Dr., Dillon 80435.

Denver is a mere 70 minutes from Lake Dillon thanks to the time-saving **Eisenhower Tunnel,** which is a story in its own right.

For a hundred years, since the days when railroads were first reaching across the continent, men had worked and dreamed of tunneling through the Continental Divide here at its narrowest point. "Nearly impossible!" a geologist said when a Colorado financier first suggested a long tunnel through the Continental Divide during the 1930s.

"Unpredictable rock!" other geologists warned in 1941. The drilling of a pilot bore already gave a clue to the unstable rock strata of this area. Steel linings buckled in the exploratory shaft. But plans were drawn, and the work began in 1968. For five years tunnel builders, sometimes as many as 1,100 men at a time, battled the mountain some 58 miles west of Denver. Lack of money, politics, explosions, fires, and, most of all, geological problems all thwarted the builders. A tunnel engineer later summed it up better than anyone else.

"We were going by the book," he said. "But the damned mountain couldn't read!"

Fortunately, the 8,941-foot-long Eisenhower Tunnel was eventually drilled despite the obstacles. The tunnel makes travel possible in all seasons, and saves the motorist 10 miles over the twisting and turning highway that crosses Loveland Pass. Since the tunnel opened in 1973, drivers need no longer expose themselves to the fierce storms and howling winds of the pass. No more jackknifed trucks, stranded cars, or vehicles swept off the highway ledges by avalanches, rock slides, or icy curves taken too fast. One of North America's best-known mountain passes was finally tamed.

> ## trivia
>
> The utility bill for the Eisenhower Tunnel runs about $80,000 a month—each tunnel (one for eastbound and one for westbound traffic) has 2,000 light fixtures, and each light fixture contains an 8-foot bulb!

The Eisenhower Tunnel is 58 miles west of Denver via I-70. Visit colorado dot.info/travel/eisenhower-tunnel for more information.

Year-Round Vacation Areas

Breckenridge is the perfect Colorado frontier town—one of the few that was rebuilt and is now well preserved and thriving.

In 1859, a group of 14 prospectors discovered gold in the Breckenridge area. A town was quickly built by miners who were hopeful that they would strike it rich. One such miner, Tom Groves, walked away a big winner when he discovered "Tom's Baby," a 136-ounce gold nugget. But, like all areas rich in minerals, the mines eventually played out. Breckenridge citizens wouldn't give up, and they found another moneymaker when Summit County's first ski area opened in 1961.

Breckenridge has a western charm that especially delights European visitors. Here are the earmarks of the old Gold Rush West: fairy-tale Victorian houses with columns, crenellations, and gingerbread trim; the clapboard structures of the miners, beautifully repainted; and store windows filled with antiques. Travelers from the Midwest and East feel the same way; they're walking through a colorful piece of American history. The ski slopes are still named for the old mines in the area: Gold King, Wellington, Bonanza,

> ## trivia
>
> Gold was first panned in Breckenridge's Blue River in 1859.

Cashier, Silverthorn—these were the monikers that excited the gold hunters more than a century ago.

Breckenridge is actually one of Colorado's oldest towns. In August 1859 the first gold seekers came streaming across the Continental Divide to pan gold in the waters of the Blue River. More than $30 million in gold was taken out of the district during its heyday. Later, a silver lode started a second boom. By 1861 some 5,000 people lived in and around Breckenridge. Summit County then extended as far as the Utah line and was one of 17 counties composing the Colorado Territory. It has since been whittled down to 600 square miles. Then, as now, Breckenridge was the county seat. As with other mountain mining towns in Colorado, the precious minerals ran out and mining came to a halt. In the early 1960s, Breckenridge became a year-round resort, at the same time maintaining its century-old status as a former mining community. Development may have brought condos and shopping centers, but it hasn't destroyed the town's historical district. Take a walk along the 6-block stretch of Main Street through the old town for a glimpse back in time. Old storefronts and original brick and wood buildings continue to serve a purpose, housing restaurants, shops, and boutiques.

But there's more. Walk east a couple of blocks from Main Street on Lincoln or Washington or Adams Avenues, and wander the grid of quiet backstreets. Many dozens of old homes sit back among the trees, lovingly restored reminders of the glory mining days of old Breckenridge. Grassy yards, flower gardens, and hummingbirds thrive, and after strolling through this lovely area you may just be tempted to drop by a real estate office or two.

Summer and fall are busy seasons in Breckenridge. Coloradans and out-of-state visitors come here to stay for a few days, renting rooms in nearby condos and lodges. This is a great base for exploring the area south toward Hoosier Pass and beyond to Fairplay. The Blue River runs through town, and several riverfront plaza areas are perfect for sitting under a tree and people-watching. Stop by *Clint's Bakery and Coffee House* at 131 S. Main St. for excellent drinks,

Breckenridge Horseback Riding

Tired of walking? *Breckenridge Stables* offers 90-minute rides along the Breckenridge Trail, which passes some of Colorado's finest scenery. Reserve all rides at least one day in advance. Ride prices are $60 for 90 minutes, with children age 3 or younger paying $25 and doubling up with an adult. Breakfast and dinner rides and lessons are also available. Call (970) 453-4438 or write PO Box 6686, Breckenridge 80454; breckstables.com.

baked goods, breakfast and lunch items. Or drop by **Crepes A La Cart,** the outdoor crepes stand at 307 S. Main St. They open at 11 a.m. offering a wide variety of savory lunch and dinner crepes, and decadent dessert crepes. There's often a line; meet other travelers and swap stories until your crepe arrives.

Breckenridge in winter is another Colorado favorite. More than 2,300 acres of skiable terrain on 155 trails offer something for every ski level. Snowboarding, snowshoeing, tobogganing, and nearby ice fishing are all part of the cold-weather scene here. Contact the Breckenridge Ski Resort, 1599-C Summit CR 3; (970) 453-5000 or (800) 789-7669; breckenridge.com.

trivia

Breckenridge features several ghost towns worth checking out: Lincoln City, Swandyke, Dyersville, and others.

Breckenridge is located 88 miles west of Denver via I-70 and Highway 9. For more information contact the Breckenridge Resort Chamber (311 Ski Hill Rd., 80424) at (970) 453-2918 or (888) 251-2417; gobreck.com.

Mining—an important part of Colorado's past—is alive and well and can be glimpsed at the **Country Boy Mine,** 2 miles from downtown Breckenridge. This working mine is one of the few that offers travelers a journey into some of the same places that hard-rock miners went more than 100 years ago when the mine was established. At the Country Boy Mine you can don a hard hat and venture 1,000 feet underground, seeing, feeling, and hearing what actual miners experienced. After the tour you can try your hand at gold panning in Eureka Creek or take a hayride past the authentic mine buildings. Sleigh rides are offered in winter. In Breckenridge turn left/east on Wellington Road and follow it to a final fork. Turn right, and then drive a mile east on French Gulch Road. Admission costs $20.95 for anyone 13 and older, $14.95 for children 4 to 12, children 3 and younger free. Open year-round. Call (970) 453-4405 for hours or visit countryboymine.com.

Vail is probably best known as a world-class ski destination, and that vibe is strong even in summer when the snow retreats to the high peaks. Where else but in Colorado would you expect to find an extensive ski museum? Founded in 1976, the **Colorado Ski and Snowboard Museum** in **Vail** reaches back to the old miners of the 19th century who raced in the Rockies surrounding their camps, competing against one another on long wooden boards while holding a long staff in one fist for braking. In the museum are photos and artifacts of skiing clergymen like Father John Lewis Dyer, who brought the gospel to Colorado's historic gold towns, as well as the stories of sheepherders and trappers who braved the snows in the 19th century on 9-foot enormous

They Almost Blew It: Vail History

Vail founders never anticipated a success of such magnitude. Although thousands of mountain troopers and skiers passed through the valley during the 1940s and 1950s, none of them saw the potential of Vail Mountain, since the best slopes were out of sight high above the highway. But Peter Seibert, an ex–Tenth Mountain man and a ski racer, knew a lot about ski areas, and he spent two years hiking, climbing, and skiing all over the Rockies to look for the ideal resort location. One day in 1957, he scaled the Vail Summit with a local prospector who lived in the valley. Upon seeing the bowls and glades and open slopes, Seibert knew he'd found the ideal site. Seibert and some friends invested their savings. But more money was needed.

Unfortunately, at that time Denver's conservative bankers wouldn't gamble on a large new ski area, with Aspen already doing well. All the same, Seibert kept looking for partners. He bought a snowcat and brought visitors to his mountain. He showed films of his powder bowls all over the country, and invited prospective investors to ski with him. Eventually he got lucky. A Michigan oilman-skier recognized the potential and found other wealthy backers who spread Seibert's gospel. They raised $5 million, formed Vail Associates, and successfully tapped the Small Business Administration and the no-longer-reluctant Denver bankers. And they sold real estate to precisely the people who had shaken their heads the hardest.

During the summer of 1962, the bulldozers started to dig in. An excellent Milwaukee architect had drawn up the plans and now supervised the frantic building activity. When the dust settled, there stood the first lodges, apartments, malls, homes, and lifts of Vail, Colorado.

wooden contraptions with crude leather straps holding their boots. Mementos of the first long-ago jumpers will fascinate viewers; photos show them taking off from knolls or flying through the air, equipment sometimes falling off high above ground. Visitors will learn much about the development of skis, bindings, boots, poles, even the first ski suits, as well as the women's fashions of earlier days when ladies skied in ankle-length black skirts.

The history of Colorado's famous Tenth Mountain Division is well illustrated; an entire room is devoted to the Mountain Troopers and their initial camps and wartime exploits. A viewing area shows ski videos. Exhibits on avalanche control, up-to-date ski racing, and the history of Vail—it's all here in the center of town. Admission is free. Open daily from 10 a.m. to 6 p.m. Colorado Ski and Snowboard Museum, 231 S. Frontage Rd. East, PO Box 1976, Vail 81657; (970) 476-1876; skimuseum.net. Winter activities range far beyond skiing and snowboarding. Inflatable tube sleds, ski-biking at night with a headlamp, dogsledding, and cross-country skiing are all available around the resort area. Famous figure skaters put on world-class shows for free in open-air rinks several times per season. Street Beat is a series of free concerts held on Thursday evenings from Dec through Apr (schedule at vvf.org). Several restaurants offer romantic, gourmet dinners in the snowy woods; try *The Cookhouse at Tennessee Pass* (719-486-8114; tennesseepass.com/the-cookhouse) or *Beano's Cabin* (970-754-3463; beanoscabinbeavercreek.com). Both restaurants are also open in the summer.

Summertime in Vail is a gentle season of greening mountainsides, flowering alpine meadows, and long, warm days. The Vail Farmers' Market and Art Show (Colorado's largest farmers' market) takes place each Sunday from 10 a.m. to 3 p.m., mid-June through mid-September. Enjoy cool jazz concerts while browsing locally grown produce, fresh baked goods, clothing, jewelry, and handmade items. Golf, kayaking, biking, fishing, and hiking are all popular here in summer. A full calendar of festivals, concerts, and events, many of them free, runs through the summer. For details go to vail.com.

After a day of play, take the gondola ride up the mountain after dark and see Vail far below glittering like a little jewel box.

Two hours west of Denver lie some of the state's most impressive mountains—the *Gore Range.* In Vail itself you'll see the Gore Creek, especially in summer. *Gore Mountain,* Gore Wilderness—who in the world was Gore? No, it's not a former vice president. George Gore was one of the more interesting visitors who ever roamed through Colorado. The best place to get acquainted with him might be north of Vail on *Gore Pass,* near Kremmling. Here a bronze plaque is visible beside the highway, at an elevation of 9,000 feet. The words on the bronze give a brief version of his time here:

> HERE IN 1854 CROSSED SIR ST. GEORGE GORE. AN IRISH BARONET BENT ON SLAUGHTER OF GAME AND GUIDED BY JIM BRIDGER. FOR THREE YEARS HE SCOURED COLORADO, MONTANA AND WYOMING ACCOMPANIED USUALLY BY FORTY MEN, MANY CARTS, WAGONS, HOUNDS, AND UNEXAMPLED CAMP LUXURIES.

Sylvan Lake State Park—Quintessential Colorado

Peaceful and unhurried, Sylvan Lake State Park is an alpine retreat down the road from Vail and just south of Eagle. Surrounded by the White River National Forest, Sylvan Lake is a lovely spot for camping, picnicking, or enjoying a quiet lake surrounded by more than 1,500 acres of parkland. Campgrounds, cabins, and yurts are available for overnight stays. For more information contact park headquarters at 10200 Brush Creek Rd., Eagle 81631; (970) 328-2021; or visit parks.state.co.us/parks/sylvanlake.

Vail Day Trip

In Vail you're surrounded by the Rockies, and there are day trip options in every direction. One sure bet is the drive from the top of Vail Pass to the summit of Shrine Pass. The road is open only in summer and has great views of Mount of the Holy Cross. Leave your car and hike around the area for some of the best wildflower displays and scenery in Colorado. Continue about 7 miles to the old mining town of Red Cliff for lunch at Mango's (166½ Eagle St.; 970-827-9109; mangosmountaingrill .com). Return on Highway 24, passing an amazing suspension bridge as you make your way to Minturn and back to Vail.

Lord Gore's party, we learn, dispatched "more than 2,000 buffalo, 1,600 elk and deer, and 100 bears," among others. Hunting was nothing new in a land where European trappers and fur traders had already scoured all of Colorado for beaver. But Lord Gore set a record; besides, no one matched his style. The baronet traveled with his retinue of hunters and porters from Ireland; his safari caravan eventually accumulated 112 horses, 21 carts, 30 wagons, and 4 dozen hunting dogs. He roamed the mountains for many months, shooting grizzly bear, antelope, and other animals and making elegant camp at night, complete with silver service and rare wines. His Lordship could afford the "unexampled camp luxuries." For one thing, his income exceeded $200,000, which was quite a sum during the mid-1850s. For another, the Irish nobleman had a taste for gourmet cuisine and rare wines—and the cooks and servants to attend his needs. Lord Gore had gone to school in Oxford, and his aristocratic tastes included various mansions in Ireland and houses in East Sussex.

Lord Gore's hunt and his exploits are still studied by local children. And thanks to the *Historical Society of Colorado,* future visitors to the region will be reminded of the Irishman by means of the bronze plaque on Gore Pass.

The summit of Gore Pass and the plaque are 17 miles west of Kremmling and can be reached from Denver via US 40. There are picnic grounds on the pass. Return to I-70 by driving south on Highway 9.

Botanists have identified thousands of different flower species in the Rockies. The first sign of spring at lower elevations brings forth a rush of daisies, mountain marigolds, wild sweet peas, fairy trumpets, pink rockhill phlox, and others in a rainbow of hues. Wander up in early summer to Colorado's 8,000- or 9,000-foot levels. Here, almost overnight, you'll see leafy cinquefoils, arnicas, yellow monkey flowers, and the official state flower, the blue Rocky Mountain columbine. (The latter also grows in the foothills.) In July, you'll be welcomed by the star gentians, wood lilies, the mountain aster, and several kinds of larkspur. After the snow has melted in the alpine zone above tree line, the next wave of color arrives, brightening the rocky slopes and high valleys with lavender, crimson, azure, butter yellow, pink, and pure white.

Perhaps the most amazing aspect of these annual displays is the fact that any plant producing such delicate beauty can survive under the freezing winter blizzards, blazing high-altitude sun, blasting winds, and generally harsh climate that occur above timberline. Their existence up here seems miraculous.

In the tundra at high elevations, you'll notice that all the plants are small. Many have short stems or none at all. That helps; the tinier the leaves and lower to the ground they are, the less resistance to the wind. At the same time, roots go deep into the soil, anchoring plants so they don't get ripped away in the stiff gusts. Mountain flowers protect themselves against the elements with protective tiny umbrellas of growth, or hairs, or fine layers of woolly matter or waxy leaves that hold in moisture. And many flowers close their petals at night to hold on to the day's warmth.

Colorado is renowned for its wildflowers. Hike just about any place in the mountains from June through August and you will find flowers, often in unlikely places. Different elevations and habitats support entirely different species. The growing season is short, but the state's flora makes up for that brief window of time by putting on one of nature's loveliest of shows. When you're outdoors enjoying the flowers, keep in mind that the vegetation is fragile, often barely holding on under extreme growing conditions. Watch where you're walking and stay on trails. Don't pick wildflowers. They often spread their seeds through their blossoms, so picking the flowers now means there will be fewer flowers next year. Picking flowers is against the law in all national parks, forests, and monuments. And they don't last long, often wilting within an hour. Leave the flowers alive and thriving for everyone to enjoy.

At 8,200 feet, the ***Betty Ford Alpine Gardens*** are billed as the world's highest botanic garden, with a lush array of high elevation perennials, rock gardens, and waterfalls in an already spectacular setting. Open from dawn to

Shrine Ridge Hike

Shrine Ridge is an easy hike that can be accomplished in 2 to 3 hours. Climb through open meadows with abundant wildflowers, then up the steepest part of the trail to the 11,089-foot summit. While atop the mountain, look for "Lord Gore," a man-shaped rock to the northwest. To reach the trailhead, take I-70 to Vail Pass, exit 190. Proceed on Road #709 to Shrine Pass Summit. Turn left here and drive to Shrine Mountain Inn, where you can park.

Vail Hikes

More than 20 scenic trails around Vail take hikers into beautiful backcountry landscapes. Here are a few of them. Local hotels, sports stores, and residents can direct you to trailheads.

- *Beaver Lake* (good workout with some elevation gain to a pretty mountain lake)

- *Berry Picker* (up Vail Mountain, lots of berries in season; you can hike to top and ride a gondola back down)

- *Booth Creek/Booth Falls* (pleasant hike through aspen groves, colorful in fall)

- *East Vail Hikes* (three trailheads starting at the end of old I-70)

- *Piney Lake* (several trails start from the lake, with a nice picnic spot)

dusk, there is no charge to visit the gardens, but donations are accepted. The gardens are located at 183 Gore Creek Dr., Vail; (970) 476-0103; bettyfordalpine gardens.org.

As you continue past Vail and Eagle on I-70 heading west, you'll soon find yourself surrounded by spectacular canyon walls. Welcome to **Glenwood Canyon.** Remarkable for its breathtaking geologic features and lovely scenery, the canyon is rendered even more extraordinary by the fact that the interstate running through it was constructed with a mind to retaining the canyon's wild and natural beauty. Though it's unfortunate a large interstate had to be put in this incredible setting, it is nonetheless encouraging that those in charge of building the road worked hard to make it as environmentally friendly as possible.

trivia

By the time Glenwood Canyon interstate construction was completed in 1992, more than 150,000 native trees, plants, and shrubs had been replanted in an effort to restore the area. In addition, engineers were careful to plan the route around large old trees instead of chopping them down, and the freshly made rock cuts fit right in with the natural canyon scenery—they had been stained so that they'd appear weathered.

The interstate swoops and bends with the canyon as it drops deeper into the earth. Between the river and the canyon wall, 16-mile long **Glenwood Springs Recreation Trail** parallels the highway. You can catch occasional glimpses of it from the road. Four rest stops along I-70 allow access to the trail within the canyon. The trail starts behind the Yampah Spa and Vapor Caves in Glenwood Springs. This paved trail and the river attract not only hikers and sightseers, but also in-line skaters, cyclists, runners, rafters, and kayakers. For more information call (888) 4-GLENWOOD, or contact the Eagle Ranger District at PO Box 720, Eagle 81631; (970) 328-6388; glenwoodchamber.com.

One of the hidden treats of Glenwood Canyon is *Hanging Lake.* Pull off of I-70 when you see the sign; the turnoff is well-marked, but if you're not in the correct lane, you will miss the exit. It's a short hike (only 1.2 miles), but in that distance it climbs 1,020 feet up the mountain. The trail follows Deadhorse Creek past box elders, cottonwoods, and lush fern gardens. Your reward at the top is a spectacular natural lake that was formed long ago when a geological fault caused the hillside to fall away. A nearby stream deposited carbonates over the fault, which hardened and formed a rim. Today the lake is 25 feet deep, crystal clear, and filled with large trout. There is no fishing, so these lunkers have grown uninterrupted by anglers. A boardwalk circles part of the lake, and the mist from the waterfalls is cooling in summer. It's a fragile, pristine place, well worth the short but strenuous uphill hike.

Glenwood Springs is the gateway to some of Colorado's most dramatic and most photographed peaks, like the Maroon Bells near Snowmass and lone, spectacular *Mount Sopris,* which is visible from almost everywhere in the region. The immense *White River National Forest* offers backpackers plenty of wilderness for roaming around. Anglers find world-class fishing for trout (rainbows and browns) in the surrounding rivers—the Roaring Fork, the Frying Pan, and the Colorado. Rivers attract rafters and kayakers as well; guiding

Touring Glenwood Springs

Glenwood Springs is 42 miles northwest of Aspen off Highway 82. "Glenwood," as residents call it, sits in the White River National Forest, which is a 3-hour drive from Denver. Glenwood's two million acres are renowned for all manner of outdoor sports. Flat Tops Wilderness, a huge 117,000-acre plateau north of Glenwood Springs, is a popular destination for anyone seeking quiet and solitude.

Glenwood was named for its hot-spring mineral baths, which are open all year. In the 1880s, silver baron Walter Devereaux decided to convert the springs, which had been used by the Utes for centuries, into a health resort for the rich. He built the 2-block-long swimming pool, intended for the guests of the posh adjacent hotel. By the early 1900s, so many wealthy and famous people came to the spa that a rail siding was installed next to the hotel for private railroad cars. Teddy Roosevelt made Glenwood his "Summer White House" in 1901 and hunted bear in the nearby hills.

The mineral baths and vapor caves are open to visitors. Massages are also available. Locals say the water is a healthy way to ease visitors' aching muscles and stiff joints after days in the nearby wilderness, on long hikes, or on Aspen's ski slopes.

services are available in Glenwood Springs. Hiking is plentiful, and hunters flock to the region for elk, deer, grouse, and waterfowl.

Despite the wealth of outdoor pursuits surrounding the town, the attraction that brings most visitors to the area is the 2-block-long *Glenwood Hot Springs* pool. No matter the season or the weather outside, the therapeutic waters are perfect for easing sore, tired muscles. With views over the conifers to the nearby peaks, the scenery and the heated pool conspire to relax even the most road-weary warrior. The Ute Indians used these springs centuries before the first explorers arrived, claiming they had miraculous healing powers. A famed architect, imported from Vienna, Austria, built the bathhouses here in 1890, and before long assorted American presidents such as Truman, Taft, Hoover, and Teddy Roosevelt came to visit Glenwood's mineral spa and "Natatorium."

trivia

Doc Holliday, the famous—or infamous—cowboy, died in Glenwood Springs in 1887; his grave marker epitaph declares only this: HE DIED IN BED.

Today the recreational swimming—and walking—part of the pool is kept at 90–93°F (29–32°C); hotter outdoor waters at 100–104°F (38–40°C) are also available, fed by more than 3.5 million gallons. The hot springs contain a cornucopia of elements, including magnesium, calcium, sulphates, bicarbonates, phosphates, and silica. Swimmers relish the almost unlimited space in the pool, while those recuperating from injuries enjoy the medical benefits.

Some guests spend much of the day in deck chairs around the pool—Colorado's version of *la dolce vita*. But no Roman bath could match Glenwood's pure air and mountain views. For additional pampering, the nearby vapor baths feature massages and natural saunas. The pool is open daily, year-round, until 10 p.m., opening at 7:30 a.m. in summer and 9 a.m. in winter. Rates vary from $8.50 to $18.75 depending on age, season, and time of day or evening. Contact the pool at (970) 947-2955; hotspringspool.com.

Glenwood Springs has plenty of lodging, but the most convenient one for soakers is the *Hot Springs Lodge.* It's a short walk from the pool to your room. The 107-unit Hot Springs Lodge is contemporary and ideally located. Rates are not as high as you might expect. For reservations call (800) 537-7946 or (970) 945-6571. For more information about the pool or lodgings write to the Hot Springs Lodge and Pool, PO Box 308, Glenwood Springs 81602; hotsprings pool.com. Glenwood Springs may be one of the state's more interesting destinations—historically, economically, scenically—yet it never gets the kind of attention accorded to trendy Aspen (41 miles to the southeast), glitzy Vail (59

Kayaking the Colorado

For an unforgettable experience, book a 2-day novice kayak river trip with the **Boulder Outdoor Center.** The trips take you down the Colorado River as it winds through Glenwood Canyon. Accompanied by accredited instructors, you learn how to read the river and maneuver a kayak safely through Class II+ rapids, eddies, and through the scenery of Glenwood Canyon. They even show you how to roll yourself upright. Participants must have some previous kayaking experience and be at least 12 years old. Trips run from May through Sept. Call (303) 444-8420 or (800) 364-9376 for details or visit boc123.com.

miles), or cosmopolitan Denver (some 158 miles to the east). Both the town and the area are blessed with accommodations for every pocketbook. Economy travelers welcome the numerous campgrounds and inexpensive little cabins flanking the soothing rivers. Large and small motels abound. Annual festivals, yearly fishing contests, *rodeos,* and mountains all around the town give Glenwood Springs a true western atmosphere while preserving its small-town feel.

Glenwood can lay claim to another local attraction found nowhere else in the state. *Strawberry Days,* held in June, brings parades, carnivals, top-notch entertainment, an art and crafts market, and sporting events. Strawberry Days, now more than 100 years old, is Glenwood Springs's oldest and most beloved annual event. The festival is Colorado's oldest civic celebration, dating back to 1898. Things have changed since the strawberry picnics of those early days, but the town's enthusiasm for this celebration is stronger than ever. The celebration goes for three days, with an estimated 30,000 people showing up to enjoy the party each year. For more information call (970) 945-6589 or visit strawberrydaysfestival.com.

The *Fall Art Festival,* held in September, is the largest nonjuried art show in the state, attracting more than 400 entries from artists throughout Colorado and the US. Professionals and amateurs compete in their own levels and media. And, of course, almost everything is for sale after the judging. Call (970) 945-2414 or visit glenwoodchamber.com for details.

While you're in Glenwood Springs, take a stroll through the stately *Hotel*

trivia

Legend has it that the Teddy Bear was born at the Hotel Colorado. One time when frequent visitor President Teddy Roosevelt had a fruitless day of bear hunting, the hotel's maids sewed a stuffed bear in an effort to cheer him up. When he did succeed in hunting down a real bear, his daughter named the bear "Teddy," a name that stuck.

Colorado, which graces the National Register of Historic Places. The 128-room hotel, one of the oldest in the state, was modeled after Italy's Villa Medici and boasts a Florentine fountain in a landscaped courtyard. The hotel's renovated lobby is one of the most attractive in the western US. The sparkling chandeliers, fireplaces, oil paintings, fountains, and potted palm trees hark back to the days of royalty and the very wealthy.

The Hotel Colorado was financed by the silver mining of the nearby Aspen region and opened officially on June 10, 1893. The cost was a staggering (at the time) $850,000; some 16 private railroad cars of the industrial barons drew up on a special Glenwood siding. Over time, leading citizens from all over the world registered at the hotel.

European millionaires arrived in droves to stay and dine here. In 1905 President Theodore Roosevelt brought his own appetite; a typical menu encouraged the presidential visitor and his entourage to consume an eight-course repast: Caviar Canapés, Spring Lamb Consommé, Rothschild Broiled Squab, Veal, Sweetbreads, Fig's Young Turkey, and Roquefort Cheese.

Eventually, Roosevelt—an avid bear hunter—made the hotel his Summer White House, complete with direct telegraph connections to Washington and special couriers bringing international news to the hunting head of state. Other famous guests included the "Unsinkable" Molly Brown, who managed to survive the *Titanic*'s sinking, gangster Al Capone, and President Taft. For more information and reservations contact Hotel Colorado, 526 Pine, Glenwood Springs 81601; (970) 945-6511 or (800) 544-3998; hotelcolorado.com.

For more information about the Glenwood Springs area, contact the Glenwood Springs Chamber Resort Association at (888) 445-3696 or (970) 945-6589; glenwoodchamber.com. Glenwood Springs is easily reached from Denver by rental car, bus, or train. Motorists use I-70. The distance from Denver is 158 miles.

Sunlight Mountain Resort

Tired of the crowds at the big resorts? Then maybe it's time to try out Sunlight Mountain Resort. With 67 named trails on more than 470 acres of terrain, plus access to plenty of Nordic trails in the adjacent White River National Forest, this resort offers a great escape. Terrific for families, almost all of the resort's ski runs come right down to the lodge. From Glenwood, head south on Highway 117. For more information contact the resort at (970) 945-7491 or (800) 445-7931; sunlight-mtn.com. Consider staying at the cozy Sunlight Mountain Inn, 9 miles outside Glenwood Springs (10252 CR 117; 970-945-5225; sunlightmountaininn.com).

Ski or Hike Vail—Hut to Hut

For an off-the-beaten-path skiing or hiking experience, try Vail's backcountry hut-to-hut system. The **Tenth Mountain Division Hut Association** was formed in 1980 to build a backcountry ski hut system in the high mountains between Aspen, Leadville, and Vail. This system of 29 huts connects 350 miles of suggested routes for a true Colorado experience. Distances between huts vary. Now you can reserve the huts for a fee as a takeoff point for day adventures or to ski or hike from hut to hut. These shelters are within the White River and San Isabel National Forests, so stunning vistas are guaranteed. The huts are rugged; bring your own food, water, and sleeping bag. The adventure isn't for everyone, however; in winter the Forest Service advises that the trails require at least intermediate skiing ability. The Hut Association also requires that someone in each group be proficient in backcountry skills, such as avalanche awareness and compass reading. The huts include wood-burning stoves, propane burners, cooking and eating utensils, kitchen supplies, and mattresses and pillows.

NOTE: With average elevations of 11,000 feet, you need to prepare for high altitude.

Reservations are required; call (970) 925-5775 or write Tenth Mountain Division Hut Association, 1280 Ute Ave., Ste. 21, Aspen 81611; huts.org.

Even by Colorado standards, the trip to **Redstone** is long, but it is worth it. The scenery along the way is classic Rockies landscape, and the distance only enhances the charms of the little hamlet of Redstone and its historic inn and castle. The imposing **Redstone Inn** and Tudor clock tower are an unexpected sight in this remote mountain landscape.

The 35 rooms are cozy and unpretentious, although some furnishings are in need of replacement. It's a quirky, one-of-a-kind place, and if you don't need four-star accommodations, this historic hotel in a beautiful setting is a nice escape from the city. The lobby and the restaurant are filled with antiques and have a Victorian atmosphere. The **Crystal River** is quiet and lovely, with fishing and horseback riding available in the warm months. In winter, the inn serves as headquarters for sleigh rides, cross-country skiing, ice climbing, and snowshoeing.

Contact Redstone Inn at 82 Redstone Blvd., Redstone 81623; (970) 963-2526 or (800) 748-2524; redstoneinn.com. Get to Redstone via I-70 west to Glenwood Springs, then Highway 82 south out of Glenwood toward Aspen; turn right at Carbondale on Highway 133—it's 18 miles to Redstone. For more information about the community and surrounding area, visit redstone colorado.com.

If you continue along Highway 82 south out of Glenwood, it won't be long until you reach **Aspen.** This pretty town is famous around the world as

Versatile Aspen

Most Colorado ski centers consist of dozens of condos, a resort, and a ski hill. By contrast, Aspen has many ski areas, and it was a full-fledged town long before skiing arrived. A pedestrian mall and flower boxes and benches invite lingering. Aspen's red, Old West–style brick buildings and Victorian gingerbread homes are periodically restored. The antique cherrywood bars shine, as do the contemporary Tiffany lamps and the stained-glass windows. Aspen outranks most North American ski resorts when it comes to the sheer number and variety of restaurants and nightlife possibilities.

There are close to a hundred eating establishments in Aspen ready to satisfy just about any craving. From American to ethnic, gourmet to down home, Aspen has enough bistros, grills, bars, saloons, pubs, subterranean dives, cafeterias, cafes, pastry shops, coffeehouses, and high-end eateries to keep even the most dedicated foodie happy for a long time. It's a cosmopolitan, polyglot, diverse town. Aspen is everything to every level of skier and, happily, to every nonskier as well; the town is ideal for couples or families where one member doesn't ski. Several hundred shops invite browsers; amusements and sports of every kind beckon.

a mountain retreat for movie stars, music moguls, and the wealthy. The gated communities in the hills above town are where the rich and famous stay and party during ski vacations or summer getaways. It's the best celebrity-spotting place in Colorado.

But Aspen is much more than glitz and glamour, and as you approach the edge of town, you will see why it's become a haven for celebrities. Aspen sits at the upper end of Roaring Fork Valley, surrounded by abundant aspen groves. The Roaring Fork River, a tributary of the Colorado River, runs through town. Mountains and wilderness rise above Aspen on three sides. Nearby Maroon Bells and Maroon Lake are among the most photographed and easily recognizable of Colorado's many natural landmarks. Mention Colorado to someone who's never been here, and the scenery around Aspen is likely the sort of place they have in mind.

trivia

One nugget from the Molly Gibson Mine in Aspen weighed 1,840 pounds. It was 93 percent pure silver.

Aspen called itself Ute City at first because it was in Ute territory. Silver gave the town its big start back in the early 1880s. Soon after news of the silver discovery broke, prospectors headed up the passes and rushed to Aspen—a hard, punishing journey, even from nearby Leadville. Some men dropped dead before they could stake their first claim. Western historians still mention the stampede of that winter in 1879. They came on burro, on foot, or on horseback.

Sometimes a man would keel over and die on the Aspen streets. Other prospectors just stuck the body into a snowbank and kept up the frantic search for silver riches. The best years were from 1885 to 1889, when mines galore—with names like the Smuggler or Montezuma—operated above the mountain town. The smelter was booked for weeks, and silver rock would pile up everywhere.

trivia

When the silver boom went bust in the 1890s, Aspen's population plummeted, and the city almost became a ghost town.

Some miners got rich fast. "The men filled their pockets and fled," wrote one observer of the era. The silver barons built the luxurious Victorian *Hotel Jerome* (330 E. Main St.; 970-920-1000; hoteljerome.com) and an opera house. Singers and musicians came from Europe to perform.

The crash came in 1893 and brought lean times. Aspen shriveled from a population of 13,000 to a mere 500. The 1930 census shows a total population of 705 residents. Many Aspen dwellings stood empty. But several investors saw potential. In the 1940s the rebirth began, and by the early 1950s skiing was well established. Aspen was on its way to a second chance, this time as a world-class ski resort.

Today the town is an eclectic mix of architectural styles: original log cabins, Victorian homes, "mineshaft" condos, and mansions in the hills. Yet despite its flaws, Aspen retains a simplicity that keeps visitors coming back. Aspen summers are a delight, with classical music, lectures, trails for hikers and bikers, rivers for anglers, and an expanded airport for private planes. The ski

Skier's Locomotion up Aspen Mountain

When the Aspen Skiing Corp. (now the Aspen Skiing Company) opened its first lifts on Aspen Mountain in 1947, it eliminated one of skiing's biggest drawbacks: climbing the hill.

Skiing 60 years ago was for the truly committed, because if you wanted to enjoy the slopes in winter, you had to hoof it. If skiers were lucky, they could catch a ride with miners up the back of Aspen Mountain.

A year later, you could ascend Aspen Mountain in a single chair. The trip took more than an hour, and you could get a free ticket by helping to "pack" the slopes in the morning. As many as 100 volunteers worked the slopes at the same time.

facilities, with four different ski areas and countless lifts, are all extraordinary, rivaling anything in the Swiss Alps. Restaurants and hotels cater to every budget. And on Red Mountain, where the movie stars live, the parties still go on most every night.

The scene is an early Saturday morning in *Ashcroft,* a remote Colorado ghost town near Aspen. The sun's first rays work their way down nearby Castle Peak and begin spilling across the snowy valley. Nothing stirs in this silent, wintry landscape until a few people assemble down the road from Ashcroft's weathered, abandoned buildings. Several more join them, all carrying snowshoes. By 9 a.m. 40 snowshoers stand ready, almost twice as many as the Colorado Mountain Club leader had expected. After a long decline in popularity, snowshoeing is back in fashion, and for several good reasons. Over the last couple of decades the equipment has evolved into lightweight, high-tech gear that makes walking in the snow easy. You don't need lessons; within minutes you will be ready to take off up the trail. And it's excellent exercise. Snowshoeing is really nothing more than winter hiking. You get to enjoy great views, stop whenever you like, and have a solid outdoor workout at a time when others are indoors hiding from Old Man Winter.

On snowshoes you can go just about anywhere, on trail or off, wherever you can find at least a few inches of snow. From the steep winter meadows of the Continental Divide, across the gentle mounds of eastern Colorado, over

Aspen Highlands

Few people know that at one point in mining history—circa 1879 to 1882—Aspen had a nearby competitor named Ashcroft. Located in an adjacent valley, Ashcroft actually boasted several hotels, numerous bars, a jail, and even a newspaper. (The Ashcroft silver riches attracted silver millionaire H. A. W. Tabor and his pretty young bride, Baby Doe.) By 1883, Aspen was famous for its silver wealth, and fortune hunters arrived by the thousands; the inhabitants of Ashcroft, meanwhile, dwindled to about 100 (from 2,600 in its heyday).

And today? Aspen is a successful ski resort, and Ashcroft is a ghost town. A half-dozen rickety buildings stand silently below Castle Peak, bleached by sun and wind, pummeled by snow and rain, slowly returning to the earth.

Yet more than 100 years after the silver boom and bust, Ashcroft still holds value. *Ashcroft Ski Touring* offers 35 kilometers of cross-country trails, along with rentals, instruction, and advice on where to ski. You reach this quiet area by driving west for half a mile on Highway 82, and then turning on Castle Creek Road. After 12 miles, you see the cross-country trails. Call (970) 925-1044 for more information or visit pinecreekcookhouse.com.

Aspen Flights

If you're ready to try something totally different, how about taking to the skies on a paraglider?

With no prior experience necessary, you can soar with an experienced certified pilot from near the summit of Aspen Mountain. Scheduled on a daily basis, these summer flights are absolutely unforgettable.

The **Aspen Paragliding School** offers an instruction course, including flights, technique, and equipment. For information, call (970) 925-7625 or visit aspenpara gliding.com.

frozen Lake Dillon, and into the dramatic deep-snow regions above Silverton and Ouray, snowshoers find many hundreds of places to explore. There are no lift lines or tickets to buy. There's no expensive outfit to buy, just standard outdoor winter clothing. Many outdoor shops in Colorado rent snowshoes; cost is around $15 per day for the first day, less for each additional day. In Denver try REI; their flagship store is at 1416 Platte St.; (303) 756-3100; rei.com/stores/18.

Summertime in the Colorado mountains is a delight to the ears. Tumbling streams, trilling birdsong, wind whistling down the canyons; it's a daily free concert. But Aspen also happens to be home to a world-famous music festival in a mountain setting unlike any other. Far from any urban center, the music at this altitude seems even more pure and lifting.

The **Aspen Music Festival** was founded in 1949 with the belief that combining art and nature encourages the growth of the human spirit. This internationally renowned festival presents some of the world's most accomplished classical musicians in a magnificent alpine setting. Over a 9-week period attendees can choose from more than 200 events, including chamber and contemporary music, orchestral concerts, classes, lectures, and kids' programs. Events are held in concert halls, churches, and a permanent tent structure with excellent acoustics. Many events are free, and there's always free seating on the lawn outside the tent. Contact the organization at 2 Music School Rd., 81611; (970) 925-3254/9042; aspenmusicfestival.com.

Nature and the outdoors are among the main reasons people visit Colorado. The first step for many is experiencing the region through road trips, camping, hiking, skiing, rafting, and biking. But many visitors seduced by the grandeur and beauty of the state are curious about the geography, flora, and fauna, and they want to learn more about the ecology and the environment that makes the area unique.

Naturalist Nights

Interesting and educational, Naturalist Nights take place every Thursday evening at Aspen Center for Environmental Studies (ACES) from 7:30 to 8:30 p.m., Jan through Mar. Naturalist Nights cover a variety of topics, such as "Survival in the Avalanche Zone," "Wolves in the West," and "Birds of the Winter Forest." Admission is $3, free for members.

The *Aspen Center for Environmental Studies* (ACES) was formed in 1968 to provide a way for an increasingly urbanized world to rediscover nature. Along with establishing a wildlife preserve in Aspen, the initial focus was to educate schoolchildren about nature and teach environmental responsibility.

Today ACES is an important part of the Aspen community. Thousands of adults and children visit every year to participate in the Naturalist Field School. Instructors from around the country come each summer to teach close to 50 different workshops and courses on the diverse Rocky Mountain ecosystem. Daily courses include hawk, eagle, and owl demonstrations; naturalist-guided walks, a variety of programs for kids, sunset beaver walks, and campground programs. Course topics include birds, plants, backcountry navigation, families in nature, geology, mushrooms, field journaling, astronomy, and farming.

In the winter, ACES leads snowshoe tours to Castle Creek Valley and Ashcroft ghost town, and ski tours at Snowmass. Each Wednesday at 7:30 p.m. during Potbelly Perspectives, weekly photo presentations by adventurers and biologists transport audiences to faraway lands. For more information and a complete list of courses contact ACES at 100 Puppy Smith St., 81611; (970) 925-5756; aces@aspennature.org; or aspennature.org.

Located just 10 miles from Aspen, *Snowmass Village* may not have the instant name recognition enjoyed by its nearby neighbor, but it compensates by offering a wide variety of activities and events throughout the year. You're

trivia

A 130-pound woman burns about 340 calories per hour of snowshoeing.

still deep in the Rockies, so expect to find miles of hiking and mountain biking, fly fishing, rafting, golf, jeep tours, and horseback riding.

But just like Aspen, Snowmass is also a cultural destination. Winter means skiing and other winter sports, but the summer and fall months bring a nonstop selection of unique festivals, concerts, and events. Summer begins with the *Chili Pepper and Brew Fest,* featuring a chili cook-off, microbrew tasting, and live music. ***Snowmass Rodeo*** begins in mid-June and stretches through mid-August. Snowmass Village puts on free music concerts featuring major acts through the summer at the Village Mall on the mountain. The ***Jazz Aspen Snowmass June Festival*** is 10 days of some of the best jazz on the planet. ***Snowmass Balloon Festival*** in September fills the sky for three colorful days with one of the highest-altitude balloon events in the country. ***Jazz Aspen Snowmass Labor Day Festival*** brings a wide variety of music to the mountain for three days.

In case this partial list isn't enough to entice you to visit Snowmass, there's much more. From late spring through fall, Snowmass hosts bike races, theater, a film festival, Octoberfest, food and wine festivals, volleyball competition, and a great July 4th party. But not all visitors come for the festivals and outdoor activities. Some visitors are drawn to Snowmass to follow their muse. Artists come here from around the country and abroad to study at ***Anderson Ranch Arts Center,*** where more than 140 workshops are offered each summer. Classes are available for all age groups, and include subjects such as ceramics, painting and drawing, photography, printmaking, furniture design, woodworking, and sculpture. Courses on the 5-acre ranch run from 2 days to 2 weeks, giving artists of all levels a place to be inspired, learn new skills, and immerse themselves in the creative process. For more information contact the ranch in Snowmass at 5263 Owl Creek Rd., 81615, or PO Box 5598, 81615; (970) 923-3181; andersonranch.org. For general information on activities and events at Snowmass call (888) 649-5982 or visit stayaspensnowmass.com or snowmass village.com.

Aspen, Snowmass, and Aspen Highlands have some of the best skiing in the country, including many advanced intermediate and expert runs. The fourth local ski area, little ***Buttermilk Ski Resort,*** would at first glance seem to be up against some tough competition. But Buttermilk has carved out a name for

Aspen Dogsledding

And you thought dogsledding only happens in Alaska! Snuggle down into a sled and be prepared for a thrilling ride though a pristine Aspen landscape. Each sled is pulled by 10 Alaskan sled dogs and guided by an experienced musher. The dogs are born and bred to run, and they are as excited as the riders to move quickly down the trail. Rides last 1.5–2 hours and are available from mid-Dec through mid-Apr depending on snow conditions. They are based at 4250 Divide Rd. in Snowmass Village, 10 miles from Aspen. For more information call (970) 923-3953 or visit krabloonikrestaurant.com.

itself in two areas. First, it focuses on beginners and skiers who don't need the heart-racing intensity of black diamond slopes. Although Buttermilk has expert runs, it's known as an excellent place for beginners with an outstanding ski school. The hills are gentle and friendly to those just starting out, or for those who want to take it easy and enjoy the slopes at a mellower pace.

Buttermilk's other specialty is snowboarding. The resort has two separate terrain parks, more than 100 features, a super pipe and a beginner's pipe, all within the world's longest (2 miles) terrain park. From beginner to Winter X Games pro, snowboarders of every skill level will find plenty to keep them happy. For more information on Buttermilk skiing, contact Aspen Skiing Company, PO Box 1248, Aspen 81612; (970) 925-1220 or toll-free (800) 525-6200; aspensnowmass.com.

Vail. Aspen. Telluride. Copper. Winter Park. Crested Butte. Snowmass. In the world of skiing, these are household names, spoken in almost reverential tones. Colorado is justifiably famous for its skiing. The snow is light, fluffy, and easy to ski. With so much of the state at high elevations, the region has the terrain, the altitude, and the weather for world-class skiing. And the western landscapes, especially when viewed from the upper slopes, are grandiose.

The state's ski meccas are deserving of their fame. None of Colorado's ski resorts look alike; each has its special character made up of a dozen variables. Century-old mining towns like Breckenridge and Crested Butte have been revived. Aspen is immense and complex. Vail is a giant in every way,

Taking It Slow in Aspen

The **Aspen/Snowmass Nordic Trail System** offers cross-country skiers numerous opportunities around the valley. This systems is unique because it links two towns (Aspen and Snowmass Village), meandering through meadows, wooded areas, and across three valleys. Choose from 60 kilometers of groomed trails or set off on your own across fresh powder. Two Nordic centers, **Aspen Cross Country Center** (970-925-2145) and **Snowmass Cross Country Center** (970-923-5700), are on the trail network, providing instruction, rentals, snacks, waxing advice, and information on choosing the right trail for your skill level. Directions and information for both centers can be found at aspennordic.com or utemountaineer.com/aspenxc.html.

A third Nordic center, **Ashcroft Ski Touring** (970-925-1044) is located up the Castle Creek Valley on the Ashcroft Trail System. They offer rentals, instruction, and trail advice, and with 35 kilometers of trail, the center has some of the prettiest routes in the valley. You can also ski or snowshoe into and out of the Pine Creek Cookhouse for a memorable gourmet meal. Visit online at skiashcroft.com or pine creekcookhouse.com.

Snowmass Summers

Snowmass summers are mellow. The rocks are warm and meadows fill with wild-flowers: anemones, bluebells, gentian, and Indian paintbrush. Hikers move into the high country. Classes begin at the arts center. Aspen's music festival is only 20 minutes away.

In summer, Snowmass is a center for picnickers, hikers, kayakers, four-wheel enthusiasts, and mountain bikers. Climbers set out for the Maroon Bells. Anglers arm themselves with flies, rods, and nets, and head out for the many trout streams. Horseback riders climb into saddles and disappear into the woods.

Miles of trails, ranging from gentle forest paths to muscle-aching switchbacks, will transport you into an alpine world of mountain blossoms, snowmelt streams, and shady aspen groves.

an American St. Moritz. Winter Park serves vacationers during the week and Denverites on weekends. Loveland Basin and Keystone yield consistent snow. Uncrowded Telluride has its fast, epic runs nestles in a beautiful box canyon.

If you come to this state anytime between late November and April, you should try to ski, even if you've never done it before. Each resort area offers excellent instruction and beginner slopes. And there are numerous other winter activities, such as cross-country skiing, snowshoeing, sledding and tubing, and sleigh rides. For more information contact Colorado Ski Country USA, 1444 Wazee St., Ste. 320, Denver 80202; (303) 837-0793; coloradoski.com.

Grand Junction is at the west end of Colorado, close to the Utah border. This is expansive, wide open country. To the south lies Grand Mesa, the largest mesa in the world. To the north are the towering Book Cliffs, stretching for nearly 200 miles. It's the largest town on the Western Slope, and this region has an entirely different feel than the mountains or eastern plains. Instead of thick forests and jagged peaks, the area around Grand Junction is all about geology. Drier than points east, this region is a land of mesas, arroyos, plateaus and pinnacles, a striking landscape sculpted by annual cycles of heat and cold, of rain, wind, sun, and snow. With little vegetation to hide the formations, this part of Colorado has a stark beauty that for many feels like the true West.

The town was named in 1881 for the nearby confluence of the Grand River and the Gunnison River. When the Grand was renamed the Colorado River in 1921, nobody bothered to change the name of the city. Today the downtown historic area retains some of that Old West charm with its Victorian-era architecture. Coffeehouses, restaurants, and shops invite lingering. And the streets of downtown Grand Junction are home to one of the country's largest sidewalk sculpture galleries with close to 100 sculptures.

The *Museum of Western Colorado* covers the history of the area, beginning with the earliest residents and displays of prehistoric pottery, Navajo paintings, and rock art. The Old West comes alive with a uranium mine, a stagecoach, a one-room schoolhouse, firearms exhibit, and the Pastime Saloon. Contact the museum at 462 Ute Ave.; (970) 242-0971; museumofwesternco.com.

Also part of the museum, the *Cross Orchards Living History Farm* recreates life as it was lived by Grand Valley pioneers in the early 1900s. A country store, blacksmith shop, bunkhouse for workers, and an extensive collection of equipment from the era are part of this 24-acre site. Costumed interpreters add authenticity and explain what life was like for early settlers. The museum is located at 3073 F Rd.; (970) 434-9814.

A third branch of the museum, *Dinosaur Journey* in Fruita, tells the story of the history of ancient dinosaur life in Colorado. This hands-on, interactive museum includes exhibits of actual dinosaur bones, fossils, rocks, minerals, and much more. At Dino Digs, spend the day with a paleontologist working in a real dinosaur quarry, digging for dinosaurs, turtles, lizards, and mammals in the 150-million-year-old badlands of the Morrison Formation. The digs fill fast and the number of participants is limited, so call ahead for reservations. Contact Dinosaur Journey at (970) 858-7282; museumofwesternco.com/visit/dinosaur-journey.

Anyone interested in beautiful cars will find plenty to admire at *Allen Unique Autos.* This museum houses more than 60 classic, rare, and iconic automobiles that have been lovingly restored to mint condition. There are cars formerly owned by celebrities and Hollywood legends, American muscle cars, customized hot rods, antiques, and European classics. The museum is located at 2285 River Rd.; (970) 263-7410; allenuniqueautos.com.

Grand Junction and the surrounding areas are known for producing some of the best fruit and vegetables in the state. And one of the best places to sample them while enjoying one of the town's signature events is at the weekly Farmers' Market Festival. Every Thursday during the summer Main Street is closed to car traffic, and farmers, artisans, vendors, musicians, and merchants gather

Safety Tips

In Colorado, state law considers bicycles to be vehicles, and they must obey the same traffic laws as automobiles. Ride single file on the right in the same direction as traffic. Always signal when stopping or turning. When you need to catch your breath, move off the road. It's also good advice to wear a helmet and protective glasses.

Rifle Falls State Park

Before you head too much farther west, consider making a side trip to Rifle Falls State Park. Though small, this unique gem of a state park offers visitors the unlikely opportunity to get downright tropical—or close to it! The triple waterfall plummets down 80 feet past limestone cliffs, keeping the lush vegetation moist. Dark, cool caves beckon to curious explorers, and interpretive signs help explain the phenomena. With its $7 per car entry fee, the park makes for a worthwhile side trip and a terrific place to have a family picnic.

From Aspen, take Highway 82 north about 41 miles. In Glenwood Springs turn left onto 6th Street then left onto North River Drive, following signs to I-70 West. Take I-70 about 25.5 miles to the Rifle exit. Go north on Highway 13 for 4 miles. Turn right on Highway 325 and drive 9.8 miles. Call (970) 625-1607 or write Rifle Falls State Park, 5775 Hwy. 325, Rifle 81650; parks.state.co.us/parks/riflefalls.

for an evening of socializing, eating, music, and fun. It's a great place to experience a community party, and everyone is welcome. The market runs from mid-June until mid-Sept, Thurs from 5 p.m. to 8:30 p.m. For more information, visit downtowngj.org.

Travelers with a penchant for sweets should make the pilgrimage to **Enstrom Candies** at 701 Colorado Ave. or 120 W. Park, Ste. 100. Enstrom's has been making candy for more than 50 years, and their almond toffee is an exquisite blend of chocolate, caramel, butter, and nuts that's gained almost mythical status in Colorado. If you're looking for a Colorado gift for the folks back home, look no further.

The region around Grand Junction doesn't seem like vineyard country. But the **Grand Valley,** stretching from Palisade to Fruita, has grown into a productive winery region. The climate here is milder than along the Front Range, with almost 300 days of sun a year. The warm, dry days and cool nights result in a microclimate that is ideal for wine grapes. The area is worth a day trip from Grand Junction to drive through the vineyards and peach orchards, stopping for lunch in Palisade. Many wineries offer tours demonstrating how the wine gets from grape to glass. The **Colorado Mountain Winefest** takes place in mid-September; (800) 704-3667; coloradowinefest.com. For more information and directions to the wineries, contact Grand Valley Winery Association at PO Box 99, Palisade 81526-0099; (970) 464-5867 or (303) 399-7586; grandvalley wine.com.

Each summer **Grande River Vineyards** hosts the **Grapevine Summer Concert Series,** musical events featuring jazz, soul, classical, rock, and blues. Guests bring picnics, and of course wine, to enjoy in the beautiful outdoor setting. For more information, 787 Elberta Ave., Palisade 81526; (970) 464-5867; granderiverwines.com.

Colorado residents also look forward to the Western Slope peach harvest. First come the Elbertas and Red Havens, followed a few weeks later by Suncrest, Sullivan, and Blake. Toward the end of summer the Redskin and Hale arrive. As each variety ripens, peach lovers search fruit markets for the peach of the week. Peach jams, cobblers, and pies show up in restaurants and kitchens. Palisade celebrates this esteemed fruit with the *Palisade Peach Festival* for four days in mid-August (970-464-7458; palisadepeachfest.com).

trivia

Despite receiving only 11 inches of rainfall annually, the area encompassed by the Colorado National Monument was continuously inhabited for thousands of years until 1881. That year, the area's most recent inhabitants, the Utes, were moved by the US military to a Utah reservation. Past inhabitants left evidence of their existence through rock art and other artifacts.

Many people drive to the orchards to buy peaches as well as apricots and cherries. Numerous fruit stands also sell local jams, preserves, salsas, and other condiments. For more information on fruit season around Palisade, contact the Palisade Chamber of Commerce at 319 Main St., 81526; (970) 464-7458; e-mail info@palisadecoc.com or visit palisadecoc.com.

Travelers in search of deep canyons, red rock walls, and sandstone spires often head to the parks of Utah. But Colorado has its own park, *Colorado National Monument,* where a world of steep plateaus, sheer drop-offs, and craggy rock spires awaits. This 31-square-mile park is easily explored via a 23-mile loop road that offers numerous overlooks across the high-desert scenery. If you're a cyclist, it's a great way to absorb the scenery. Thirteen backcountry trails lead into the far reaches of the park.

To reach Colorado National Monument, follow Monument Road out of downtown Grand Junction, which will take you to the entry gate. Fees are $10 per vehicle, $5 per motorcycle or individual biker or hiker. For more information call (970) 858-3617 or write Colorado National Monument, Fruita 81521; nps.gov/com.

Places to Stay in the Central Mountains

ASPEN

Aspen Mountain Lodge
311 W. Main St.
(970) 925-7650 or
(800) 362-7736
aspenmountainlodge.com
Moderate to Expensive
Comfortable, affordable, and within walking distance to everything in town. On the bus line to the ski resort.

Hotel Aspen
110 W. Main St.
(970) 925-3441 or
(800) 527-7369
hotelaspen.com
Moderate to Expensive
Centrally located, modern decor, daily breakfast, après-ski wine and hors d'oeuvres; Jacuzzi suites available.

Hotel Jerome
330 E. Main St.
(970) 920-1000 or
(800) 331-7213
hoteljerome.com
Expensive
Luxury historic hotel known for its authentic ambience. The hotel's J-Bar is Aspen's oldest and most famous bar.

Limelight Lodge
335 Monarch St.
(970) 925-3025 or
(800) 433-0832
limelightlodge.com
Moderate to Expensive
A classic contemporary ski lodge located steps away from Aspen Mountain and downtown hot spots. Includes nice continental breakfast.

Little Nell
675 E. Durant Ave.
(970) 920-4600 or
(888) 843-6355
thelittlenell.com
Expensive
Aspen's only ski-in/ski-out hotel, with newly renovated rooms and excellent guest service.

St. Regis Resort
315 Dean St.
(970) 920-3300 or
(888) 454-9005
stregisaspen.com
Expensive
Recently renovated luxury hotel located between Aspen Mountain's 2 base ski lifts with high-end amenities in all rooms. The hotel's Remede Spa is one of Aspen's finest.

BRECKENRIDGE

Allaire Timbers Inn
9511 S. Main St.
(970) 453-7530 or
(800) 624-4904
allairetimbers.com
Moderate to Expensive
Friendly and intimate lodge with full breakfast included, free wireless Internet, and located on a free ski area shuttle route.

Barn on the River Bed & Breakfast
303B N. Main St.
(970) 453-2975 or
(800) 795-2975
breckenridge-inn.com
Moderate to Expensive
Located on the river next to historic Main Street, with a riverside hot tub.

Lodge & Spa at Breckenridge
112 Overlook Dr.
(970) 453-9300 or
(800) 736-1607
thelodgeandspaatbreck.com
Moderate to Expensive
Boutique hotel with a mountain cabin feel located 5 minutes from town.

River Mountain Lodge
100 South Park Ave.
(970) 453-4000 or
(877) 346-4000
resortquestbreckenridge.com
Expensive
European-style lodge steps away from historic downtown and across the street from ski area. Free wireless Internet, hot tubs, heated pool.

Skiway Lodge
275 Ski Hill Rd.
(970) 453-7573 or
(800) 472-1430
skiwaylodge.com
Moderate to Expensive
Bavarian-style chalet with 10 guest rooms, all with full baths and private balconies. Ski-in/ski-out access to the Breck Connect Gondola.

FOR MORE INFORMATION

ASPEN

Aspen Chamber Resort Association
425 Rio Grande Place, 81611
(970) 925-1940 or (800) 670-0792
aspenchamber.org

BRECKENRIDGE

Breckenridge Resort Chamber
111 Ski Hill Rd., 80424
(888) 251-2417
gobreck.com

GEORGETOWN

Downtown Georgetown Community Center
PO Box 834; 613 6th St., 80444
(303) 569-2888 or (800) 472-8230
georgetowncolorado.com

GLENWOOD SPRINGS

Glenwood Springs Chamber Resort Association
1102 Grand Ave., 81601
(970) 945-6589 or (888) 445-3696
glenwoodchamber.com

GRAND JUNCTION

Grand Junction Visitor and Convention Bureau
740 Horizon Dr., 81506
(970) 244-1480
visitgrandjunction.com

IDAHO SPRINGS

Idaho Springs Chamber of Commerce
2060 Miner St., 80452
(303) 567-4382
historicidahosprings.com

PALISADE

Palisade Chamber of Commerce
319 Main St., 81526
(970) 464-7458
palisadecoc.com

VAIL

Vail Valley Chamber and Tourism Bureau
100 E. Meadow Dr., 81620
(970) 476-1000 or (800) 653-4523
visitvailvalley.com

Vail Resorts Management Company
vail.com

DILLON

Best Western Ptarmigan Lodge
652 Lake Dillon Dr.
(970) 468-2341 or
(800) 842-5939
ptarmiganlodge.com
Moderate
Affordable ski resort lodging with Jacuzzi and sauna room.

La Quinta Inn
(Summit County)
560 Silverthorne Lane
(970) 468-6200
lq.com
Moderate
Standard La Quinta accommodations with free breakfast, free wireless Internet, spa, and indoor pool.

GEORGETOWN

Mad Creek Bed & Breakfast
167 W. Park Ave., Empire
(303) 569-2003 or
(888) 266-1498
madcreekbnb.net
Inexpensive to Moderate
Victorian cottage filled with antiques, featuring full breakfast, afternoon snacks, an outdoor hot tub, and a friendly owner.

Rose Street Bed & Breakfast
200 Rose St.
(303) 569-2222 or
(866) 569-2221
rosestreetbedbreakfast
.com
Moderate
Historic home in George-
town's Historic Residential
District.

GLENWOOD SPRINGS

Hot Springs Lodge
(across from Glenwood
pool)
415 6th St.
(970) 945-6571 or
(800) 537-7946
hotspringspool.com
Moderate to Expensive
Includes unlimited access
to Glenwood Hot Springs
Pool and full breakfast.

Hotel Colorado
526 Pine St.
(970) 945-6511 or
(800) 544-3998
hotelcolorado.com
Moderate
Historic luxury hotel with
well-appointed rooms, free
wireless Internet, and spa
and massage facilities.

Redstone Inn
82 Redstone Blvd.,
Redstone
(970) 963-2526 or
(800) 748-2524
redstoneinn.com
Moderate
Rustic turn-of-the-20th-
century resort with char-
acter, charm, and friendly
staff in a small mountain
village.

GRAND JUNCTION

The Chateau at Two Rivers
2087 Broadway
(866) 312-9463 or
(970) 255-1471
tworiverswinery.com
Inexpensive to Moderate
Wine country inn with
upscale lodging, French
country chateau decor, and
breakfast included.

Grand Vista Hotel
2790 Crossroads Blvd.
(800) 800-7796 or
(970) 241-8411
grandvistahotel.com
Moderate to Expensive
Newly renovated rooms,
complimentary wireless
Internet, indoor pool and
hot tub, and restaurant and
lounge on-site.

Hampton Inn Grand Junction
205 Main St.
(970) 243-3222
hamptoninn.com
Inexpensive to Moderate
Located on historic Main
Street with free breakfast
and wireless Internet.

Los Altos B&B
375 Hill View Dr.
(970) 256-0964 or
(888) 774-0982
losaltosgrandjunction.com
Moderate to Expensive
Three miles from town, this
B&B has expansive views,
a full gourmet breakfast,
large rooms, and free wireless Internet.

GRANT

Tumbling River Ranch
PO Box 30, 80448
(303) 838-5981 or
(800) 654-8770
tumblingriver.com
Expensive
Deluxe mountain guest
lodge with hiking, horse-
back riding, fishing, swimming, rafting, and a full
dude ranch experience.

IDAHO SPRINGS

Argo Inn and Suites
2622 Colorado Blvd.
(303) 567-4473
argoinnandsuites.com
Inexpensive to Moderate
Located on Clear Creek,
clean and comfortable with
continental breakfast, free
wireless Internet, outdoor
grills, and fire pit, some
rooms with fireplace and
private deck.

H & H Motor Lodge
2445 Colorado Blvd.
(303) 567-2838 or
(800) 445-2893
hhlodge.com
Inexpensive
Clean and affordable
lodging.

KEYSTONE

Ski Tip Lodge
764 Montezuma Rd.
(970) 496-4950
Moderate
Cozy alpine B&B with good
breakfasts included, off-
site hot tubs available, and
a short shuttle ride away
from Keystone ski resort.

VAIL

Four Seasons Resort Vail
1 Vail Rd.
(970) 477-8600
fourseasons.com/vail
Expensive
Renowned Four Seasons luxury and service with a European flair at the base of Vail Mountain.

The Sebastian Vail
16 Vail Rd.
(800) 354-6908
thesebastianvail.com
Expensive
Stylish, comfortable resort hotel with mountain view pool in the heart of Vail Village and steps away from Vail Mountain.

Sonnenalp Resort of Vail
20 Vail Rd.
(866) 284-4411
sonnenalp.com
Expensive
World-class accommodations and excellent Old World service with a spa, private 18-hole golf course, and easy access to Vail Village.

Vail Cascade
1300 Westhaven Dr.
(800) 282-4183
vailcascade.com
Expensive
Luxurious yet relaxed retreat overlooking Gore Creek; the hotel restaurant, Atwater, is one of Vail's finest.

Places to Eat in the Central Mountains

ASPEN

Boogie's Diner
534 E. Cooper Ave.
(970) 925-6610
Moderate
Retro diner-style eatery with an extensive menu of hearty meals, burgers, sandwiches, salads, homemade desserts, milk shakes, and more.

Cantina
411 E. Main St.
(970) 925-3663
cantina-aspen.com
Moderate to Expensive
Fresh Mexican cuisine, popular for happy hour and après ski.

Grateful Deli
233 E. Main St.
(970) 925-6647
Inexpensive
Groovy little deli with excellent sandwiches, subs, and paninis—a local favorite.

Hickory House Ribs
730 W. Main St.
(970) 925-2313
hickoryhouseribs.com
Moderate
Extensive menu, the place to go for barbecue in Aspen.

Little Annie's
517 E. Hyman Ave.
(970) 925-1098
littleannies.com
Moderate to Expensive

Diverse selection of ribs, steak, chicken, fish, soups, stews, chilis, and salads.

Main St. Bakery & Cafe
201 E. Main St.
(970) 925-6446
Inexpensive to Moderate
Popular patisserie and cafe serving breakfast and lunch, baked goods, hot drinks.

Paradise Bakery & Cafe
320 S. Galena St.
(970) 925-7585
paradisebakery.com
Inexpensive
Delicious muffins, croissants, bagels, cookies, and more.

Takah Sushi
320 S. Mill St.
(970) 925-8588
takahsushi.com
Moderate to Expensive
Wide selection of sushi, sashimi, soups, salads, and small side dishes.

Wild Fig
315 E. Hyman Ave.
(970) 925-5160
thewildfig.com
Moderate to Expensive
European-style brasserie serving innovative Mediterranean lunch and dinner.

AVON

Ticino
100 W. Beaver Creek Blvd.
(970) 748-6792
ticinorestaurantavon.com
Inexpensive to Expensive
A gem of an Italian home-style restaurant with pizza and homemade pasta.

BRECKENRIDGE

Blue Moose
540 S. Main St.
(970) 453-4859
Inexpensive to Moderate
Local favorite for tasty, filling breakfasts. Cash only.

Breckenridge Brewery
600 S. Main St.
(970) 453-1550
breckbrew.com
Moderate
Ribs, fish-and-chips, fajitas, and more, along with excellent beer and dramatic mountain views.

Clint's Bakery and Coffee House
131 S. Main St.
(970) 453-2990
Inexpensive to Moderate
The coolest coffeehouse in town, serving fresh pastries, bagels, wraps, and an extensive menu of hot drinks. Free wireless Internet for customers.

Crepes A La Cart
307 S. Main St.
(970) 453-4022
crepesalacarts.com
Inexpensive to Moderate
Permanent crepe cart on Main Street offering a variety of savory and sweet crepes.

Giampietro Pasta and Pizzeria
100 N. Main St.
(970) 453-3838
giampietropizza.com
Inexpensive to Moderate
Cozy Italian eatery considered by many locals to have the best pizza in Summit County.

Lucha Cantina
500 S. Main St.
(970) 453-1342
luchacantina.com
Inexpensive
Homemade, healthy Mexican cuisine, burgers, and a nice tequila selection.

DILLON

Arapahoe Cafe
626 Lake Dillon Dr.
(970) 468-0873
arapahoecafe.com
Inexpensive to Moderate
Historic cafe/pub serving hearty, tasty breakfast, lunch, and dinner.

Silverheels Bar & Grill
603 Main St., Frisco
(970) 668-0345
silverheelsrestaurant.com
Moderate to Expensive
Southwestern specialties,

OTHER ATTRACTIONS WORTH SEEING IN THE CENTRAL MOUNTAINS

ASPEN
Aspen Historical Society Wheeler/Stallard Museum
(970) 925-3721
aspenhistory.org

Independence Pass
(Highway 82, closed in winter)
independencepass.org

DILLON
Copper Mountain Resort Ski Area
(866) 841-2481
coppercolorado.com

GEORGETOWN
Loveland Ski Area
(800) 736-3754
skiloveland.com

GLENWOOD
White River National Forest
(970) 945-2521
fs.fed.us/r2/whiteriver

IDAHO SPRINGS
Idaho Springs National Historic District
(303) 567-4382
historicidahosprings.com

salads, steak, seafood, and trout.

EDWARDS

Juniper Restaurant
970 Main St., E101
(970) 926-7001
juniperrestaurant.com
Expensive
New World seasonal cuisine at one of the best restaurants in the Vail Valley.

GEORGETOWN

The Happy Cooker
412 6th St.
(303) 569-3166
georgetowncolorado.com/happycooker.htm
Inexpensive to Moderate
Home-style American menu of sandwiches, salads, soups, chili, breads, desserts; breakfast and lunch only.

Lucha Cantina at Red Ram
606 6th St.
(303) 569-2300
Inexpensive
luchacantina.com
Homemade, healthy Mexican cuisine, burgers, and a nice tequila selection.

GLENWOOD SPRINGS

Daily Bread Cafe
729 Grand Ave.
(970) 945-6253
Inexpensive to Moderate
Excellent breakfasts, sandwiches, salads, and soups, popular with locals and visitors.

Florindo's
721 Grand Ave.
(970) 945-1245
Moderate to Expensive
Longtime local Italian restaurant.

Juicy Lucy's Steakhouse
308 7th St.
(970) 945-4619
juicylucyssteakhouse.com
Moderate to Expensive
Steak, seafood, lamb, pork, and elk along with daily specials and a full wine list.

River's
2525 S. Grand Ave.
(970) 928-8813
theriversrestaurant.com
Moderate to Expensive
Well-prepared beef, game, and seafood. Gluten-free menu available.

GRAND JUNCTION

Dream Cafe
314 Main St.
(970) 424-5353
Inexpensive to Moderate
Breakfast and brunch; great food with friendly service and a trendy, upbeat atmosphere.

Il Bistro Italiano
400 Main St.
(970) 243-8622
ilbistroitaliano.com
Moderate
Traditional and contemporary Italian dishes, pastas, pizzas, and small plates, prepared from fresh ingredients.

Main Street Bagels
559 Main St.
(970) 241-2740
gjmainstreetbagels.com
Inexpensive to Moderate
Artisan bakery and espresso cafe with soups, salads, hot panini, and sandwiches.

Pablo's Pizza
319 Main St.
(970) 255-8879
pablospizza.com
Moderate
Creative, award-winning pizza, warm panini sandwiches, and homemade soups. Pleasant patio area.

626 on Rood
626 Rood Ave.
(970) 257-7663
626onrood.com
Expensive
Modern American cuisine, highly rated on Trip Advisor, with an extensive wine list.

IDAHO SPRINGS

Beau Jo's
1517 Miner St.
(303) 567-4376
beaujos.com
Moderate
Legendary among Coloradans for serving some of the best pizza in the state.

Two Brothers Deli
1424 Miner St.
(303) 567-2439
twobrothersdeli.com
Inexpensive to Moderate
Quality deli with great sandwiches and soups, good service, free wireless.

MINTURN

The Minturn Saloon
146 N. Main St.
(970) 827-5954
minturnsaloon.com
Moderate
Get down with politicians, actors, misfits, and locals, then indulge in good Mexican food, ribs, and the house specialty: quail. Housed in a century-old building, Minturn Saloon is one of a kind.

RED CLIFF

Mango's
166½ Eagle St.
(970) 827-9109
mangosmountaingrill.com
Inexpensive to Moderate
Lively mountain grill with plenty of local color and tasty food.

VAIL

Atwater
1300 Westhaven Dr.
(970) 479-7014
vailcascade.com/atwater/
Moderate to Expensive
Creative American cuisine, specializing in craft beer and food/dessert pairings. Try the beer and home-made ice cream float.

Bart & Yeti's
551 E. Lionsheads Circle
(970) 476-2754
Moderate
Homey, economical, and tasty American comfort food. Think burgers, chili, ribs.

Blu's
193 E. Gore Creek Dr.
(970) 476-3113
blusrestaurant.com
Inexpensive breakfast and lunch, Expensive dinner
Diverse menu, with excellent breakfast and lunch served until 5 p.m. in Vail Village.

Larkspur
Golden Peak Lodge
458 Vail Valley Dr.
(970) 479-8050
larkspurvail.com
Expensive
Sophisticated New American cuisine with weekly menu changes reflecting the offerings of the season.

Left Bank
183 Gore Creek Dr., #4
(970) 476-3696
leftbankvail.com
Expensive
Authentic French cuisine and an extensive wine list; a Vail Valley favorite for more than 40 years.

Pazzo's Pizzeria
122 E. Meadow Dr.
(970) 476-9026
pazzospizzeria.com
Moderate
Popular pizza palace, service can be variable but pizza is good.

Sweet Basil
193 E. Gore Creek Dr.
(970) 476-0125
sweetbasil-vail.com
Expensive
Creative contemporary American cuisine with an extensive wine list; popular with locals and travelers for over 30 years.

Terra Bistro
352 E. Meadow Dr.
(888) 794-0410
terrabistrovail.com
Expensive
Gourmet green restaurant blending southwestern, Mediterranean, and Asian cuisines, with a 100 percent all-natural, largely organic menu. Excellent small plates of entrees and well-mixed drinks during "Appy Hour" in the bar.

SOUTHERN COLORADO →

Colorado Springs & Beyond

Southern Colorado is far from the Front Range, and in many ways it's another world. Too far from Denver for a day trip or short weekend getaway, the area escapes the crowds that can congregate at destinations farther north. No interstates cross the region, which somehow translates to a slower pace of life in this corner of the state. That's all good news for anyone wanting to explore this varied landscape, because many of the state's highlights lie in this area. Mountain ranges such as the Sangre de Cristo, San Juan, La Plata, and San Miguel are home to Colorado's most rugged peaks and largest wilderness tracts. The San Luis Valley and Great Sand Dunes are unexpected and imposing in their vastness. Mining ghost towns, plunging canyons, and alpine meadows jam-packed with wildflowers wait to be explored. Friendly western towns offer a mix of mountain biking, ranching culture, and brewpubs that bring together eclectic communities. The region contains well-preserved evidence of the ancient Puebloans who lived in the area for centuries before the first Europeans rode up on horseback.

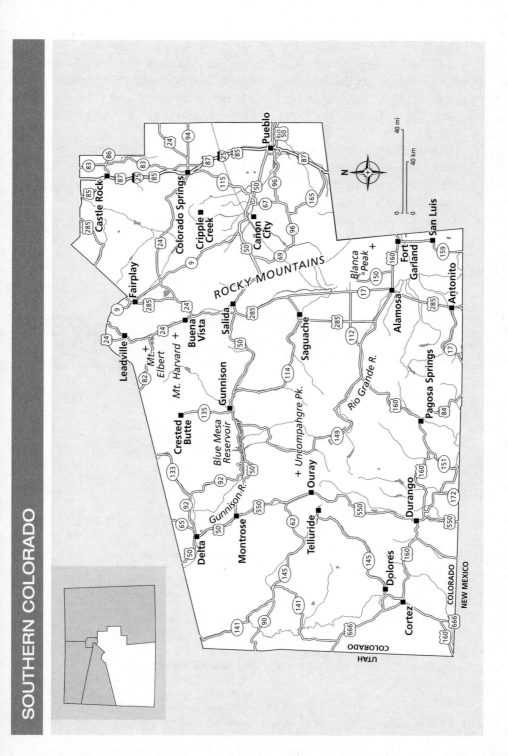

Dozens of different vacations await visitors to southern Colorado. Take your pick of Victorian mountain towns, red rock canyons, local festivals, alpine ski villages, challenging mountain biking, counterculture communities, ancestral cliff dwellings, rodeo, and some of the best scenery, hiking, camping, skiing, fishing, and other outdoor pursuits to be found on the planet.

The **Devil's Head Lookout Trail,** in the Rampart Range west of the little community of Sedalia (south of Denver) offers a 360-degree view of surrounding Pike National Forest. On clear days you can see mountain peaks over 100 miles away. It got its name from the red rock formations that stick out like two horns. The trail winds through deep pine forests interspersed with aspen, past giant red cliffs. The trail's length—just 1.375 miles—doesn't sound like much; it climbs steeply, though, and includes a 950-foot vertical elevation gain, beginning at 8,800 feet.

AUTHOR'S FAVORITES IN SOUTHERN COLORADO

Black Canyon of the Gunnison
(970) 641-2337
nps.gov/blca

Cumbres & Toltec Scenic Railroad
(888) 286-2737
cumbrestoltec.com

Durango & Silverton Narrow Gauge Railroad
(970) 247-2733 or (877) 872-4607
durangotrain.com

Garden of the Gods
(719) 634-6666
gardenofgods.com

Great Sand Dunes National Park
(719) 378-6300 or (719) 378-6399
nps.gov/grsa

Manitou and Pikes Peak Cog Railway
(719) 685-5401 or (800) 745-3773
cograilway.com

Mesa Verde National Park
(970) 529-4465
nps.gov/meve

Royal Gorge Bridge and Park
(719) 275-7507 or (888) 333-5597
royalgorgebridge.com

Shelf Road
(719) 269-8500
co.blm.gov, then do a search for Shelf Road

Town of Salida Downtown and Riverfront
(877) 772-5432 or (719) 539-2068
salida.com or salidachamber.org

Town of Telluride
(888) 605-2578
visittelluride.com

Ute Mountain Tribal Park
(970) 565-3751 ext. 330 or (970) 565-9653
utemountainute.com/tribalpark.htm

Along the way, you get views of **Pikes Peak,** a number of "fourteeners" (peaks over 14,000 feet high), some of the peaks in Rocky Mountain National Park, and the Great Plains. Benches for the tired line the uphill paths. Bring water since there is none along the trail.

To reach the trailhead, from Denver take Santa Fe (US 85) south to Sedalia (13 miles); turn west toward Deckers (Highway 67) for 10 miles and make another left turn onto the **Rampart Range Road** (Highway 5); go another 8.5 miles until you see the Devil's Head sign. For more information contact the South Platte Ranger District, 19316 Goddard Ranch Ct., Morrison 80465; (303) 275-5610; funcoloradohikes.com/devils_head.html.

En route from Denver to Colorado Springs via the interstate, you may see a modest sign that says **Larkspur.** Few travelers have ever heard of it. Even many Denver residents are unfamiliar with this hamlet.

Yet on weekends from mid-June through July, tiny Larkspur comes alive with a bang. Cannon shots can be heard from afar. When your car draws closer to the hillside, the cannons are followed by medieval trumpets played in unison.

For more than 35 years, the zany, lively **Colorado Renaissance Festival** has entertained summer visitors on a wooded Colorado hillside above Larkspur. Part theater, part learning experience, part petting zoo for children, and part artisans' market, its Renaissance theme begins when you enter the walled compound and you're greeted as "My Lord" or "My Lady." Artisans galore demonstrate their craft: Blacksmiths hammer away, glassblowers regale onlookers with their art, potters shape at their wheels, leatherworkers show their stuff. Bands of costumed musicians wander up the mountainside. Harpists, flutists, bagpipers, and minstrel singers materialize and harmonize.

Several times a day, "King Henry" and his "Court" introduce you to knights jousting on horseback at a gallop, doing tricks with their lances. The stages are busy with storytellers and merrymakers; the pubs dispense barrels of beer and huge turkey legs. Processions of celebrities—Shakespeare, Anne Boleyn—promenade among the visitors, while a few yards away, you can be a medieval archer or knife thrower or dart artist. Encounter the unexpected: Youngsters ride real camels and elephants; jugglers and puppet masters dazzle onlookers. A good time is had by everyone.

There is no charge for parking weekends June through July. To reach Larkspur, take exit 172 from I-25 and follow the signs. Open 10 a.m. to 6:30

trivia

The Devil's Head Lookout Tower at the end of the Devil's Head Lookout Trail sits atop the highest point in the Rampart Range. It is the last operational lookout on the Front Range.

p.m. Sat and Sun. Admission costs $18.95 for adults and teenagers 13 and older and $8 for children 5 to 12; children under 5 are free. For more information contact the festival at 409F S. Wilcox St., Castle Rock 80104; (303) 688-6010; coloradorenaissance.com.

A 10-minute drive south of Larkspur on Country Road 105 brings you to quiet, photogenic **Palmer Lake.** Almost no travel guide mentions it, and most people bypass it via I-25. Palmer Lake was once a refueling stop for steam railroad engines; now it's almost forgotten. Its colorful history includes gold mines, Indian raids, the occasional scalping, posses hunting murderers, and saloon shootings. Several trailheads in town lead into the hills, and there are good restaurants, shops, and a historical museum. People come here to get away from the city, walk around the lake, or take their young children to the small playground. Traffic is minimal, and it's a fine place to relax. For more information contact the Town Offices at 42 Valley Crescent, Palmer Lake 80133; (719) 481-2953; ci.palmer-lake.co.us.

For those who like to hike or bike, the 15-mile **Santa Fe Regional Trail,** one of the largest continuous trails in El Paso County, begins at **Palmer Lake Recreation Area.** It goes through the town of Monument to the south, ending at the southern boundary of the **US Air Force Academy.** For more information call (719) 520-6375 or visit traillink.com.

trivia

The US Air Force Academy's Cadet Chapel received a 1996 American Institute of Architects' award. The chapel conducts services for Protestant, Catholic, Buddhist, Muslim, and Jewish worshippers.

The Air Force Academy north of Colorado Springs is one of eastern Colorado's most recognized landmarks. Whether you hike, bike, or drive, consider a stop at the academy's visitor center, located at exit 150B off I-25. A nature trail and the **Cadet Chapel** are open for visitors. The stunning chapel was completed in 1963 and is considered to be the architectural centerpiece of the academy's campus with its 17 silver-hued spires that sweep to heights of more than 150 feet. It is open Mon through Sat, 9 a.m. to 5 p.m.; Sun from 1 to 5 p.m. Sunday services are open to all; call (719) 333-2636 for times.

When visiting the academy, ask for a map at the gate. The visitor center is open from 9 a.m. to 5 p.m. daily. For more information call (719) 333-2025 or visit usafa.af.mil.

Continuing south on I-25 from the US Air Force Academy, you'll come to your next stop—the **ProRodeo Hall of Fame and Museum of the American Cowboy,** which presents the West's unique cowboy heritage in a facility that is both entertaining and educational. The cowboy played a vital role in opening the West to the expansion of the 19th century, and his reputation for courage and individualism has become part of our national folklore and culture.

Families with children will enjoy the outdoor corral with its live animals. Inside, dioramas and exhibits display saddles, boots, buckles, spurs, ropes, chaps, branding equipment, and other paraphernalia, all telling the story of rodeo's history in this country. Rodeo as a sport comes alive through the mementos of America's major rodeo champions.

Visitors can learn about such colorful rodeo champs as bull rider Warren G. "Freckles" Brown, reputed to be the oldest man in ProRodeo history to win a riding event. His long career was interrupted by a broken neck, as well as by World War II. With typical spirit during wartime parachute jumps into China, Brown put on a rodeo using army mules and native cattle and declared himself the Orient's all-around champion of 1942.

Over the years, rules and equipment were standardized, judging was streamlined, prize money increased, and the freewheeling entertainment of the 1800s evolved into the modern sport of professional rodeo.

Here the visitor can learn the fine points of saddle bronc riding and how to judge a rider's performance, and can get the jolting sensation, through film with stereo sound, of what it's like to ride a bucking Brahma bull. Other films trace the historical development of rodeo.

The ProRodeo Hall of Fame is located just north of Colorado Springs on I-25 at exit 148. Hours are 9 a.m. to 5 p.m. daily except for major holidays. Entrance is $6 for adults, $5 for seniors, $4 for military, and $3 for children 6 to 12. Free for children under 6. Call (719) 528-4764 or write 101 ProRodeo Dr., Colorado Springs 80919; prorodeohalloffame.com.

The wonders of nature blend together at the **_Garden of the Gods_** in Colorado Springs to create one of the most unusual natural settings in Colorado. Established as a free city park in 1909, the almost 1,370 acres are filled with silent and spectacular red sandstone rock formations, including **_Gateway Rocks, Cathedral Spires,_** and the **_Balanced Rock._** Grasslands meet mountain forests to provide contrasts of scenic beauty. A common resident of the park is the great horned owl, whose keen, light-gathering eyes and superior hearing make it an effective nighttime hunter. Hike, picnic, and horseback ride to fully appreciate the park's natural beauty. But most of all, bring your camera and photograph these wonders (especially at sunset or sunrise when the low sun accents the naturally colorful red stone).

trivia

The Garden of the Gods was once sacred ground to Native Americans.

The park is open daily from November 1 through April 30 from 5 a.m. to 9 p.m. and May 1 through October 31 from 5 a.m. to 11 p.m. The Garden of the Gods Visitor and Nature Center is open from 9 a.m. to 5 p.m. in the winter months and 8 a.m. to 8 p.m. Memorial Day weekend through Labor Day weekend. The center offers free color maps of the park and free entrance to the *Museum of Natural and Cultural History.* Arrive via exit 146 off I-25. Go west on Garden of the Gods Road, and then south on North 30th Street. The visitor center will be on your left at Gateway Road. For more information contact Garden of the Gods Visitor and Nature Center, 1805 N. 30th St., Colorado Springs 80904; (719) 634-6666; gardenofgods.com.

If you want to vacation in luxury, consider the five-star *Broadmoor,* which has 14,110-foot Pikes Peak for a backdrop. The Broadmoor actually began in the 1850s with a Silesian count. He hoped to create another Monte Carlo against the backdrop of Colorado's mountainscape. Eventually, two Philadelphians, Charles Tutt and Spencer Penrose, took over. They'd become rich in Cripple Creek mining and real estate, and as world travelers, they knew what they wanted—a regal, Renaissance-style hotel.

The Broadmoor's doors opened on June 29, 1918; among several notables, the first to register was John D. Rockefeller Jr. Since that day, there has been a stream of industrialists, diplomats, movie moguls, film stars, and titled ladies and gentlemen. They mingle nowadays with anyone who can afford this pricey, year-round retreat. It is among the largest, plushest, and most elegant in Colorado, offering every conceivable amenity. For more information call (866) 837-9520 or (719) 634-7711 or visit broadmoor.com.

Seven Falls is 10 driving minutes west of the Broadmoor resort. "The Grandest Mile of Scenery in Colorado" lives up to its slogan: A 1,000-foot-high granite canyon leads to seven waterfalls flanked by healthy forests of juniper, blue spruce, Douglas fir, and ponderosa pine. Not far from the dramatic, perpendicular "pillars of Hercules," you can climb several hundred steep steps to platforms from which you view these scenic wonders.

You can reach Seven Falls via Cheyenne Boulevard and Mesa (exit 140B off I-25). Hours are 9 a.m. to 5 p.m. daily. Daytime admission ranges from $9.25 for adults to $5.75 for children 6 to 15. Children under 6 are free. For more information contact Seven Falls Company, 3850 S. Cheyenne Canyon Rd., Colorado Springs 80906; (719) 632-0765; sevenfalls.com.

Located on Cheyenne Mountain just above the Broadmoor resort is the *Cheyenne Mountain Zoo.* With 146 acres and 172 species, the zoo mirrors the natural habitats of animals from Africa, Australia, Asia, and North America. A petting zoo and oversize garden are a delight for kids. To reach the zoo, from I-25 go south on Nevada Avenue. Turn right on Lake Avenue. Turn onto Mirada

Road and follow signs to 4250 Cheyenne Mountain Zoo Rd. Admission prices range from $12.25 to $17.25 from May 1 through Labor Day depending on age. After Labor Day through April, prices are $2–3 cheaper. Military discounts are available. Children 2 and younger free. For more information call (719) 633-9925 or visit cmzoo.org.

The year was 1806; the discoverer of Colorado Springs's "Great Mountain" was Lieutenant **Zebulon Montgomery Pike.** Neither he nor any of his party got even close to the top, due to bad weather and perhaps a lack of planning. At that time, it certainly wasn't conceivable that one of America's most unusual railroads ever constructed would carry thousands to its summit.

Today you can journey on the country's highest railroad to the apex of famous Pikes Peak. The **Manitou and Pikes Peak Cog Railway,** which is 46,158 feet long, climbs from an elevation of 6,571 feet at the **Manitou Springs** station to one of 14,110 feet at the summit. This is a vertical gain of 7,539 feet, or an average of 846 feet per mile. The distance is longer than any covered by the famous cogwheel rails in Switzerland.

Along the entire route you'll be treated to a continuous panorama. At the 11,578-foot level, the train emerges from a sea of quaking aspen into the windswept stretches of timberline and climbs into the Saddle, where you get

trivia

Some of the bristlecone pine trees along the Manitou and Pikes Peak Cog Railway are estimated to be almost 2,000 years old, making them among the oldest living things on earth.

an unparalleled view of Manitou Springs and of the Garden of the Gods in the valley below. You also see the vast expanses of the **Great Plains** stretch toward the horizon.

On clear days, you can spot Denver 75 miles to the north of Colorado Springs and the dramatic **Sangre de Cristo Mountains** in southern Colorado. The view to the west is astounding; mile upon mile of snowcapped giants rise into the blue Colorado sky.

The Steamer Stop Shop (clothing and curios) is a good place to pick up gifts at the Manitou Springs station. You can purchase a box lunch at the cafe to eat on the patio or take on the train ($9 per lunch). The Cog Railway runs year-round. Depending on the season, tickets run $26 to $35 for adults and $14.50 to $19 for children 3 to 11, and children younger than 2 ride free if held on a lap throughout the ride. Reservations are highly recommended. The round-trip takes 3 hours and 10 minutes; call for departure times. Take exit 141 (US 24) off I-25. Head west on US 24 for 4 miles to the Manitou Springs exit. Go west on Manitou Avenue for 1.5 miles. Turn left on Ruxton Avenue. The station is

Some Little-Known Facts about Manitou Springs

- It was actually from Manitou Springs's mineral springs that Colorado Springs got its name.

- "Manitou" is a Native American word for "Great Spirit."

- Native Americans attributed supernatural powers to Manitou Springs's waters and temporarily reserved the surrounding area as a sanctuary.

three-quarters of a mile up the road. For more information call (800) 745-3773 or (719) 685-5401, or visit cograilway.com.

Back in 1891, the *Cripple Creek* gold strike proved to be the last major gold rush in North America. Within a few years, those mines in the mountains west of Colorado Springs yielded almost a billion dollars' worth of the valuable mineral. By 1900 Cripple Creek had grown to some 50,000 inhabitants. The miners could patronize 75 saloons, 40 grocery stores, 17 churches, and 8 newspapers. Every day a dozen passenger trains steamed into the depot. Eventually, 500 gold mines operated in the area. Some 8,000 men brought on a gambling, carousing, and whoring boom.

Ironically, the man who discovered the first gold vein sold his claim for $500 and proceeded to drink it all away. Colorado Springs owes part of its existence to the prospectors. In time, celebrities came and went. Adventurer Lowell Thomas was born in nearby Victor, now nearly a ghost town. Groucho Marx once drove a grocery wagon in Cripple Creek, and he performed here as well. Jack Dempsey, for a brief bout a miner, trained and boxed in the region. Financier Bernard Baruch worked as a telegrapher here. Teddy Roosevelt, after a Cripple Creek visit, told the world that "the scenery bankrupts the English language." Politicians arrived in droves to see for themselves.

trivia

Mining experts considered Cripple Creek worthless despite frequent reports of gold; still, novice prospectors, mining with pitchforks, eventually developed the "300-million-dollar cow pasture."

Over the years, gold prices dropped. Production began to slip, and the miners scattered. By 1920 fewer than 5,000 people lived here.

And today? Cripple Creek attracts lots of summer tourists. They come for the narrow-gauge train rides. They pan for gold on Main Street and browse the antiques and souvenir shops housed in historic buildings. They play blackjack, poker, and the slots in more than a dozen casinos. The Cripple Creek District Museum, Jail Museum, and Old Homestead (former bordello) Museum offer a glimpse back in time to life during an untamed era. Small cafes serve home-cooked food.

Each summer the renovated **Historic Butte Opera House** puts on a full program of summer theater productions. This building, originally constructed in 1896, has had many uses throughout its history. Before its renovation in the late 1990s, the building served as a storage facility for the Cripple Creek Fire Department located below.

Extensive renovations by the city of Cripple Creek restored the theater's splendor. The Butte theater now seats 174 people and has a 1,350-square-foot stage, state-of-the-art sound equipment and movie projectors, and a snack bar. For more information and performance dates, contact the Opera House at (719) 689-6402; butteoperahouse.com.

The old railroad depot has become the **Cripple Creek District Museum,** along with an old assay office and the Colorado Trading and Transfer Company building, constructed in 1893. These three buildings are crammed with mementos of the mining age. Superbly maintained, the museum is well worth a visit. Hours are 10 a.m. to 5 p.m. daily mid-May through mid-Oct; Sat and Sun 10 a.m. to 4 p.m. for the rest of the year. Call (719) 689-2634 or (719) 689-9540 or visit cripple-creek.org. The museum is on Bennett Avenue in Cripple Creek.

Not many visitors venture beyond the town and into the surrounding hills. This leaves plenty of room on the miles of hiking and biking trails leading through stunning scenery in Pike National Forest. Several local outfitters offer horseback riding trips ranging from 1 hour to all day. The mountains are studded with old abandoned mines that can be reached by hiking up old mining roads past rusting machinery and old wooden trestles. View the mines from outside only; they are dangerous and unstable inside, and should not be entered.

Some Little-Known Facts about Cripple Creek

- In its heyday, the Cripple Creek area produced $25 million in gold in one year.

- Famous Cripple Creek workers included Jack Johnson and Jack Dempsey. Dempsey once fought a bloody, drawn-out battle here in Cripple Creek . . . for 50 dollars.

- Speakeasy hostess "Texas" Guinan started in Cripple Creek. Perhaps this is one of the reasons why the city is now best known for its Las Vegas–style gambling.

Take a Ride on the Railroad

For an unusual perspective, explore the area from a car on the *Cripple Creek & Victor Narrow-Gauge Railroad.* It takes about 45 minutes to complete the winding 4-mile ride behind a coal-burning steam locomotive. The train travels through the historic gold mining district, passing abandoned mines, and stopping at several points of interest and photo opportunities. The railroad is open daily from mid-May through the second week of October. Call (719) 689-2640 for departure times. The fare is $13 for adults and teenagers 13 and older, $12 for senior citizens 65 and older, and $8 for children 3 to 12; children 2 and younger ride free; cripplecreekrailroad.com.

The story of the **Mollie Kathleen Gold Mine** is a Cripple Creek legend. Back in 1891, Mollie Kathleen Gortner moved to the area with her family, including her attorney husband, Henry. On an excursion by herself to see a herd of elk (she'd never seen them before), Mollie Kathleen came upon an outcropping of quartz that was veined with gold. Upon attempting to file her claim in town, she was informed that as a woman, she had no right to do so. Not to be deterred, Mollie Kathleen seized the papers and signed them anyway, declaring that the issue could be taken up with her husband if there was a problem. Thus Mollie Kathleen Gortner became the first woman in the area to stake a gold claim. Her mine continued to produce gold uninterrupted for the next 70 years, with the exception of a period of time during World War II when all gold production ceased due to a nationwide ban. Today the gold that came out of the mine would be worth more than $100 million.

trivia

The Cripple Creek Mining District, made up of roughly 25 towns in the Cripple Creek area, was once known as "The World's Greatest Gold Camp."

The Mollie Kathleen Gold Mine stopped producing long ago, but now visitors can descend 1,000 feet below ground on the country's only historic gold mine tour. Learn about the life and working conditions of the hard rock gold miner. The tour begins with a ride on a skip (elevator) down to the lower levels of the mine. There you can see equipment used to mine at these depths and ride on the last air-powered Tram-Air Locomotive. Appropriate for all ages (there are no steps or ladders to climb), the 40-minute tours of the Mollie Kathleen Gold Mine depart at frequent intervals during the peak season. The mine is open for tours daily from mid-Mar through Oct. Call ahead for times since they vary depending on the season. Rates are $18 for adults and $10 for children 3 to 12; children under 3 tour free. For more information call (719) 689-2466 or (888) 291-5689. When using the toll-free phone number, you must enter a PIN number (9101). You can also visit goldminetours.com.

Many people come to Cripple Creek just for gaming at the dozen or more casinos. But regardless of whether you enjoy gambling, the wealth of historical sites and the plentiful outdoor activities are well worth a visit. Cripple Creek is 45 miles west of Colorado Springs. From there it can be reached via US 24 west, then Highway 67. For more information write the Cripple Creek Welcome Center, PO Box 430, Cripple Creek 80813; call (877) 858-4653; or check out visit.cripplecreek.com.

trivia

Cripple Creek's Mollie Kathleen Gold Mine, the longest continually operating gold mine tour in the world, boasts the only vertical-shaft gold mine tour in the US.

Pueblo, located some 40 miles south of Colorado Springs, hosts the yearly ***Colorado State Fair & Exposition,*** the largest single event in the state. Every summer, the fair delivers an action-packed 17-day experience for all who visit. Come to see the PRCA Championship Rodeo and stroll the largest carnival and midway in the state. In the agricultural section, view prize lambs, hogs, steers, horses, and other animals. Young animals are available to pet in the children's barnyard. Competition for the best baked goods, jams and pre-serves, quilting, and scores of exhibits and creative arts displays give visitors literally hundreds of things to see. At night there are performances by some of the nation's top entertainers.

trivia

Pueblo is known to many as the home of the Federal Citizen Information Center, where Americans can write to "Pueblo, Colorado 81009" for information on thousands of subjects.

Pueblo's El Pueblo History Museum

Designed to be the gateway to Historic Arkansas Riverwalk of Pueblo (HARP), the El Pueblo History Museum includes a permanent gallery covering the history of Pueblo along with an atrium gallery and a children's gallery. A recreated 1840s adobe trading post, archaeological excavation site, and more, the museum also serves as a central location for tourist information. Contact the museum at (719) 583-0453 for details or visit historycolorado.org/museums/el-pueblo-history-museum-0. The museum is located at 301 N. Union St. in Pueblo. Hours are Tues through Sat 10 a.m. to 4 p.m.

TOP ANNUAL EVENTS IN SOUTHERN COLORADO

JANUARY

Ouray Ice Festival
Ouray
(970) 325-4288
ourayicepark.com

FEBRUARY

Pagosa Springs Winter Fest
second weekend in Feb
(800) 252-2204
visitpagosasprings.com

MARCH

Monte Vista Crane Festival
Monte Vista National Wildlife Refuge
(719) 852-3552
cranefest.com

Music and Blossom Festival
Cañon City
Spring
(719) 239-1743
ccblossomfestival.com

MAY

Mesa Verde Country Indian Arts & Cultural Festival
late May to early June
(970) 565-8227
mesaverdecountry.com

Pikes Peak or Bust Rodeo
Colorado Springs
Summer
(719) 635-1101
coloradospringsrodeo.com

Royal Gorge Rodeo
Cañon City
(719) 252-3707
horsestop.net/royalgorgerodeo.htm

JUNE

Colorado Renaissance Festival
Larkspur
June and July
(303) 688-6010 or (877) 259-3328
coloradorenaissance.com

Donkey Derby
Cripple Creek
late June
(877) 858-4653
visitcripplecreek.com/donkeyderbydays

Gunnison River Festival
Gunnison and Altmont
(970) 596-7094
gunnisonriverfestival.com

Telluride Bluegrass Festival
late June
(303) 823-0848 or (800) 624-2422
bluegrass.com/telluride

General admission to the state fair is $10 Fri through Sun and $7 Mon through Thurs; children 6 and younger get in free. Hours run 10 a.m. to midnight throughout the course of the fair, with many exhibits closing at 10 p.m. From I-25, take exit 97A west (Central Avenue). This will take you to Northern Avenue. Follow Northern west; the state fairgrounds will be on your right. Call (719) 561-8484 or (800) 876-4567 for details, or visit coloradostatefair.com.

For more information on visiting the Pueblo area, contact the Greater Pueblo Chamber of Commerce, 302 N. Santa Fe Ave., Pueblo 81003; (800) 233-3446 or (719) 542-1704; pueblochamber.org.

JULY

Cattlemen's Days Rodeo and County Fair
Gunnison
mid-July
(970) 641-1501
gunnisoncrestedbutte.com

Cherry Days
Paonia
early July
(970) 527-3886
paoniachamber.com

Crested Butte Wildflower Festival
(970) 349-2571
crestedbuttewildflowerfestival.com

AUGUST

Boom Days and Burro Race
Leadville
first full weekend of Aug
(719) 486-0197
leadvilleboomdays.com

Buena Vista Gold Rush Days
Buena Vista
mid-Aug
(719) 395-6612
fourteenernet.com/goldrush/index.htm

Colorado State Fair & Exposition
Pueblo Fairgrounds
late Aug–early Sept
(719) 561-8484 or (800) 876-4567
coloradostatefair.com

Crested Butte Arts Festival
early Aug
(970) 349-1184
crestedbutteartsfestival.com

SEPTEMBER

Colorado Springs Balloon Classic
Labor Day weekend
(719) 471-4833
balloonclassic.com

Telluride Film Festival
(510) 665-9494
telluridefilmfestival.com

OCTOBER

Durango Cowboy Poetry Gathering
Durango
first week of Oct
(970) 749-2995
durangocowboygathering.org

From Pueblo, head west on US 50 to *Cañon City,* known as Colorado's Prison Capitol for the abundance of prisons in the area. One of the nearby attractions is *Shelf Road.* Shelf Road makes up part of the *Gold Belt Tour,* a designated Colorado Scenic Byway. From stunning limestone cliffs that attract rock climbers from all over the world to the sheer drop-offs on the side of the road (hence the name) into lush green valleys, the views and the isolation encountered along Shelf Road are idyllic. Abundant wildlife viewing potential rounds out the area's special charm—possible sightings include mule deer, foxes, hawks, American black bears, and owls.

trivia

Pueblo was originally a crossroads for travelers, including Spaniards, fur traders, and Native Americans.

Some of the driving is on rough roads (it's not for the faint of heart) and should be avoided in wet or icy weather; furthermore, four-wheel drive is recommended for portions of Upper Shelf Road. However, any two-wheel-drive vehicle can navigate the scenic portion of Shelf Road that leads out of Cañon City. The road becomes narrow once it turns to dirt, so drive carefully and slowly, watching for oncoming traffic. Plan ahead where you are going to turn around; a good place is at mile marker 14. The entire Gold Belt Tour encompasses 131 miles of driving and takes roughly 5 hours.

To get there from Cañon City, drive north on Raynolds, and then head north again on Fields after Raynolds swings west. Nine miles along Fields takes you directly to Shelf Road. For more information call (719) 269-8500 or visit co .blm.gov/ccdo/canon.htm.

After a jaunt along Shelf Road, another scenic wonder awaits at the **Royal Gorge Bridge and Park.** The gorge, at 1,200 feet deep, has been compared to the Grand Canyon. With its striking reds, mauves, browns, and yellows, the deep and narrow gauge stopped Lieutenant Zebulon Pike (of Pikes Peak fame) in his tracks back in 1806. He couldn't forge the gorge (and he didn't climb Pikes Peak, either).

In 1929 the Royal Gorge Bridge opened up to traffic after 7 months of construction. The bridge is able to support more than two million pounds, so don't worry about your car's weight! Today people flock from all over to drive across this mighty suspension bridge, allegedly the highest of its kind in the world.

The 2,200-foot-long **Aerial Tram** offers another viewing option as it takes visitors for a ride across this remarkable canyon. Painted a fiery red, the 35-passenger tram cabin comes with a guide-conductor who assures timid passengers that the tram will not plunge into the Arkansas River, which rages and roars below. Three braking systems and an extra motor guarantee your safety. In the terminals, a total of about 100 tons of concrete and steel anchor the conveyance's enormous cables, providing reassurance with their heftiness. In fact, a helicopter had to string the tram's pilot cable, and more than $350,000 was needed to rig up this tourist attraction.

trivia

The Royal Gorge Bridge cost more than $10 million to construct.

After looking at it from above, hop aboard for a 5.5-minute ride on the **Incline Railway** to the bottom of the gorge. The world's steepest conveyance of its kind, the Incline Railway gives you a view from below as you look back up at the gorge and bridge above you. Built by the same crew who constructed the bridge, the railway opened in 1931 and has been operating ever since.

These days there is much more to the gorge than the aerial tram and the railway. Horse and donkey rides, a roller coaster, carousel, petting zoo, wildlife pavilion, cliff walk, scale-model railway, and mule team wagon rides are just a few of the many activities that keep families busy. Park admission is $26 for adults and teenagers and $19 for children 4 to 11; children 3 and younger are admitted free. Senior and military discounts are available. Park hours vary throughout the year. Admission offers unlimited access to all park attractions, although some attractions are seasonal. Call for details. The Royal Gorge Bridge and Park is 12 miles west of Cañon City on US 50. Call (719) 275-7507 or (888) 333-5597 or visit royalgorgebridge.com. The Cañon City Chamber of Commerce can be reached at 403 Royal Gorge Blvd.; (719) 275-2331 or (800) 876-7922; canoncitychamber.com.

US 50 west from Cañon City takes you to **Salida.** There are few more outdoorsy places in Colorado. With the Arkansas River running along the edge of town, and an excellent white-water course created by the city, Salida is famous for whitewater rafting, kayaking, and fishing. Locals bring their kids to the river to laze on the warm boulders and splash in the shallows. Mountain bikes and road bikes are popular modes of transportation. And the historic district, several blocks of century-old redbrick buildings, is filled with casual cafes and coffeehouses, fine dining, art galleries, a bookstore, and unique boutiques. Stop by the Salida Cafe just a block from downtown, grab a coffee or a bite to eat, and sit out on the deck overlooking the Arkansas River. The town often shows up on those "Best Places to Live in America" lists. Spend a few hours walking the streets and strolling along the river, and you'll see why.

For more information on Salida visit salida.com or contact the Salida Chamber of Commerce, 406 W. Hwy. 50, Salida 81201; (719) 539-2068 or (877) 772-5432; salidachamber.org.

Driving north on Highway 24 from Salida to **Buena Vista,** travelers have panoramic views of the **Collegiate Peaks** to the west. Nine of the state's 14,000-foot peaks and a handful of 13,000-foot peaks are clustered together in a dramatic backdrop to the valley. Both the Continental Divide Trail and Colorado Trail cross through here, and the area is rich with hiking trails and campgrounds. Anyone interested in climbing some of those fourteeners or just wandering into the backcountry will find a convenient base in Buena Vista. Several motels and a variety of cafes, cantinas, pubs, and coffeehouses make this a popular overnight spot prior to heading into the wilderness.

Each August Buena Vista hosts of one the state's most colorful small-town festivals. **Gold Rush Days** combine a celebration of the area's history with contemporary entertainment and a few wacky events thrown into the mix. During the 13.5-mile Pack Burro Race, runners leading burros loaded with 35 pounds of mining equipment race along a loop that begins and ends in town. A duck race, toilet seat race, and an abundance of infamous "madams," storytelling, beer and wine gardens, food, and live entertainment round out the weekend. For more information contact the Chamber of Commerce at (719) 395-6612 or go to fourteenernet.com/goldrush/index.htm.

Buena Vista preserves an intriguing bit of Colorado history at the **Turner Farm and Apple Orchard.** This early 1900s apple farm has been restored and repurposed as a living museum. Around 50 apple trees, a farmhouse, mother-in-law cabin, homestead cabin, and other buildings give visitors a glimpse into a way of life from another century. On Sunday during the summer a farmers' market is held here. The farm is located at 829 W. Main St. For more information call (719) 395-8458 or go to buenavistaheritage.org/turner-farm.

Going north on US 285 toward Denver from the Buena Vista area, the road enters **South Park,** a sprawling series of valleys and hills where antelope roam the grassy fields and the landscape is largely undeveloped. Up the road is the town of **Fairplay,** home to one of Colorado's best-preserved historical sites.

The **South Park City Museum** is a restored 1880s mining town with over 40 authentic buildings. As you walk through the streets, you'll pass the saloon, barber shop, dentist office, brewery, chapel, morgue, schoolhouse, doctor's office, narrow-gauge train, and countless other buildings and exhibits. Inside these structures are more than 60,000 artifacts from frontier boomtown life. The museum is open from May 14 to October 16. For more information call (719) 836-2387 or visit southparkcity.org.

An easy nearby hike leads to an ancient forest of strangely beautiful trees. The **Limber Grove Trail** takes hikers to a stand of thousand-year-old limber pines, twisted and tortured by centuries of wind, rain, snow, and sun. From Fairplay, go south on US 285 1 mile to Fourmile Road, CR 18. Turn west and drive 8 miles to Fourmile Campground. The Limber Grove trailhead is about half a mile farther west on the south side of the road. The trailhead is well marked with good parking. Allow about 2 hours round-trip for this leisurely hike.

Continuing north on Highway 24 from Buena Vista to *Leadville,* it's time now for a story of love and power, of wealth and poverty, of joys and tragedy, of a Colorado mining town whose fortunes flourished and then vanished. A story so extraordinary that it became the subject of an opera, a play, and many biographies, some good and some bad.

The characters were bigger than life. Begin with Horace Austin Warner Tabor, a onetime Vermont stonecutter, and his straitlaced hardworking wife, Augusta. The couple gave up a Kansas homestead to try their luck first in Denver, then under Pikes Peak, then at Oro City. They arrived in Leadville with a rickety wagon and an old ox during the 1860s, some years after the first gold had been discovered in California Gulch.

The Tabors established themselves as best as they could—Augusta with a tiny rooming house and a small bakery, Horace with a store and later a part-time job as mayor. The Tabors' first break came on April 20, 1878. Two destitute miners, new in town, dropped into Horace's shop. Could he help out with some tools and a basket of groceries? The accommodating mayor agreed to help for a third of whatever minerals they might find. A few days later, some hard digging produced a rich silver vein.

The Tabors were launched. By summer that first mine—the Little Pittsburgh—lavished $8,000 a week on its owners. Before long there was $100,000 worth of silver per month; this was followed by other Tabor ventures, all successful. In time, Tabor invested in many mines, controlled a good chunk of the local bank, built the Leadville Opera House, and erected

Some Little-Known Facts about Leadville

- As the highest incorporated city in the US, Leadville is just below the timberline.
- Legend says that in the old days, a barrel of Leadville whiskey was worth as much as $1,500.
- Tents were once pitched along the main street, and it was boasted that each was "the best hotel in town."
- "Unsinkable" Molly Brown made her fortune here; also David May, Charles Boettcher, Charles Dow, and Meyer Guggenheim.

mansions in the mining town and in Denver. He owned a lot of real estate and a hotel. By 1879 Leadville had 17 independent smelters; it took 2,000 lumberjacks to provide enough wood to fire the machinery that processed the silver riches. Thanks to Tabor's new wealth and almost daily discoveries of more ore, the immigrants flooded to Leadville in droves. Celebrities like the "Unsinkable" Molly Brown showed up, as did various Dows, Guggenheims, and Boettchers.

Tabor soon bought an additional mine—the Matchless. He prospered while Leadville grew to a city of 30,000. Oscar Wilde appeared in the famous **Tabor Opera House.** The Chicago Symphony Orchestra and the Metropolitan Opera came there, to faraway Colorado. Well-known singers, ballet dancers, actresses, and entertainers arrived to perform.

H. A. W. Tabor became a millionaire many times over. He was a tall man, mustached, kindly, and, as a local historian writes, "outgoing, gregarious, and honest as the falling rain." By contrast, Horace was married to a woman who, although she worked hard, brought Tabor no happiness. She allegedly nagged; she was described as prim and humorless. Perhaps Colorado's richest man thought he deserved better.

Horace Tabor's luck changed one day in 1882. That evening the 50-year-old silver magnate saw Elisabeth Doe-McCourt in the restaurant of Leadville's Clarendon Hotel.

"Baby" Doe was 22—a beauty with shining blue eyes and curly, dark blonde hair. Round-faced and charming, she'd been born into an Irish immigrant family of 14 children. Baby Doe had just emerged from a brief, unhappy marriage with an unsupportive miner in Central City. Recently divorced, she had the good sense to look for a better partner in booming Leadville. She was a respectable young woman. And her search was crowned by success.

What began as a simple flirtation deepened into an abiding love that scandalized people in the Rockies and became the celebrated story of Colorado's opera **The Ballad of Baby Doe,** by Broadway veterans John Latouche and Douglas Moore.

Horace and Baby Doe were snubbed by Denver high society when Tabor divorced his wife, Augusta, who allegedly received a $500,000 settlement. Tabor soon married his new love. The wedding took place in Washington, DC, in the presence of President Chester Arthur and other dignitaries. Baby Doe received a $90,000 diamond necklace, and she wore a $7,500 gown.

Although young, she actually had greater substance than most of her biographers gave her credit for. She was honest and loyal, helpful to others, and interested in a variety of things. Best of all, she was in love with her much older Colorado husband. Her love was returned.

The Tabors lived the lavish life of luxury to the hilt. Most historians estimate that the Tabors spent some $100 million. Horace Tabor made few new worthwhile investments. For a brief time he was elected to the US Senate.

In 1893 disaster struck Leadville. Silver was replaced by paper money. The nation experienced a financial panic. The Tabors were ruined. The mines began to fail. Real estate was sold to satisfy creditors.

The couple moved to Denver, still in love. Thanks to some contacts, Horace got a postmaster's job for a short time. But the financial plunge must have been too much for him. Soon he was ailing. His final hours came on April 10, 1899, at Denver's Windsor Hotel. His wife, Baby Doe, was by his side, holding his hand.

As legend has it, before Horace Tabor died, he once more spoke about his **Matchless Mine** in Leadville. It had long played out after yielding some $1 million during its 14 years of operation. "Hold on to the Matchless," Tabor whispered. "It'll make millions again." His wife nodded.

Baby Doe kept her promise. She moved back to Leadville. Penniless, she lived in a shack beside the mine pit for 36 years. She remained faithful to Tabor.

During the winter of 1935, while in her seventies, she shopped at a local grocery for some food. The grocer gave her a ride home in his truck. Baby Doe was dressed in tatters. Her feet were sheathed in sackcloth instead of shoes. The cabin next to the Matchless Mine was squalid, but she kept a rifle in it, protecting her mine.

Leadville's altitude is more than 10,000 feet. It gets cold there on winter nights. Baby Doe Tabor was found in her shack on March 7, 1935. She had frozen to death. No one knows how long the body had been there. Ironically, there were some unopened boxes with new blankets sent by some Leadville sympathizers, which the dying woman had refused to use.

trivia

Leadville, at 10,152 feet above sea level, is North America's highest incorporated city.

The Tabors are buried side by side in Denver. *The Ballad of Baby Doe* was added to the New York City Opera's repertoire shortly after its 1956 debut in Central City. The role of Baby Doe was among the first that Beverly Sills sang for a company she was to head many years later.

And how about the current Leadville? Thanks to the town's solid mining history, there is a 70,000-square-foot **National Mining Hall of Fame & Museum.** This museum should be essential for rock hounds, mining school students, and history buffs. Located in a restored Victorian schoolhouse, the

Leadville Visit

While in Leadville, well-conditioned adventurers won't want to miss a chance to hike Colorado's highest mountain, *Mount Elbert* (14,433 feet).

Depending on time and ability, hikers can choose one of the mountain's two main trails:

North Mount Elbert Trail is a 5-mile hike to the summit. From 6th Street in Leadville, head south on US 24 for about 4 miles. Go west on Highway 300 for three-quarters of a mile, and then south (left) on Lake County Road 11 for 1.25 miles. Head west (right) on FR 110 for 5 miles, which will take you to the parking area at Halfmoon Campground.

South Mount Elbert Trail can be serene; it is seldom crowded. It is 5.5 miles to the summit with a trailhead near Lakeview Campground. Go south on US 24, and then head west on Highway 82 for about 3.5 miles. Go north on Lake County 24 for just over a mile to reach the parking area, just north of the campground.

With a 4,500-foot elevation gain, both trails should be attempted only by hikers who are in good shape and are knowledgeable about safety in hiking.

For more information contact the San Isabel National Forest, Leadville Ranger District, 810 Front St., Leadville 80461; (719) 486-0749; fs.fed.us/r2/psicc/leadville.

facility retraces the entire Leadville history; you can also view old equipment, assorted rocks and crystals, various artifacts, and dioramas. The Hard Rock Mine is a realistic replica of a hard-rock mine tunnel. Stretching more than 120 feet, the "rock" walls have exposed ore veins. Mine-gauge rail tracks are underfoot on the rock-strewn floor. Dripping water adds to the illusion of being underground in a real mine. Admission to the museum is $7 for adults and teenagers 12 and older, $6 for seniors 62 and older, and $3 for children 6 to 11; children 5 and younger are admitted free. Hours are 11 a.m. to 6 p.m. daily during winter, 9 a.m. to 5 p.m. summer. For more information call (719) 486-1229 or visit mininghalloffame.org.

Several other museums in Leadville are also worth visiting. The Heritage Museum displays Victorian furniture, dioramas, and various mining and boomtown paraphernalia as it depicts the western flavor of Leadville's past. A replica of the Leadville Ice Palace and Tenth Mountain Division memorabilia from Camp Hale are also here.

The Matchless Mine and Baby Doe's Cabin are the site of the last chapter in the Tabor-Doe saga, and both are open to visitors. The Tabor Opera House on Harrison Avenue was once the largest and grandest opera house west of the Mississippi. The Tabor Home on 5th Street is also open for tours.

The Healy House Museum and Dexter Cabin provide a glimpse of life in a booming silver mining camp. Daniel Healy was an engineer who ran a boardinghouse, and James Dexter was a rakish resident who built this luxury cabin as a social club.

More than 70 square blocks of Leadville have been designated as a National Historic Landmark District of Victorian architecture, making it one of the largest such districts in Colorado. You can enjoy the town's history at any time of year by going on a short historic walking tour through this district. Start your free, self-guided tour at *Ice Palace Park* in the 100 block of West Tenth. Plenty of parking can be found here. The park commemorates the ill-fated Ice Palace, built nearby in 1896. The palace, constructed of 5,000 tons of ice and 307,000 board feet of lumber, lasted only a few months before going under. From the park, you walk southeast to Harrison Avenue, where most of the tour's attractions await your exploration, including the *Heritage Museum,* the *Hyman Block* (where the infamous Doc Holliday shot—but failed to kill—his last victim), the saloon visited by Oscar Wilde, and the *Tabor Opera House.*

For a map of the walking tour, visit leadville.com/walktour or call the Leadville/Lake County Chamber of Commerce at (800) 933-3901. For general information about Leadville go to leadville.com or leadville.org. To reach Leadville from Denver, take I-70 west, turning off at Highway 91 (exit 195, Copper Mountain).

Due west of Salida is *Crested Butte,* a laid-back mountain town with a scenic ski center. Thirty minutes up the road from Gunnison, Crested Butte is too far from Front Range cities to attract crowds. (Denver is 199 miles to the northeast.) The town is surrounded by almost two million acres of pristine wilderness, giving everyone plenty of elbow room to find his or her own private Eden. Crested Butte has become a major mountain-biking destination with hundreds of miles of trails outside of town. The sport is celebrated during Crested Butte Bike Week each June. An entire week is devoted to racing, guided tours, clinics, and fun competitions like the Chainless World Championships, where spectators have as much fun as riders. A concert at the base of the ski area livens things up. For more information call the Chamber of Commerce at (800) 545-4505 or (970) 349-6438 or visit ftbw.com.

trivia

Two thousand miles of trout-fishing streams and Colorado's largest lake are within driving range of Gunnison—excellent fishing!

In a state filled with beautiful mountains, the scenic peaks around Crested Butte rank among the best. The town sits at the end of a long valley, up the road from Gunnison. As the crow flies, it's not far from Aspen, just over the

Elk Mountains. And like Aspen, the town retains some of its mining-town past with restored Victorian houses and buildings.

But the similarities end there. Crested Butte never became a playground for the wealthy and famous. The town is mountain-hip without being pretentious. There may be more bikes than cars here. And some of the locals would probably have fit in just fine back in the old mining days. A marketing campaign for the ski area some years back said it best: "Aspen like it used to be, and Vail like it never was."

The skiing here is as good as it gets in Colorado. But summer is a magical time in Crested Butte. One of the state's major festivals is the ***Crested Butte Wildflower Festival.*** The wildflower displays here are among the best in the state. In fact, Crested Butte is recognized by the Colorado legislature as the Official Wildflower Capital of Colorado. All mountain towns have wildflowers, but the climate in this sheltered valley seems to produce more floral quantity and variety than other places around the state. And the festival is scheduled right around the peak wildflower season each summer in mid-July.

Guided hikes and bike rides, 4x4 tours into the backcountry, photography and art classes, home garden tours, medicinal plant classes, wildflower gardening, and birds and butterflies are some of the ways to enjoy the festival. Call (970) 349-2571 for more information or visit crestedbuttewildflowerfestival.com.

Crested Butte was the site of the first mountain biking in Colorado. In the mid-1970s, after a motorcycle group rode their Harley Davidsons from Aspen over the rough Pearl Pass jeep road, some "Butte" locals decided to one-up the bikers by doing the same route on bicycles. They hopped on their basic clunkers and rode the 40 miles back over the mountain. With that, a sport was born and so was the annual Pearl Pass Mountain Bike Tour from Crested Butte to Aspen.

Since then these bikes have evolved from one-speed clunkers into sophisticated machines of lightweight carbon alloy with up to 27 gears. Crested Butte

Florissant Fossil Beds

One of the richest and most diverse fossil deposits in the world lies in this grassy mountain valley. Once a primeval rain forest, the area was covered by volcanic ash 30–40 million years ago, perfectly preserving insects, plants, and redwood stumps up to 14 feet wide. The visitor center with exhibits and a brief film is a good first stop before exploring the monument. There are 14 miles of trail and hourly ranger talks at the amphitheater during the summer. The monument is 2 miles south of the town of Florissant. For directions and more information, contact (719) 748- 3253; nps.gov/flfo.

Highway of the Fourteeners

From Buena Vista, this 19-mile stretch of US 24 along the Collegiate Peaks Scenic Byway offers dramatic, close-up views of 10 of Colorado's 14,000-foot mountains. Nowhere else in the US will you see so many high peaks in one place. Allow about 30 minutes for the drive, more if you stop for photos. In Buena Vista, drop by Bongo Billy's Cafe (713 US 24; bongobillyscafe.com) for coffee, sandwiches, soups, and pastries.

has a wealth of trails available to mountain bikers. Keep in mind that most of these trails are open for public use. Cyclists are required to yield to hikers and horses. If this means you have to get off your bike and move off the trail, then do it. Around the US, failure of cyclists to yield has caused some popular trails to be closed to them.

Crested Butte celebrates the sport with the *Mountain Bike Hall of Fame and Museum,* which documents the people and events that helped shape the sport of mountain biking. You can see vintage bikes and components, classic photos, memorabilia, and press clippings and highlights from historic races and events. The hall of fame is located in the Crested Butte Mountain Heritage Museum at 331 Elk Ave., open daily 10 a.m. to 8 p.m. in summer, noon to 6 p.m. in winter; (970) 349-1880; mtnbikehalloffame.com. Since the museum is closed some weeks during the off-season, call to verify hours.

The *Crested Butte Mountain Heritage Museum,* housed in an 1883 building formerly used as a gas station and hardware store, has interesting collections and displays depicting early mining, ranching, skiing, and settler life around Crested Butte. Open daily 12 p.m. to 7 p.m.; 331 Elk Ave.; (970) 349-1880; crestedbuttemuseum.com.

Artistic types have been drawn to the area for decades, and as a result, Crested Butte offers a diverse and rich calendar of cultural activities throughout the year. The *Crested Butte Center for the Arts* at 606 6th St. hosts concerts, art displays, classes, films, events, and more. Call (970) 349-7487 or visit crested buttearts.org.

The *Crested Butte Mountain Theatre* is located at 403 2nd St. in the 1880s-era Old Town Hall. Since 1972 this group has entertained locals and visitors with live theatrical performances ranging from drama and musicals to comedy and beyond. It's a delightful way to spend an evening. For more information, contact (970) 349-0366; cbmountaintheatre.org.

Three miles up the road from town is *Crested Butte Mountain Resort,* another of Colorado's premier ski destinations. The majority of the mountain

Bureau of Land Management & US Forest Service

The Bureau of Land Management (BLM) administers millions of acres of public lands around the country, including 8.4 million acres in Colorado, while the US Forest Service (USFS) manages 14.3 million acres in the state. State offices for both organizations can direct you to specific regional and local offices, many of which are listed throughout this book as well. For more information, look on the USFS website—fs .fed.us—or contact the USFS Rocky Mountain Regional Office at (303) 275-5350. For information about BLM lands in Colorado, visit co.blm.gov/index.htm or contact the BLM Colorado state office at (303) 239-3600.

(57 percent) is for the intermediate skier, with the remaining 43 percent almost equally divided between beginning and advanced runs. There are numerous long, intermediate runs, as well as gentle, rolling meadows with plenty of places to go at your own pace. The trail network is well-planned, and an excellent children's ski school and child-care facility make this an attractive family ski resort.

For many, though, the big draw at Crested Butte is extreme skiing and snowboarding. Both can be found at the Extreme Limits, more than 580 acres of ungroomed, double-black diamond terrain. It's no coincidence that the US Extreme Skiing Championships are held here. Steep bowls, narrow chutes, cliff drops, and through-the-trees skiing await adrenaline junkies who are ready for some of the steepest lift-served runs in North America. Tours are available for expert skiers who want a taste of the mountain's wild side.

For slightly tamer winter fun, there are snowshoe tours, snowcat driving experiences, sleigh ride dinners to Uley's Cabin, and an Adventure Park with lift-served tubing, bungee trampolines, rock climbing, and miniature golf. The Crested Butte Zip Line Tour at the resort is one of the few zip lines in the country that runs in winter as well as spring and fall. For more information call (970) 349-2222 or visit skicb.com.

Crested Butte's ski season runs from the week of Thanksgiving through early April. The ski slopes are open from 9 a.m. to 4 p.m. daily. Prices vary throughout the season. For more information call (800) 810-7669 or visit skicb .com.

Located at the edge of town, the **Crested Butte Nordic Center** is unique. No other cross-country center in Colorado offers in-track skiing so close to a town. An extensive, 55-kilometer network of trails spreads out from three nearby trailheads, making it easy to ski a few morning hours, ski into town for lunch, then take off into the woods again in the afternoon. Choose trails ranging from novice to advanced. The Nordic Center offers lessons, rentals, backcountry tours, ice skating, sledding, snowshoeing, brunch and dinner at the yurt, and many races and events. For information contact (970) 349-1707; cbnordic.org.

When the snow melts and warm weather returns to Crested Butte, the summer season kicks into high gear. Between the Evolution Bike park, mountain biking and hiking trails, chairlift rides (for hiking, biking, picnics, sightseeing), Adventure Park (minus the tubing in the summer), and the Crested Butte Zip Line Tour, there's no shortage of outdoor activities. Free outdoor concerts happen each Wednesday in July and August at the base of the ski mountain. And in addition to the Wildflower Festival and Bike Week, there's a full schedule of summer festivals, including Bluegrass in Paradise and the Crested Butte Land Trust Wine & Food Festival.

Crested Butte is 28 miles north of Gunnison on Highway 135. For more information contact the Gunnison-Crested Butte Tourism Association at (800) 814-7988 or visit gunnisoncrestedbutte.com. The visitor centers are located at 601 Elk Ave. in Crested Butte and next to the bus stop at Mountaineer Square (the ski area base) in Mt. Crested Butte.

Between Crested Butte and Gunnison, where the East and Taylor Rivers meet to form the Gunnison River, lies the small community of *Almont.* Winter visitors on their way to the resort stop here at places like the Three Rivers Resort for a variety of lodging and skiing packages. In warm-weather months the area is a good base for nearby camping, canoeing and kayaking, 4x4 driving, hiking, rock climbing, horseback riding, fishing, rafting, and exploring nearby Taylor Canyon. Ranch resorts and riverside cabins offer a quieter, simpler vacation where you can slow down and enjoy the western landscape. The wildflowers along this route are spectacular from late June through mid-Aug. For information call (800) 814-7988 or visit gunnisoncrestedbutte.com/area-tour/almont.

Gunnison County Facts

- Gunnison County is part of two byways: West Elk Loop Scenic & Historic Byway and Silver Thread Scenic & Historic Byway.

- Crested Butte has the largest aspen grove in the US; see it when traveling over Kebler Pass, a gravel road that is closed in winter.

- Crested Butte is one of the birthplaces of mountain biking along with Marin Country, California.

Don't overlook *Gunnison* on your way to Crested Butte. With its legacy of ranching and farming, the town and surrounding area are as authentically western as it gets in Colorado. Cowboy boots and wide-brimmed hats are worn as work clothes. Western State College adds a subtle college-town feel to the community. And nature lovers use Gunnison as a base for excellent nearby fishing, boating, rafting, camping, and mountain biking.

If you want to learn about early life in the area, visit the *Gunnison Pioneer Museum* at 803 E. Tomichi Ave. These 6 acres contain an antique car collection, a narrow-gauge train, two rural schoolhouses, a log cabin chapel, carpenter shop, blacksmith shop, print shop, and displays of pioneer life. Open Memorial Day weekend through mid-Sept 9 a.m. to 5 p.m. Mon through Sat and 1 to 5 p.m. Sun; (970) 641-4530.

Tap into the local cultural scene with a visit to the *Gunnison Arts Center* (102 S. Main St.; 970-641-4029; gunnisonartscenter.org). Along with its three gallery exhibit spaces, this community arts center has a busy schedule of performance artists, literary events, movies, music, classes, and a theater. The area attracts artists of all kinds, and the center is a window into that community.

The *Gunnison Valley Observatory* houses the largest public telescope in Colorado. Located off Gold Basin Road at the base of "W" Mountain, just southwest of town on US 50, the observatory houses a 30-inch reflector telescope, taking advantage of the unpolluted atmosphere here to scan the skies. The observatory is open to visitors every Friday and Saturday evening at dusk from mid-June to mid-Sept. For more information call (970) 642-1111 or visit gunnisonobservatory.org.

trivia

In December 1999, the city of Pueblo was astonished to find 17 trees on its Historic Arkansas Riverwalk of Pueblo (HARP) destroyed within a matter of days. The culprit? A Colorado beaver whom officials affectionately deemed "Bandit" before they relocated the creature to a place a little farther out of town.

For those who enjoy whitewater sports and for those who enjoy watching them, *Gunnison Whitewater Park* is a pleasant place to spend a few hours. A series of rock structures along a several-hundred-foot section of the Gunnison River creates a paddling playground for kayaking, canoeing, and rafting. A walking path and picnic area offer good vantage points to watch the action. For more information, call (800) 814-7988 or visit gunnisoncrestedbutte.com/whitewater-park.

Hartman Rocks Recreational Area, located just 5 minutes from downtown Gunnison, has more than 20 trails on 8,000 acres of public land. This

St. Elmo

Far up a dirt road, deep in the mountains of Chaffee County, lies the ghost of St. Elmo. This weathered ghost town, where creaking wooden sidewalks meander past splintered wooden buildings with false fronts, is among Colorado's best preserved.

Once a rollicking mining town, St. Elmo sits quietly in a wooded valley, home to hummingbirds and chipmunks. From Buena Vista take US 24 south for 8 miles to Nathrop, then CR 162 west for 16 miles. For more information see coloradoghosttowns .com/st-elmo-area.htm.

network of trails welcomes hiking, single-track and double-track mountain biking, rock climbing, and horseback riding. In winter the area is popular for cross-country skiing and snowshoeing. The routes pass through rolling hills of sagebrush with granite rock outcrops and occasional cottonwood groves. To get there, drive west on Highway 50 about 1.5 miles from downtown, and turn left/south on Gold Basin Road (City Road 38 just before the twin bridges). Go for about 2.2 miles and turn right for Hartman Rocks.

Nine miles west of Gunnison along Highway 50 is *Curecanti National Recreation Area,* a series of three reservoirs set in a starkly beautiful volcanic landscape. One of them, Blue Mesa Reservoir, is the largest body of water in the state, and from its depths have come several state record lake trout. Swimming, camping, boat rentals, sailboarding, and other activities are available.

Continuing along US 50, an hour out of Gunnison you will come to the dramatic *Black Canyon of the Gunnison National Park,* which became a national park in 1999. In the sunlight, the massive black granite towers, pillars, and stone blocks turn mauve. In all, the Black Canyon of the Gunnison National Park comprises some 30,385 acres. Carved by the river, the canyon measures 53 miles long and 2,722 feet from the rim to the bottom at its deepest point.

There are three roads in the park: East Portal, North Rim, and South Rim. Each offers spectacular views, but only East Portal allows access to the bottom by car. The South Rim Visitor Center offers exhibits detailing the geology and history of the canyon. This is a good place to learn about the scenic overlooks along each drive, and to find out about the hiking trails, from easy to moderate, leading to different vistas. The area can be hot in summer, so come prepared with water and a hat. Two campgrounds offer tent and RV camping, but vehicles more than 35 feet long are discouraged. The closest lodging outside the park is in Montrose, 15 miles southwest.

Eat a Peach

Each summer from July through October, local farmers offer apples, cherries, peaches, pears, and apricots, often organically grown, at numerous roadside stands across Delta County. Delta and the nearby towns of Cedaredge and Paonia each host farmers' markets through the summer.

Rock climbing in the canyon is considered one of Colorado's best big-wall destinations and is only for experienced climbers. Some routes can take several days to complete, requiring climbers to overnight on narrow ledges or in hammocks slung from the rock wall.

The national park is open year-round. The entrance fee is $15 per vehicle or $7 per pedestrian, bicyclist, and motorcyclist (no charge for visitors age 16 or younger). The North and South Rim stations are open daily, but access is limited in winter. The campground is open all year, although two of the three loops are closed in winter. To get to the South Rim take US 50 from Montrose for 15 miles to Highway 347. The visitor center is at the South Rim. The North Rim is 11 miles south of Crawford via US 92 and North Rim Road, which is closed during winter. Contact Park Headquarters, 102 Elk Creek, Gunnison 81230; (970) 641-2337; nps.gov/blca.

Nearby **Montrose** is a convenient base for exploring the Black Canyon of the Gunnison and surrounding public lands. Almost 300 miles from Denver, this city on the Western Slope is a mecca for outdoor activities ranging from hiking and camping to mountain biking, cross-country skiing, and snowmobiling. The historic downtown, Museum of the Mountain West, Montrose County Historical Museum, and Ute Indian Museum all offer insights into life in the Old West.

North of Montrose, the town of **Delta** has many buildings on the National Historic Register. Visit the **Fort Uncompahgre Living History Museum** at pretty **Confluence Park** to see a reconstruction of the original trading post used by trappers, traders, and Native Americans. More than 200 years old, the **Ute Council Tree** at the entrance to Delta is a majestic cottonwood where Chief Ouray met with white settlers in an effort to keep peace with the Utes. The **Delta County Historical Museum** in the old firehouse recounts the cultural heritage and natural history of the area. When you need a break from history, head to some of Delta County's 13 wineries and 5 tasting rooms. Visit deltacountycolorado.com/activities_attractions/wineries.aspx.

Southwestern Colorado

As you drive toward the southwestern corner of Colorado from the northeast, you have the chance to visit one of the most geologically unique areas on the continent. **Great Sand Dunes National Park** is on the short list of "don't miss" places that both residents and visitors return to year after year, and for good reason. These dunes, the tallest in North America at 750 feet high, run 8 miles in length at their longest point, covering 30 square miles in the main dune field.

The 150,000-acre park offers hiking, overnight camping, and bird watching here and in nearby wetlands such as in the San Luis State Wildlife Area. But most visitors come to climb the dunes. There are few experiences that can compare with being on them. Climb to the top of a ridge and take in the view of golden sandy waves stretching for miles to the distant Sangre de Cristo Mountains, then drop into a trough until you are in a valley surrounded by towering hills of sand. Stop and listen to the silence broken only by the wind as it pushes thousands of the tiny grains. Climb back several ridges into the dunes and you will be alone.

Most visitors come during the hot months of July and August. Make sure you wear shoes to climb the dunes during this season—the sand can reach temperatures of 140°F. Save the bare feet for wading across the soft, water-cooled sand of **Medano Creek.** Flowing at the base of the dunes during the spring snowmelt, Medano Creek is one of the few places in the world to experience "surge flow" where creek water comes in rhythmic waves. The best times to experience surge flow depend on annual snow levels. The creek often begins flowing in March and may last until July or longer after a heavy snowfall winter. After dry winters the creek may not even reach the main parking area.

Great Sand Dunes National Park is located on Highway 150 in the south-central part of the state, just 16 miles off US 160, the main east-west highway through southern Colorado. Individuals age 17 or older pay a $3 entry fee. The site is open daily. The visitor center is also open daily except for federal holidays. Visitor center hours are 9 a.m. to 6 p.m. in summer, and 9 a.m. to 4:30 p.m. or 5 p.m., as staffing permits, the rest of the year. The 88-site campground is available on a first-come, first-served

trivia

For amateur geologists, most sand at Colorado's Great Sand Dunes is between 0.2 and 0.3 mm in diameter, composed of 51.7 percent volcanic rock fragments, 29.1 percent quartz, 8.9 percent feldspar, 2.5 percent sandstone, 0.7 percent magnetite, 3.4 percent other minerals, and 3.7 percent other rocks.

basis, and fills up fast on summer weekends. Campers should come prepared to face gnats and hungry mosquitoes in late spring and early summer. For more information contact Great Sand Dunes National Park, 11500 Hwy. 150, Mosca 81146; (719) 378-6300; nps.gov/grsa.

Thirty-eight miles southwest of the park is *Alamosa,* a good overnight base for exploring the sand dunes. Each spring the town fills with birders eager to see the sandhill cranes and thousands of ducks and other water-fowl that stop at the Alamosa and Monte Vista National Wildlife Refuges just southeast of town. The birds are celebrated during the *Monte Vista Crane Festival* (cranefest.com) held in early March. The *Luther Bean Museum and Art Gallery* (719-587-7827; adams.edu/lutherbean) in Richardson Hall at the Adams State College displays Native American and Hispanic pottery and textiles, European porcelain and furniture, and a changing exhibit of regional arts and crafts.

Twenty-six miles east of Alamosa on US 160 is *Fort Garland Museum* in a compound built in 1858 to protect settlers from Ute Indian resistance. Frontier scout Kit Carson was a post commander here, and the famous Buffalo Soldiers were stationed here from 1876 to 1879. The fort has been restored, and its rich history is depicted in the parade grounds, adobe buildings, and displays. The folk art and culture of southern Colorado's Hispanic community are also high-lighted. The museum is open Thurs through Mon throughout the year; from 9 a.m. to 5 p.m. April 1 to October 31, and 10 a.m. to 4 p.m. November 1 to March 31. For more information call (719) 379-3512 or visit museumtrail.org/fortgarlandmuseum.asp.

Drive south from Fort Garland on CO 159 for 16 miles and you'll come to *San Luis,* established in 1851 and the state's oldest town. The local Hispanic population worships at the original Sangre de Cristo Parish church, and one of the former residences has been transformed into the El Convento Bed and Breakfast at 512 Church Place. Of special interest to visitors and a famous Catholic pilgrimage site are the *Stations of the Cross,* a set of 15 bronze sculptures on the *Hill of Piety and Mercy* in town, representing the last hours in the life of Christ. The lifelike statues line a cactus-strewn path leading up the hill to the domed, adobe *Chapel of All Saints.* The short but steep walk is peaceful, the sculptures are exquisite, and the surrounding scenery of juniper, piñon, and yucca is typical of the area. For more information drop by the visitor center at 408½ Main St.

From San Luis, drive west for 31 miles on Highway 142 to the village of *Manassa,* the home of 19th-century boxing champion Jack Dempsey. A small museum containing artifacts from his career is housed in the cabin where Dempsey was born.

When Highway 142 ends 3 miles farther west at Highway 285, turn left and travel south for 7 miles to Antonito. By now you're just a few miles from the New Mexico border. You're also at the start of one of America's most scenic narrow-gauge rail trips. The **Cumbres & Toltec Scenic Railroad** travels between Antonito and Chama, NM, encountering tunnels, loops, trestles, gorges, rivers, forests, meadows, and spectacular scenery as it crosses the state border 11 times. This is the country's highest and longest coal-fired, steam-operated, narrow-gauge railroad, combining a great train ride with a truly historic artifact of the Old West. For more information call (888) 286-2737 or visit cumbrestoltec.com.

If you're traveling north from Alamosa, drive 13 miles north on Highway 17 to Mosca for one of Colorado's more unexpected wildlife encounters. The **Colorado Gators Reptile Park** (719-378-2612; gatorfarm.com) is a working tilapia fish farm and reptile sanctuary, and they serve as an animal rescue facility for unwanted or abused reptile pets. The geothermal pools here attract a variety of bird species, making it a popular spot for birders.

Located a few miles east of Highway 17 and nestled against the edge of the San Isabel National Forest just north of Great Sand Dunes National Park is a town unlike any other in Colorado. Formerly a small mining burg, **Crestone** and the surrounding area have developed into a spiritual and New Age center with representatives of a variety of world religions. Several Tibetan centers, a Zen Buddhist center, Hindu temple, Carmelite monastery, and a regular schedule of New Age events bring spiritual pilgrims to Crestone. Ecotourists come to hike the adjacent mountains. The town is popular with day-trippers who visit the temples, wander around the few shops, browse the Saturday market, and walk through the village. The area is known for its experimental, alternative architecture and art scene. There's a higher-than-average number of body-work specialists in town, so it's a good place to get a massage. The Lotus Cafe and Desert Sage Restaurant are popular local eateries. While some visitors are quickly bored, others are content to slow down and delight in the ambience of this unique village. To reach Crestone take Highway 17 through the San Luis Valley to Moffat and turn east on the local county road. For more information visit crestonecolorado.com.

trivia

Although Pagosa Springs water is used primarily for bathing, some of the hotter springs, at 153°F, are used for energy to heat houses and buildings.

Farther west on scenic US 160 and south of Wolf Creek Pass is **Pagosa Springs.** Named for the Ute word *Pagosa,* meaning "boiling water," Pagosa Springs has a continual supply of natural geothermal energy. Many a weary

Hot Springs

Set along the banks of the San Juan River, Pagosa Springs offers numerous therapeutic, mineral-rich pools for soaking weary muscles after a long day of skiing,
backpacking, golfing, or driving. Two spas in the middle of town offer day rates and
overnight accommodations. For more information, call (970) 264-5236 or visit pagosa
.com; pagosahotsprings.com.

traveler has stopped for a day or more to soak in these healing waters at The
Springs Resort and Spa and to enjoy nearby San Juan National Forest and
Weminuche Wilderness. Nearby stables rent horses and lead trips. Fishing,
mountain biking, and hiking are all options.

Another water wonder near Pagosa is *Treasure Falls.* This is the longest
waterfall in the entire San Juan National Forest. The short hike is a perfect place
to break up a long drive and stretch the legs. To get there, follow US 160 east
for 15 miles toward scenic Wolf Creek summit. The parking lot and trailhead
are on the right (east) side of the road. A short quarter-mile well-worn trail
climbs 300 feet up the canyon through dense pine and oak forest to Colorado's
mini-version of Niagara. For more information write to Pagosa Ranger District,
180 Pagosa St., PO Box 310, Second Springs 81147; (970) 264-2268; fs.fed.us/
r2/sanjuan.

To the west of Pagosa Springs stands a man-made wonder built a thousand years ago. The stone ruins of *Chimney Rock* were home to the ances-
tors of the modern *Pueblo Indians* and are of great spiritual significance to
these tribes. More than 200 homes and ceremonial buildings were constructed
around the area, and archaeologists have found hundreds of individual sites.
Named for the towering twin spires of natural stone that dominate the landscape, Chimney Rock provides expansive views to the far distance.

The Chimney Rock Interpretive Program leads tours four times daily and
operates the visitor center during the open season (May 15 through September 30). Tour costs are $10 for adults and teenagers 12 and older and $5 for
children 5 to 11; children 4 and younger get in free. Fees are paid at the visitor center, which is open from 9 a.m. to 4:30 p.m. daily during the season.
Chimney Rock is located 17 miles west of Pagosa Springs via US 160, and then
southwest on Highway 151.

For more information contact Chimney Rock Interpretive Program, PO Box
1662, Pagosa Springs 81147; (970) 883-5359 (May 15 through September 30)
or (970) 264-2287 (off-season, October 1 through May 14); chimneyrockco.org.
For more information about the Pagosa Springs area write to Pagosa Springs

Area Chamber of Commerce, 402 San Juan St., Pagosa Springs 81147; (970) 264-2360 or (800) 252-2204; pagosa-springs.com.

Another 17 miles south past Chimney Rock on Highway 151, ***Navajo State Park*** is Colorado's version of Lake Powell. Sprawling Navajo Reservoir is surrounded by piñon and juniper hillsides that look more like New Mexico than Colorado. That's no surprise, since the reservoir extends 35 miles across the state line. Boating, fishing, hiking, biking, and camping keep visitors busy during the day, while quiet nights under starry skies promise a good night's sleep. For more information call (970) 883-2208 or visit parks.state.co.us/parks/navajo.

The chute opens, and the cowboy holds on to the horse's riggings with one hand. The horse rears wildly, resenting the man on his back, hooves flailing in all directions, a bucking, pitching, twisting, snorting, wild-eyed animal. The cowboy's hat flies off and lands in the dust. He has been on the horse for five seconds now, and he still hangs on. Leaning back until his shoulder blades graze the animals back, the man's outstretched arm hits the horse's flank. Six seconds now. Seven. Eight.

The buzzer sounds and the cowboy jumps safely to the ground. Eight seconds of bareback riding can seem like 8 hours. In the early days of rodeo, the rider stayed in the saddle "until the horse was rode or the cowboy throwed."

Southwest Colorado Overview

In the San Juan Range of southwest Colorado, piñons and junipers yield to spruce and aspen as you go up in elevation. The weather in towns like Durango and Cortez is remarkably mild year-round, despite copious snowfall in the heights. The mountains are always cooler than the lower, drier elevations, but usually comfortably so, especially in summer when days are short-sleeves warm, and a light blanket is de rigueur for sleeping at night.

As is common throughout Colorado, summer is the main tourist season in southwest Colorado, followed by the ski months of winter. Caution: Skiing through waist-deep, soft powder in the high, dry air on a typical sunny winter day may be addictive. The sun always comes out after a storm, so skiers sans jackets by noon are another common sight.

Colorado's legendary outdoor world has much to do with its geography. The state has 1,143 mountains rising to an altitude of at least 10,000 feet above sea level—and 1,000 are 2 miles high or more. Fifty-four often snow-crowned peaks towering above 14,000 feet give the state more than six times the mountain area of Switzerland. For more information on hiking and climbing the mountains, contact the Colorado Fourteeners Initiative at (303) 278-7650; 14ers.org.

Today, the saddle bronc rider must stay aboard 8 seconds, while at the same time not disqualifying himself in any number of ways. It takes a tough person to ride at the rodeo.

These western riding competitions are an important income source for some Colorado cowboys. Rodeo began in the 1700s with the vaqueros, Spanish cattlemen in the American West. In the 1800s, American cowboys would hold informal riding, roping, and cattle driving competitions. The sport caught on and became commercialized with the early efforts of entrepreneurs such as Buffalo Bill Cody and Will Rogers. By the 1970s rodeo turned professional, and today it is a big business, earning the top performers a comfortable living.

Every summer Colorado towns such as Leadville, Brush, Walden, Steamboat Springs, La Junta, Las Animas, Durango, Gunnison, Kiowa, Kremmling, Salida, and others are part of the rodeo circuit for a few days. Each offers a standard mix of bull riding, steer wrestling, bareback, team roping, and other events that comprise this slice of true Americana. As you drive around the state, ask locally; there's bound to be a rodeo not too far away. For more information contact the **Colorado Pro Rodeo Association** at (719) 647-2828; coloradopro rodeo.com.

Durango lies in the Animas River Valley against a backdrop of the San Juan Mountains. It's the largest town in southern Colorado, but with only 16,000 people, you'll quickly fall under its small-town charm. The lovingly preserved historic downtown area is filled with restaurants, art galleries, coffeehouses, and shops. Wander south from the intersection of 13th Avenue and Main past elegant buildings from the 1800s, then head east to 3rd Avenue, where an eclectic mix of period homes and mansions line the street. With more restaurants per capita than San Francisco, the town takes pride in cuisines ranging from French and American southwestern to sushi and Himalayan. Four brewpubs keep the town supplied with handcrafted, award-winning beers. The **Rocky Mountain Chocolate Factory** is based here, sending premium chocolate candies across the US and Canada. Held every Saturday morning from spring through fall, the **Durango Farmers' Market** is one of the best in the state.

But as inviting as the culinary scene may be, there's much more to do and see in the area. Start with a walk along the 7-mile long Animas River Trail that goes through town and watch rafters, kayakers, and canoeists navigate the rapids. A 2-mile stretch of the Animas south of downtown is designated Gold-Medal water for fishing. Outside of town, more than 350 miles of trails await hikers, horseback riders, mountain bikers, wildflower enthusiasts, and anyone who enjoys stunning outdoor scenery.

With its mild climate and close proximity to some of the state's most stunning scenery, Durango is also known for the many festivals that fill the calendar. Ranging from bike races, river fests, and bluegrass gatherings to celebrations of beer, coffee, film, and motorcycles, the town is host to a wide variety of local festivals and community parties that welcome visitors. For a complete list go to durango.org.

Housed in America's oldest surviving coal-fired, steam-generated AC power plant, the *Durango Discovery Museum* is filled with hands-on science and energy exhibits, historic interpretation exhibits, labs, workshops, a museum store, and more. The museum provides an entertaining, inspiring look at energy, guaranteeing something here for all ages. For more information call (970) 259-9234 or visit durangodiscovery.org.

Durango is the departure point for the *Durango & Silverton Narrow Gauge Railroad,* a heritage railway that takes passengers on a 45-mile, 7-hour round-trip to the historic mining town of *Silverton.* These steam-powered trains date back to the 1920s and before, and the nicely restored coaches and open-air cars allow you to enjoy the changing scenery. It's easily one of the classic Colorado sightseeing journeys. The train has both summer and winter schedules, as well as special event trains, with a range of prices depending on the class and several departures a day in summer. For more information contact the railroad at 479 Main Ave., 81301; (970) 247-2733 or (877) 872-4607; durangotrain.com.

Colorful Locals

In the early days in Durango, there was a rowdy local set that went by the name of the Stockton–Eskridge Gang. These boys and a group of local vigilantes once fought an hourlong gun battle on the main street through town.

In 1885, locals set out on an expedition to New Mexico. Their goal? To "dig up Aztecs." Included in the supplies were five cases of tobacco, three cases of beer, 10 gallons of "heavy liquids," four burro-loads of "the stuff that busted Parliament," seven reels of fuse, soap, cigars, one fish line, rubber boots, bread, lard, and a pound of bacon.

Newspaperman "Dave" Day, the witty, often profane editor of the *Durango Herald-Democrat* in the 1890s, once had 42 libel suits pending against him.

In 1922, after the paper had split into two papers, William Wood, city editor for the *Durango Herald,* was shot dead in front of the barber shop by Rod Day (son of former editor "Dave" Day), editor of the *Durango Democrat,* after a long squabble that started over Prohibition and reached a peak over the printing of a scandal. Ah, the good old days.

While traveling on the train, a number of guests get off at a stop partway to Silverton in order to experience one of Colorado's more thrilling activities. **Soaring Tree Top Adventures** is the largest canopy tour zip line course in the world, and the only way to get here is via the train. With 27 spans and more than 1.5 miles of zip line, the course takes guests through old-growth forests and over the Animas River on this daylong experience. The train ride, zip line experience, and a gourmet lunch are included in the price. Soaring Tree Top Adventures is open from mid-May through late Oct. For more information call (970) 769-2357 or visit soaringcolorado.com.

Anyone interested in experiencing an authentic western rodeo should head to **La Plata County Fairgrounds** in Durango. Each summer the fairgrounds hosts a series of rodeos where spectators enjoy a variety of events, including bareback riding, saddle bronc riding, barrel racing, and the most dangerous sport in the world, bull riding. For information on summertime rodeos, contact the Durango Area Tourism Office at (800) 525-8855; durango.org.

Located 18 miles north of Durango on US 550, the year-round **Durango Mountain Resort** remains a secret to many Coloradans. This remote oasis has everything—nature, atmosphere, and amenities. In the summer months, guided horseback expeditions depart each day from the stables, bringing you into the one-million-acre San Juan National Forest. Fishing, river rafting, jeep tours into the high country, mountain biking, golfing, an alpine slide, and a day camp for kids are just a few of the activities. In winter, Purgatory at Durango Mountain Resort is one of the state's classic ski mountains with 88 trails, 5 terrain parks, 1,360 skiable acres, and an average of 240 inches of snowfall each year. As you ski around the mountain, you're surrounded by the spectacular scenery of the rugged San Juans. Other fun winter activities include snow tubing, Nordic skiing, snowshoeing, horse-drawn sleigh rides, zip-lining, snowbiking, backcountry skiing, and snowmobiling. For more information contact Durango Mountain Resort, 1 Skier Place, Durango 81301; (970) 247-9000 or (800) 982-6103; durangomountainresort.com.

For more information about Durango and surrounding areas contact the Durango Area Tourism Office, 111 S. Camino del Rio, PO Box 2587, Durango 81302; (800) 525-8855 or (970) 247-3500; durango.org.

Located 25 miles southeast of Durango in Ignacio, the **Southern Ute Cultural Center and Museum** depicts the history and culture of the Ute people through their eyes. Early rock art, a re-created camp scene, and the tumultuous time of reservations and boarding schools are a few of the subjects covered here. Priceless artifacts, permanent exhibits, a museum store offering Native American art and crafts, and a changing temporary gallery round out the center's offerings. Admission is $7 for adults, $4 for seniors, and $3 for children 3

Agritourism

The Ancestral Puebloans of Mesa Verde were the first farmers in southwestern Colorado, laying the foundation for today's farmers and ranchers. These days the region produces a delectable variety of edibles, and visitors can choose from a wide range of activities to experience the agricultural products produced nearby, including farm and ranch visits and stays, farmers' markets, and restaurants. Here are a few to get you started:

Farm and Ranch Stays:

Canyon of the Ancients Guest Ranch, Cortez; (970) 565-4288; canyonofthe ancients.com
East Pines Ranch, Cortez; (970) 565-6439; eastpines.com
Never M/T Circle Ranch, Cortez; (970) 564-1669; nevermtcircleranch.com
Turning Beyond Ranch, Mancos; (970) 215-0536; turningbeyondranch.com

Farm and Ranch Visits:

Crabapple Tree Farm, Mancos; (970) 739-1172
Dragonfly Farm, Dolores; (970) 565-2644; localharvest.org/dragonfly-farm-M19765
Flippin' Eggs, Dolores; (970) 882-3240
Pelican Acres Alpacas, Cortez; (970) 882-2412
Shadow Ranch Alpacas, Dolores; (970) 882-1296 or (970) 564-9792; alpacanation .com/shadowranch.asp

Locally Produced Food Sources:

Carver Brewing Co., Durango; (970) 259-2545; carverbrewing.com
Dolores River Brewery, Dolores; (970) 882-4677; doloresriverbrewery.com
High Desert Foods, Durango; (886) 248-6584; highdesertfoods.com
J. Fargo's Microbrewing, Cortez; (970) 564-0242; jfargos.com
Metate Room, Mesa Verde N.P.; (800) 449-5210; visitmesaverde.com
The Farm Bistro, Cortez; (970) 565-3834

to 14. Children under 3 are free. For more information call (970) 563-9583 or visit succm.org.

Just 35 miles west of Durango is ***Mesa Verde National Park.*** With more than 4,700 archaeological sites in the park, this is an extraordinary place, made even better by the restraint with which the national park service has limited development. Aside from the narrow road, the museum and visitor center, a small restaurant and shop, and trails leading to the cliff dwellings, almost nothing here hints at the 21st century. Ravens and vultures drift across the ridges. Coyotes yip and howl on moonless nights. The fragrance of piñon and juniper sweetens the dry mesa air after a summer squall. The only things missing are the hundreds of people who called this place home some 800 years ago.

Mesa Verde is best known for its Ancestral Puebloan cliff dwellings. A UNESCO World Heritage Site, these structures represent an astonishing culture that thrived for 700 years in this harsh land. A good place to begin your visit is at the *Chapin Mesa Archeological Museum,* where you can see baskets, pottery, agricultural tools, and exhibits describing these first residents. At Far View Visitor Center you can purchase tickets for ranger-guided tours of the three main cliff dwelling areas. Self-guided tours to two of the cliff dwellings as well as several hiking trails are available for further exploration. Drive across Wetherill Mesa through the ponderosa, spruce, and juniper, stopping to explore the mesa-top sites and admire the views from various overlooks. Dawn and dusk offer quiet moments when the cliffs are bathed in warm, golden light.

Devote at least a full day to the park, two if possible. It is an 8-hour drive southwest of Denver and is about an hour and a half west of Durango on US 160, midway between Mancos and Cortez. About 500,000 visitors come here each year, with most of them visiting during the summer months. The park is open all year, with some activities closed during winter.

Mesa Verde National Park is open daily year-round. The park entry fee is $10 per vehicle; the fee is waived from Jan through Feb. The Chapin Mesa Archeological Museum is open daily at 8 a.m., closing at 6:30 p.m. in summer and fall and at 5 p.m. in winter and spring. The Far View Visitor Center is open from mid-Apr through mid-Oct from 8 a.m. to 5 p.m. For park information call (970) 529-4465 or visit nps.gov/meve. Camping is available at Morefield Campground, 4 miles inside the park, on a first-come, first-served basis. The campground is never full. Lodging is available at Far View Lodge. For more information on both options call (888) 896-3831 or visit visitmesaverde.com.

When visiting Mesa Verde you're not far from the Four Corners area of Colorado, Utah, New Mexico, and Arizona. The sky seems even bluer here against the red rock buttes, mesas, and canyons. Mesa Verde was the major population center for the Ancestral Pueblo people, but there were many communities scattered for hundreds of miles across the four-state area of Colorado, Utah, New Mexico, and Arizona. The remains of many are hidden in remote areas and can only be reached on foot. But others are vehicle accessible, and exploring them will increase your fascination for the culture that flourished here long ago.

A quieter, less known site west of Cortez is *Hovenweep National Monument.* Six Puebloan-era villages lie in a landscape of arroyos, mesas, and sage, straddling the Colorado-Utah border. With artistic skill that would rival a stonemason's today, ancient Pueblo Indians built these towers in several configurations. Round, square, and oval structures dot the canyon edge. Each rock was trimmed to fit exactly with its neighbor, and the lines of the buildings are straight and almost smooth. Small peepholes and keyhole entrances could have provided views of a possible enemy approaching or just been a way to keep an eye on the rest of the community. Hiking and interpretive trails link most structures. These towers and buildings were constructed around the same time as Mesa Verde, but the monument's solitude and fewer visitors make for a very different experience from the better-known park to the east. Allow at least a half-day to explore the monument.

The ranger station is open year-round and operates a bookstore and a small museum. Bring your own food; there is none available. A small campground with picnic tables and water offers overnight stays. A $3 entry fee per person or $6 per vehicle is charged. Call for directions; the only paved entrance is from Utah. Hovenweep is open year-round. The visitor center is open from 8 a.m. to 6 p.m. daily Apr through Sept, and 8 a.m. to 5 p.m. the rest of the year (closed Thanksgiving, Christmas, and New Year's Day). For more information call (970) 562-4282 or visit nps.gov/hove.

For those with an interest in Native American culture, the city of **Cortez** is the gateway to both the **Southern Ute** and **Ute Mountain Ute Indian Reservations.** The **Ute Mountain Utes** are one of seven original Ute bands that once inhabited the entire state of Colorado. The Ute Mountain Tribal Park, set in a classic southwestern landscape of mesas and canyons, contains an impressive collection of Ancestral Puebloan cliff dwellings, ruins, **petroglyphs,** and pictographs. Access is restricted to tours with Ute guides, who provide interpretation of the culture and history of these homelands.

The half-day tour visits petroglyphs, pictographs, scenic landmarks, and some surface archaeological sites. All sites on this tour are within easy walking distance of the gravel road. The full-day tour is more strenuous, including

Farmers' Markets

In southwestern Colorado farmers' markets are a friendly introduction to the community. Locals gather to peruse fresh produce, cheeses, jams, and meats, browse locally made products, and enjoy a hot drink and fresh pastry while socializing with neighbors and listening to live music. Markets are open from June through Oct. Start with these:

Cortez, Saturday 7:30 to 11 a.m.; cortezfarmmarket.com

Dolores, Wednesday 4 to 6 p.m.

Durango, Saturday 8 a.m. to noon; durangofarmersmarket.org

Mancos, Thursday 4:30 to 6:30 p.m.; mancoscolorado.com/farmmarket.htm climbs up rock faces via a series of ladders and a 3-mile walk on unpaved trails. The reward is a visit to four well-preserved cliff dwellings.

Tours begin at the Visitor Center/Museum, 20 miles south of Cortez at Highway Junction 160/491. For more information contact the Ute Mountain Tribal Park, PO Box 109, Towaoc 81334; (970) 565-3751 ext. 330 or (800) 847-5485; or the Visitor Center at (970) 749-1452; utemountainute.com/tribalpark.htm.

Highway 550 from Durango to Ouray passes though some of the state's most stunning mountain scenery. Climbing over Red Mountain Pass, the road switchbacks down into *Ouray,* often referred to as "The Switzerland of America." As you drive into town and gaze up at the soaring mountain peaks on all sides, you'll understand why. Nestled in a narrow river valley, the town is also blessed with hot springs. The *Ouray Hot Springs and Pool* (1230 Main St.; 970-325-7073) has a large pool partitioned into different sections, each with a different temperature. Every area comes with views of the surrounding peaks. The *Weisbaden Hot Springs* (625 5th St.; 970-325-4347; wiesbadenhotsprings .com) is a small natural hot springs spa and lodge with an outdoor swimming pool, private outdoor spa with soaking pool, and vapor cave.

Ouray is also known for the many jeep trails in the mountains surrounding town. Four-wheel routes such as Imogene, Engineer, and Black Bear Passes are so popular that during the colorful autumn foliage season traffic jams sometimes develop. You don't need to be an off-road expert to enjoy these high altitude trips; several companies in town offer tours into the backcountry to experience some of Colorado's most dramatic mountain terrain. When the tour is over, return to town for an ice-cream cone while browsing the many boutiques, galleries, and restaurants along Main Street.

At the edge of town, *Box Canyon Waterfall & Park* (CR 361; 970-325-7080) has several short trails leading into a deep box canyon carved out of limestone by Canyon Creek. It's a nice place to picnic and exhibits at the visitor center explain the geology, wildlife, and history of the area.

Down the road in Ridgeway, *Orvis Hot Springs* (CR 3; 970-626-5324; orvishotsprings.com) is a clothing-optional natural hot springs resort with four

Telluride

Telluride is renowned for its breathtaking alpine beauty, but many people don't realize that the town lies in the center of the greatest diversity of geology and archaeology in the nation. This area, known as the *Grand Circle,* encompasses four states, numerous state and national parks, and a variety of topography from the Rocky Mountains to the Painted Desert.

outdoor soaking pools, an indoor pool, and two private tubs. Lodging is also available here, and room guests have access to the pools all night. One of the valley's many pleasures is lying in the hot pools at night under a sky filled with sparkling stars.

Whenever the Rio Grande Southern rolled into the **Telluride** station back in the boomtown days of the early 1900s, legend has it the conductor would yell, "To hell you ride!" reminding passengers of the jarring, dusty journey they'd just completed. These days most people arriving at this former gold-mining town think they've pulled into paradise. Nestled in a box canyon where waterfalls roar down from surrounding peaks, Telluride sparkles as one of Colorado's crown jewels.

The town has two personas. In winter, heavy snowfall makes it a deep-powder ski destination. But when the snows melt each spring, wildflowers bloom, hummingbirds return, and Telluride becomes a sun-drenched alpine village where festivals, fun, and a funky mountain atmosphere drive away winter's chill.

At less than a mile long, the place is made for walking. Victorian buildings line Main Street. While the brothels and gambling dens are gone and the saloons have lost their rough edges, the town offers delights and distractions those miners never imagined. Throughout the summer, festivals celebrate everything from jazz, blues, and bluegrass to wine, film, and mushrooms.

Colorful shops, cafe bakeries, galleries, and bookstores provide plenty of low-volume entertainment. But sometimes paradise means nothing more than a morning latte and a comfortable bench along Main Street to watch the local color and wonder whether it's true that there are more dogs than residents in Telluride.

With rugged mountains on all sides, there are plenty of reasons to leave the pavement. The **San Miguel River Trail** follows the river for 2.7 easy miles.

Bridal Veil Falls, the tallest free-falling waterfall in Colorado, can be reached via a steeper hike of 1.8 miles. For an easier route and a panoramic view, ride the free, 12-minute gondola from town up to **Mountain Village,** Telluride's upscale sister hamlet. Once there, ogle the sky-high real estate, or take off on one of many hiking and biking trails that start here.

Telluride's gold-rush era left numerous high country roads, and today those tracks lead to weathered mining ruins. Local companies offer jeep tours to Tomboy and Alta ghost towns, Imogene and Ophir Passes, and points beyond.

Experienced 4x4 enthusiasts can buy a detailed map and take off on their own past flower-filled meadows to panoramic vistas. For more information call (888) 605-2578 or check out visittelluride.com.

The name says bluegrass, but don't let that fool you. The famous *Telluride Bluegrass Festival* may be one of the country's most progressive bluegrass gatherings, but expect to hear folk, rock, blues, country, pop, Celtic, world beat, and just about everything in between. Set in the box canyon amid soaring mountains, the 4-day event takes place at one of the most spectacular locations in America. When it's time for a break from the music, Telluride is a short stroll away, where eclectic eateries, galleries, coffeehouses, quirky shops, and bars await in the Victorian-era historic district. As a true Colorado tradition with stunning scenery, superb music, and plenty of friendly folks, this festival is a national treasure. Call (303) 823-0848 or (800) 624-2422 or visit bluegrass .com/telluride.

Places to Stay in Southern Colorado

ALAMOSA

Hampton Inn Alamosa
710 Mariposa St.
(719) 480-6023
hamptoninn.hilton.com, then type Alamosa in search field.
Moderate
Among Alamosa's newest hotels, clean, with free wireless Internet and breakfast.

Holiday Inn Express
3418 Mariposa
(877) 859-5095
Moderate
Newer hotel with upgraded rooms, free wireless Internet, and breakfast. Pets allowed.

ALMONT

Almont Resort
10209 Hwy. 135
(970) 641-4009
almontresort.com
Moderate to Expensive
Historic lodge and cabins at the headwaters of the Gunnison River offering fishing, horseback riding, rafting, skiing, mountain biking, and more on 90 acres.

Harmel's Ranch Resort
CR 742
(970) 641-1740 or
(800) 235-3402
harmels.com
Moderate to Expensive
Dude ranch at the confluence of 3 rivers offering rafting, fly fishing, horseback riding, and gourmet meals.

Three Rivers Resort
130 CR 742
(970) 641-1303 or
(888) 761-3473
3riversresort.com
Inexpensive
Cabins on the Taylor River with fishing, rafting, kayaking, and mountain relaxation.

BUENA VISTA

Best Western Plus Vista Inn
733 US 24 North
(800) 809-3495 or
(719) 395-8009
bestwestern.com/vistainn buenavista
Moderate
Breakfast included, friendly staff, free high-speed Internet, dependable Best Western amenities, and pool.

Buena Vista Super 8 Motel
530 N. US 24
(866) 944-0808 or
(719) 395-4090
bvsuper8.com
Inexpensive to Moderate
Affordable, clean accommodations, recently remodeled, with hot breakfast and hot tub.

Cottonwood Springs Hot Springs Inn & Spa
18999 CR 306, 5.5 miles west of Buena Vista
(719) 395-6434
cottonwood-hot-springs.com
Inexpensive to Moderate
Lodge and cabin room rates include use of hot springs pools.

Liars' Lodge
3000 CR 371
(719) 395-3444
liarslodge.com
Moderate
Attractive, modern log lodge offering a hearty breakfast, free wireless Internet, and views of the Collegiate Range and Arkansas River.

CAÑON CITY

Arkansas River Inn & Suites
1925 Fremont Dr.
(719) 275-3377
arkansasriverinn.net
Inexpensive
Affordable, hot tub, complimentary wireless Internet.

Parkview Inn Motel
231 Royal Gorge Blvd.
(719) 275-0624
parkviewinnmotel.com
Inexpensive
Located across from the Royal Gorge Route Railroad, this place is clean, quiet, and a good value, with free wireless Internet and friendly owners.

Quality Inn and Suites
3075 E. US 50
(719) 275-8676
qualityinn.com
Inexpensive to Moderate
Near the Arkansas River and rafting trips, this place has a hot breakfast, free wireless Internet, and a whirlpool. Pet-friendly.

COLORADO SPRINGS

Antlers Hilton Colorado Springs
4 S. Cascade Ave. at Pikes Peak Avenue and Cascade Avenue
(719) 955-5600
antlers.com
Moderate
Four-diamond hotel in downtown within walking distance to restaurants, shops, museums, and clubs, with complimentary wireless Internet and a fully equipped health club.

The Broadmoor
1 Lake Ave.
(719) 577-5775 or
(866) 837-8520
broadmoor.com
Expensive
Among Colorado's top resort hotels, historic, luxurious, with a championship golf course and a choice location nestled against the foothills of the Rockies.

Garden of the Gods Motel
2922 W. Colorado Ave.
(719) 636-5271
gardenofthegodsmotel.pikes-peak.com
Inexpensive
Affordable, centrally located, with heated indoor pool.

Holden House 1902 Bed & Breakfast Inn
1102 W. Pikes Peak
(719) 471-3980 or
(888) 565-3980
holdenhouse.com
Expensive
Long-established B&B with 6 guest suites on a residential street, free wireless Internet, and afternoon wine social.

Old Town Guesthouse Bed & Breakfast
115 S. 26th St.
(719) 632-9194 or
(888) 375-4210
oldtown-guesthouse.com
Moderate
Clean and contemporary lodging in a centrally located historic building, with an evening wine/beer reception.

Rodeway Inn & Suites Garden of the Gods
1623 S. Nevada Ave.
(719) 623-2300 or
(877) 424-6423
rodewayinn.com, then enter Colorado Springs in search field
Inexpensive to Moderate
Affordable, free wireless Internet, pet-friendly.

CORTEZ

Best Western Turquoise Inn and Suites
535 E. Main St.
(970) 565-3778 or
(800) 547-3376
bestwesternmesaverde.com
Moderate
Spacious, clean rooms in a pet-friendly inn, with outdoor heated pool, complimentary breakfast, and free wireless Internet.

Holiday Inn Express
2121 E. Main St.
(970) 565-6000 or
(877) 859-5095
hiexpress.com
Moderate
Clean, comfortable, and friendly, with on-site restaurant serving southwestern cuisine.

CRAWFORD

Smith Fork Ranch
45362 Needle Rock Rd.
(970) 921-3454
smithforkranch.com
Expensive
All-inclusive luxury guest ranch in Gunnison National Park with gourmet cuisine, amid mountains, rivers, lakes, and stunning views.

CRESTED BUTTE

Cristiana Guesthaus
621 Maroon Ave.
(800) 824-7899
cristianaguesthaus.com
Moderate
Cozy bed-and-breakfast lodge located 1 block from shops and restaurants in the main business district.

Elk Mountain Lodge
129 Gothic Ave.
(970) 349-7533 or
(800) 374-6521
elkmountainlodge.com
Moderate
Historic hotel, completely renovated, includes full breakfast, wireless Internet, indoor hot tub, bar, and sunroom.

Inn at Crested Butte
510 Whiterock Ave.
(970) 349-2111 or
(877) 343-2111
innatcrestedbutte.net
Moderate to Expensive
Boutique hotel in town with outdoor Jacuzzi, continental breakfast, free wireless Internet, and afternoon wine hour. Dog-friendly.

Lodge at Mountaineer Square
12 Snowmass Rd., Mt. Crested Butte
(970) 349-2222 or
(800) 810-7669
skicb.com/cbmr/
mountaineer-square-lodge
.aspx
Moderate to Expensive
Centrally located, steps away from ski lifts, hiking, biking, and nearby restaurants and shopping.

Nordic Inn
14 Treasury Rd., Mt. Crested Butte
(970) 349-5542 or
(800) 542-7669
nordicinncb.com
Inexpensive to Moderate
Family-owned lodge with outdoor hot tub, free wireless Internet, a fireplace in

lobby, and a continental breakfast.

Old Town Inn
210 N. 6th Ave.
(970) 349-6184 or
(888) 349-6184
oldtowninn.net
Moderate
Good-value lodging with hearty continental breakfast, an outdoor hot tub, close to historic downtown shops and restaurants. Free wireless Internet, pet-friendly.

Purple Mountain Lodge Bed and Breakfast
714 Gothic Ave.
(877) 349-5888
purplemountainlodge.com
Moderate to Expensive
Quiet 6-room B&B, with hot tub and day spa. The owner happily offers recommendations on local activities. No children under 12.

The Ruby of Crested Butte
624 Gothic Ave.
(970) 349-1338 or
(800) 390-1338
therubyofcrestedbutte.com
Moderate to Expensive
Luxury B&B decorated with posh western antique furnishings, offering free wireless Internet and a full breakfast.

West Wall Lodge
14 Hunter Hill Rd., Mt. Crested Butte
(970) 349-9404
westwalllodge.com
Expensive
Luxury condos with ski-in/ski-out convenience, close to lift-served hiking and

biking trails in summer, and free town shuttle.

CRIPPLE CREEK

Carr Manor
350 E. Carr Ave.
(719) 689-3709
carrmanor.com
Moderate to Expensive
Luxury historic inn with full breakfast, evening coffee, tea, and cookies, free wireless Internet, and 14 uniquely decorated rooms.

Gold King Mountain Inn
601 E. Galena Ave.
(719) 689-2600 or
(800) 445-3607
playwildwood.com/gold-king.html
Moderate
Part of Wildwood Casino, so discount packages are available for breakfast, dinner, and casino gaming.

Imperial Casino Hotel
123 N. 3rd St.
(719) 689-2561 or
(877) 546-0925
imperialhotelrestaurant.com
Moderate
Restored historic Victorian hotel and restaurant with authentic Old West atmosphere.

J.P. McGill's Hotel and Casino
232 Bennett Ave.
(719) 689-2446 or
(800) 635-5825
triplecrowncasinos.com
Moderate
Located above the casino floors, this place is newly remodeled, with free wireless Internet and plush pillow top mattresses.

DELTA COUNTY

Best Western Sundance
903 Main St., Delta
(970) 874-9781
bestwesternsundance.com
Moderate
Recently redecorated, offering free full breakfast, hot tub, and wireless Internet in rooms.

The Bross Hotel B&B
312 Onarga Ave., Paonia
(970) 527-6776
paonia-inn.com
Moderate
Turn-of-the-twentieth-century hotel richly appointed with period antiques and remodeled with modern amenities. Full breakfast, expansive views from guest rooms.

The Cedaredge Lodge
810 N. Grand Mesa Dr. (Hwy. 65), Cedaredge
(970) 856-3728
thecedarlodge.com
Inexpensive to Moderate
Relaxing, cozy lodge with hot tub, loaner bikes, an outdoor cooking space, massage service, and creekside lounging areas.

Fresh and Wyld Farmhouse and Garden
1978 Harding Rd., Paonia
(970) 527-4374
freshandwyld.com
Moderate
Historic B&B complete with vegetable gardens, chickens, a berry patch, and heirloom apple trees. Massage available.

DURANGO

Bear Paw Lodge at Vallecito Lake
18011 CR 501, Bayfield
(970) 884-2508
bearpawlodge.com
Moderate
Affordable cabins on a scenic lake in the San Juan National Forest with easy access to fishing and hiking.

Durango Mountain Resort
1 Skier Place
(970) 247-9000 or
(800) 982-6103
durangomountainresort.com
Expensive
Located at Purgatory Ski area, wide variety of year-round outdoor activities.

General Palmer Hotel
567 Main Ave.
(970) 247-4747 or
(800) 523-3358
generalpalmerhotel.com
Moderate
Victorian-style hotel blending antique furnishings with modern amenities.

Iron Horse Inn
5800 N. Main St.
(970) 259-1010 or
(800) 748-2990
ironhorseinndurango.com
Inexpensive to Moderate
Renovated rooms, outdoor pool, continental breakfast.

Lightner Creek Inn
999 CR 207
(970) 259-1226 or
(800) 268-9804
lightnercreekinn.com
Moderate
Luxury mountain B&B with 9 rooms.

FOR MORE INFORMATION

ALAMOSA

Alamosa Convention and Visitors
Bureau
610 State Ave., 81101
(800) 258-7597
alamosa.org

CAÑON CITY

Cañon City Chamber of Commerce
403 Royal Gorge Blvd., 81212
(719) 275-2331 or (800) 876-7922
canoncitychamber.com

COLORADO SPRINGS

Colorado Springs Convention and
Visitors Bureau
515 S. Cascade Ave., 80903
(719) 635-7506 or (800) 368-4748
experiencecoloradosprings.com

CRESTED BUTTE

Gunnison-Crested Butte Tourism
Association
202 E. Georgia Ave., Gunnison 81230
(800) 814-7988
gunnisoncrestedbutte.com

CRIPPLE CREEK

Cripple Creek Heritage Center
5th and Bennett Ave.
PO Box 430, 80813
(877) 858-4653
visitcripplecreek.com

DELTA

Delta Area Chamber of Commerce
301 Main St., 81416
(970) 874-8616
deltacolorado.org

DURANGO

Durango Area Chamber Resort
Association
111 S. Camino del Rio
PO Box 2587, 81302
(800) 525-8855 or (970) 247-3500
durango.org

GUNNISON

Gunnison-Crested Butte Tourism
Association
202 E. Georgia Ave., Gunnison 81230
(800) 814-7988
gunnisoncrestedbutte.com

LEADVILLE

Leadville/Lake County Chamber of
Commerce
809 Harrison Ave.
PO Box 861, 80461
(719) 486-3900
leadvilleusa.com

**Rochester Hotel/Leland
House Bed & Breakfast**
721 E. 2nd Ave.
(970) 385-1920 or
(800) 664-1920
rochesterhotel.com
Expensive
Two restored properties
on same street block,
both include full gourmet
breakfast at Rochester
Hotel. Quiet area 1 block
from Main Street galler-
ies, shops, restaurants,
museums.

The Strater Hotel
699 Main Ave.
(970) 247-4431 or
(800) 247-4431
strater.com
Moderate to Expensive
Beautifully restored his-
toric downtown hotel with

MANITOU SPRINGS

Manitou Springs Chamber of
Commerce & Visitors Bureau
354 Manitou Ave., 80829
(800) 642-2567 or (719) 685-5089
manitousprings.org

MESA VERDE COUNTY

Cortez Chamber of Commerce
928 E. Main St., 81321
(970) 565-3414
cortezchamber.org

Mesa Verde Country Visitor
Information Bureau
(800) 530-2998 or (970) 565-8227
swcolo.org

Mesa Verde National Park
PO Box 227, Mancos, 81328
(800) 449-2288
visitmesaverde.com

MONTROSE

Montrose Chamber of Commerce
1519 E. Main St., 81401
(970) 249-5000 or (800) 923-5515
montroseact.com

MOSCA

Great Sand Dunes National Park
11999 Hwy. 150, 81146
(719) 378-6300 (main) or (719) 378-6399 (visitor center)
nps.gov/grsa

MT. CRESTED BUTTE

Gunnison-Crested Butte Tourism
Association
Next to the bus stop at ski area base
(800) 814-7988
gunnisoncrestedbutte.com

PAGOSA SPRINGS

Pagosa Springs Area Chamber of
Commerce
PO Box 787, 81147
(970) 264-2360 or (800) 252-2204
visitpagosasprings.com

PUEBLO

Greater Pueblo Chamber of
Commerce
PO Box 697, 81002
302 N. Santa Fe Ave., 81003
(800) 233-3446 or (719) 542-1704
pueblochamber.org

SALIDA

Salida Chamber of Commerce
406 W. Hwy. 50, 81201
(877) 772-5432 or (719) 539-2068
salidachamber.org

TELLURIDE

Telluride Tourism Board
PO Box 1009, 81435
(888) 605-2578
visittelluride.com

adjoining eating options at Diamond Belle Saloon, Office Spiritorium, and Mahogany Grille.

Wilderness Trails Ranch
23486 CR 501, Bayfield
(970) 247-0722 or
(800) 527-2624
wildernesstrails.com
Expensive

All-inclusive dude ranch experience with hearty ranch meals, horseback riding, hiking, mountain biking, fishing, nightly entertainment, and more.

GREAT SAND DUNES

Great Sand Dunes Lodge
7900 Hwy. 150 North
(Mosca)
(719) 378-2900
gsdlodge.com
Inexpensive to Moderate
Conveniently located by
park entrance, with heated
indoor pool and free wireless Internet.

GUNNISON

Holiday Inn Express Hotel & Suites
910 E. Tomichi Ave.
(970) 641-1228 or
(877) 859-5095
hiexpress.com
Moderate
Dependable Holiday
Inn standards, with free
breakfast, a fitness center,
heated indoor pool and
whirlpool, and complimen-
tary wireless Internet.

Island Acres Resort
38339 W. Hwy. 50
(970) 641-1442
islandacresresort.com
Inexpensive
Cabin-like motel units in a
relaxed atmosphere on 3
acres filled with large cottonwood trees. Individually
decorated rooms combine
1950s charm with Gunni-
son's history. Green motel
facility, pet-friendly.

Lost Canyon Resort
8264 Hwy. 135
(970) 641-0181
lostcanyonresort.com
Inexpensive to Moderate
Quiet, rustic cabins on
the Gunnison River, fully

supplied with bedding,
linens, and kitchen uten-
sils. Free wireless Internet,
pet-friendly.

Quality Inn
400 E. Tomichi Ave.
(970) 641-1237
qualityinn.com
Inexpensive to Moderate
Within walking distance of
historic downtown, offer-
ing free hot breakfast and
wireless Internet in this pet-
friendly establishment.

The Seasons Inn
412 E. Tomichi Ave.
(866) 641-0700
gunnisoninn.com
Inexpensive
Affordable rooms and
kitchenette cottages, with
continental breakfast, hot
tub, and free wireless
Internet.

Super 8
411 E. Tomichi Ave.
(970) 641-3068
super8.com
Inexpensive
Affordable and clean, with
a convenient location.

Water Wheel Inn
37478 W. Hwy. 50
(970) 641-1650 or
(800) 642-1650
waterwheelinnatgunnison
.com
Inexpensive to Moderate
Affordable pet-friendly
lodging with 49 rooms,
continental breakfast, on-
site massage available, and
free wireless Internet.

Wildwood Resort and Cabins
1312 W. Tomichi Ave.
(970) 641-1663
wildwoodmotel.net
Inexpensive to Moderate
Quiet and clean modern
motel units with kitchens,
equipped with wireless
Internet.

LEADVILLE

Grand West Village Resort
999 Grand West Dr.
(800) 691-3999 or
(719) 486-0702
grandwest.com
Expensive
Lodge-style condomini-
ums with fully equipped
kitchens, fireplaces, and
laundry.

McGinnis Cottage Bed and Breakfast
809 Spruce St.
(800) 288-1775
mcginniscottage.com
Moderate
Fully restored Victorian-
style inn, offering full
breakfast and free wireless
Internet.

MANITOU SPRINGS

El Colorado Lodge
23 Manitou Ave.
(719) 685-5485 or
(800) 782-2246
elcolorado.pikes-peak.com
Inexpensive to Moderate
Historic lodge with
southwestern-style adobe
cabins, heated swimming
pool, hot tub, outdoor
recreation.

Red Crags Bed-and-Breakfast Inn
302 El Paso Blvd.
(719) 685-4515 or
(800) 685-4515
redcrags.com
Moderate
Historic Victorian mansion B&B located on a bluff with expansive views of Manitou Valley. All room have king beds, most have fireplaces. Outdoor Jacuzzi, private picnic area, and barbecue pit.

Rocky Mountain Lodge and Cabins
4680 Haerman Ave., Cascade
(719) 684-2521 or
(888) 298-0348
rockymountainlodge.com
Moderate
Six bedrooms, separate cottage and cabin lodging, with a great room with massive fireplace, an outdoor hot tub, and gourmet breakfast.

Town-N-Country Cottages
123 Crystal Park Rd.
(719) 685-5427 or
(800) 366-3509
townncountryc.com
Moderate
Quaint cottages in a quiet, tree-filled setting, with a heated pool and hot tub.

MESA VERDE
Far View Lodge
At Navajo Hill; in the park 15 miles from entrance
(602) 331-5210 or
(800) 449-2288
visitmesaverde.com

Inexpensive to Moderate
Breathtaking views, private balcony with all rooms, western decor, excellent dining at adjacent Metate Room. Book in advance.

MONTROSE
Best Western Red Arrow
1702 E. Main St.
(970) 249-9641 or
(800) 468-9323
bestwesterncolorado.com/hotels/best-western-red-arrow
Moderate
Nice complimentary breakfast, spacious rooms with free wireless Internet.

Black Canyon Motel
160 E. Main St.
(970) 249-3495 or
(800) 348-3495
blackcanyonmotel.com
Inexpensive to Moderate
Complimentary breakfast, hot tub, free wireless Internet.

Country Lodge
1624 E. Main St.
(970) 249-4567
countrylodgecolorado.com
Inexpensive
Individually decorated rooms, hot tub, free wireless Internet.

Uncompahgre Bed-and-Breakfast
21049 Uncompahgre Rd.
(970) 240-4000 or
(800) 318-8127
uncbb.com
Moderate
Country inn with 8 guest rooms.

Western Motel
1200 E. Main St.
(970) 249-3481 or
(800) 445-7301
westernmotel.com
Inexpensive
Affordable, with free continental breakfast, hot tub, and wireless Internet.

MT. CRESTED BUTTE
Crested Butte Lodging
Various properties
(970) 349-2400 or
(888) 412-7310
crestedbuttelodging.com
Inexpensive to Expensive
Wide range of lodging from studio condos to resort properties.

Crested Butte Retreat
39 Whetstone Dr.
(970) 349-1701
crestedbutteretreat.com
Expensive
Ten rooms in luxury boutique mountain lodge on hillside above town with panoramic views.

Elevation Hotel & Spa
500 Gothic Rd.
(800) 810-7669 or
(970) 349-2222
elevationhotelandspa.com
Expensive
Luxury ski-in/ski-out resort property combines cozy ski lodge feel with hip urban decor.

Grand Lodge Crested Butte
6 Emmons Loop
(800) 810-7669
grandlodgecrestedbutte.com
Moderate

Full-service affordable and pet-friendly hotel close to ski lifts, with spacious rooms, heated indoor and outdoor pools, hot tub.

Lodge at Mountaineer Square
500 Gothic Rd.
(800) 810-7669
mountaineersquare.com
Moderate
Luxury ski resort accommodations for winter or summer.

Nordic Inn
14 Treasury Rd.
(970) 349-5542 or
(800) 542-7669
nordicinncb.com
Inexpensive to Moderate
Family-owned lodge with outdoor hot tub, free wireless Internet, a fireplace in the lobby, and continental breakfast.

West Wall Lodge
14 Hunter Hill Rd.
(970) 349-9404
westwalllodge.com
Expensive
Luxury condos.

OURAY

Best Western Plus Twin Peaks Lodge & Hot Springs
125 3rd Ave.
(970) 325-4427
bestwesterncolorado.com
Moderate
Hot springs soaking pool, full hot breakfast, pet-friendly, and wireless Internet.

Ouray Antlers Motel
405 Main St.
(970) 325-4589
antlersouray.com
Inexpensive
Convenient, retro-style motel in the center of town.

St. Elmo Hotel
426 Main St.
(970) 325-4951
stelmohotel.com
Moderate
Historic hotel lovingly restored with turn-of-the-twentieth-century furnishings, sauna, and hot tub. Breakfast included.

Timber Ridge Lodge
1550 Main St.
(970) 325-4856
timberridgelodgeouray.com
Inexpensive to Moderate
Near downtown and Ouray hot springs, recently renovated, with free wireless Internet. Pets allowed.

Wiesbaden Hot Springs Spa & Lodging
625 5th St.
(970) 325-4347
wiesbadenhotsprings.com
Moderate
Rooms include access to hot springs, vapor cave, outdoor pool, and discounts on spa services.

PAGOSA SPRINGS

High Country Lodge
3821 E. Hwy. 160
(970) 264-4181 or
(800) 862-3707
highcountrylodge.com
Moderate
Casual lodge rooms and comfortable log cabins on 20 wooded acres.

The Pagosa Lodge
3505 W. Hwy. 160
(970) 731-4141
pagosalodge.com
Moderate
Heated indoor pool, hot tubs, free wireless Internet, and hot breakfast.

The Springs Resort & Spa
165 Hot Springs Blvd.
(970) 264-4168 or
(800) 225-0934
pagosahotsprings.com
Expensive
All rooms come with 24-hour complimentary access to the soaking pools.

Wyndham Pagosa
42 Pinon Causeway
(800) 625-1649
wyndhampagosaresort.com
Inexpensive to Moderate
One- and two-bedroom fully furnished condos with kitchen, washer, dryer, and free wireless Internet.

PUEBLO

Days Inn
4201 N. Elizabeth
(719) 543-8031
daysinn.com
Inexpensive to Moderate
Affordable, with continental breakfast and free wireless Internet.

Edgar Olin House Bed and Breakfast
727 W. 13th St.
(719) 544-5727
olin-house.com
Inexpensive to Moderate
Victorian-style inn with afternoon refreshments,

antique furnishings, and free wireless Internet.

Guest House Inn
730 N. Santa Fe Ave.
(719) 543-6530
guesthousepueblo.com
Inexpensive
Complimentary breakfast, newly remodeled rooms, seasonal pool, free wireless Internet, pet-friendly.

RIDGWAY

Chipeta Solar Springs Resort
304 S. Lena St.
(800) 633-5868
chipeta.com
Moderate to Expensive
Adobe-style boutique resort retreat with unique rooms, hot pools, spa, yoga and fitness center, and Four Corners Cafe.

SALIDA

Days Inn
402 E. Hwy. 50
(719) 539-6651
daysinnsalida.com
Inexpensive to Moderate
Outdoor hot tub, continental breakfast, free wireless Internet, and a natural hot springs pool (nominal fee).

Tudor Rose Bed-and-Breakfast
6720 CR 104
(719) 539-2002 or
(800) 379-0889
thetudorrose.com
Moderate to Expensive
Large guest rooms and outdoor hot tub, located 1.5 miles from Salida, surrounded by 37 acres

of piñon pine. They offer stabling for those traveling with horses.

Woodland Motel
903 W. 1st St.
(719) 539-4980 or
(800) 488-0456
woodlandmotel.com
Inexpensive to Moderate
Close to downtown historic district, clean, pet-friendly accommodations with free wireless Internet. Some units have kitchens.

SAN LUIS

El Convento Bed and Breakfast
512 Church Place
(719) 672-4223
Inexpensive
Simple, clean, quiet, affordable rooms in a converted convent.

TELLURIDE

Hotel Columbia
301 W. San Juan Ave.
(970) 728-0660 or
(800) 201-9505
columbiatelluride.com
Expensive
Modern boutique hotel offering luxury accommodations with excellent hospitality, good location across the street from main ski resort gondola, and excellent complimentary European-style hot breakfast.

Lumiere Telluride
118 Lost Creek Lane
(970) 728-4224 or
(866) 530-9466
lumieretelluride.com
Expensive

Luxury boutique hotel with plush furnishings, designer decor, and free wireless Internet.

Mountain Lodge
457 Mountain Village Blvd.
(970) 369-5000
mountainlodgetelluride.com
Moderate to Expensive
Upscale hotel suites and condo rentals at the ski slope, with an outdoor deck with a heated pool and Jacuzzi, concierge services, and free wireless Internet.

New Sheridan
231 W. Colorado Ave.
(970) 728-4351 or
(800) 200-1891
newsheridan.com
Moderate
Telluride's newest "old" hotel with rich historic ambience and renovated guest rooms, home to the New Sheridan Bar and Chop House restaurant.

Places to Eat in Southern Colorado

ALAMOSA

Cavillo's Mexican Restaurant
400 Main St.
(719) 587-5500
Inexpensive to Moderate
Authentic Mexican cuisine and occasional mariachi music at this local favorite.

Milagro's Coffeehouse
529 Main St.
(719) 589-9299
milagrosalamosa.com
Inexpensive
Friendly local coffeehouse with all proceeds going to a local shelter. Excellent coffee, breakfast, and pastries.

San Luis Valley Brewing Co.
631 Main St.
(719) 587-2337
slvbrewco.com
Inexpensive to Moderate
Good selection of handcrafted beers and a diverse menu of quality pub entrees, salads, and appetizers.

San Luis Valley Pizza Company
2069 1st St.
(719) 589-4749
sanluisvalleypizzacompany .com
Inexpensive to Moderate
Traditional and gourmet pizzas, pasta, Italian dishes, salad and potato bar.

ALMONT

Almont Resort
10209 Hwy. 135
(970) 641-4009
almontresort.com
Inexpensive to Moderate
Two dining rooms offering fireside dining and homemade food in a friendly atmosphere.

Harmel's Ranch Resort
(seasonal)
CR 742
(970) 641-1740
harmels.com

Moderate to Expensive
A wide range of western ranch-style cuisine is available for breakfast, lunch, and dinner to guests not staying at the resort.

Three Rivers Resort Smokehouse
(seasonal)
130 CR 742
(970) 641-1303 or
(888) 761-3474
3riversresort.com
Moderate
Breakfast, lunch, and dinner served indoors or on the outside patio.

BUENA VISTA

Bongo Billy's Cafe
713 US 24
(719) 395-2634
bongobillyscafe.com
Inexpensive
Local coffeehouse with good coffee and teas, excellent baked goods, sandwiches, and soups.

CAÑON CITY/ROYAL GORGE

Merlino's Belvedere
1330 Elm Ave.
(719) 275-5558
belvedererestaurant.com
Moderate to Expensive
Family-owned Italian and American food.

Pizza Madness
509 Main St.
(719) 276-3088
mypizzamadness.com
Inexpensive to Moderate
Award-winning, handcrafted pizza, fresh salads, calzones, fresh

baked sandwiches, and microbrews.

COLORADO SPRINGS

Carlos Bistro
1025 S. 21st St.
(719) 471-2905
Expensive
Italian/Mediterranean bistro with excellent food and service, praised by locals.

Edelweiss
34 E. Ramona Ave.
(719) 633-2220
edelweissrest.com
Inexpensive to Moderate
Authentic Old World German dishes including schnitzel, bratwurst, and sauerbraten along with traditional continental fare.

Flying W Ranch
3330 Chuckwagon Rd.
(719) 598-4000 or
(800) 232-FLYW (3599)
flyingw.com
Expensive
Chuck wagon supper and musical show in a western atmosphere.

La Baguette French Bistro
4440 N. Chestnut St.
(719) 599-0686
labaguettefrenchbistro.com
Inexpensive
European deli and bakery.

La Casita Mexican Grill (3 locations)
3725 E. Woodmen Rd.
(719) 536-0375
4295 N. Nevada Ave.
(719) 599-7829
306 S. 8th St.
(719) 633-9616
Inexpensive to Moderate

Award-winning, made-from-scratch Mexican food using fresh ingredients.

Marigold Cafe & Bakery
4605 Centennial Blvd.
(719) 599-4776
marigoldcoloradosprings
.com
Moderate
French bistro-inspired menu coupled with an in-house bakery make this a local favorite.

Summit at Broadmoor
1 Lake Ave.
(719) 577-5733
broadmoor.com
Expensive
This American brasserie, with an eclectic menu and an innovative wine and cocktail list, uses the best available ingredients and produce from across the US.

CORTEZ

Metate Room
(Mesa Verde National Park)
(602) 331-5210 or
(800) 449-2288
visitmesaverde.com/dining/
metate-room.aspx
Moderate to Expensive
Award-winning restaurant serving contemporary cuisine inspired by Ancestral Puebloan regional heritage foods and flavorings.

Nero's Restaurant
303 W. Main St.
(970) 565-7366
nerocortez.com
Moderate
Fine traditional Italian cuisine.

Silver Bean Coffee Shop
410 W. Main St.
(970) 946-4404
Inexpensive
Tastefully kitschy roadside attraction and coffee shop in an Airstream trailer.

CRESTED BUTTE

Donita's Cantina
332 Elk Ave.
(970) 349-6674
donitascantina.com
Moderate
Lively local eatery serving a wide variety of Mexican specialties.

Izzy's
218 Maroon Ave.
(970) 349-5630
Inexpensive to Moderate
Popular local spot for excellent breakfasts. Open breakfast and lunch only.

Le Bosquet
6th and Belleview, Majestic Plaza
(970) 349-5808
Expensive
Country French cuisine; seasonal menu includes fresh seafood, chicken, beef, lamb, and vegetarian entrees.

Lil's Sushi Bar & Grill
321 Elk Ave.
(970) 349-6233
lilssushibarandgrill.com
Moderate to Expensive
Fresh fish, full sushi menu, and Japanese-style grilling and tapas.

Marchitelli's Gourmet Noodle
411 3rd St.
(970) 349-7401
Moderate to Expensive
Wide variety of Italian pastas and entrees.

Paradise Cafe
303 Elk Ave.
(970) 349-6233
paradisecafecrestedbutte
.com
Inexpensive to Moderate
Longtime local favorite serving breakfast and lunch.

Pitas in Paradise
212 Elk Ave.
(970) 349-0897
pitasinparadise.com
Inexpensive
Mediterranean-style cafe with gyros, rice bowls, salads, milk shakes, and a wide range of pitas.

Secret Stash
21 Elk Ave.
(970) 349-6245
thesecretstash.com
Moderate
Gourmet pizzeria, exotic specialty drinks, and cool local ambience.

Slogar Bar & Restaurant
517 2nd St.
(970) 349-5765
Moderate to Expensive
American comfort food served family style.

Soupcon Bistro
127A Elk Ave.
(970) 349-5448
soupconcrestedbutte.com
Expensive
Artful blending of French regional cuisine with

OTHER ATTRACTIONS WORTH SEEING IN SOUTHERN COLORADO

COLORADO SPRINGS

Flying W Ranch
(719) 598-4000 or (800) 232-3599
flyingw.com

Old Colorado City
(719) 577-4112
shopoldcoloradocity.com

US Olympic Visitor Center
(888) 659-8687
teamusa.org/About-the-USOC.aspx

CORTEZ

Trail of the Ancients
(800) 530-2998
trailoftheancients.com

DELTA COUNTY

Delta County Historical Museum
251 Meeker St., Delta
(970) 874-8721
deltacountycolorado.com

Delta County Tourism
(970) 874-2100 or (970) 874-9532
deltacountycolorado.com

Grand Mesa Scenic and Historic Byway
(970) 856-7554
grandmesabyway.org

DURANGO

Durango Mountain Resort
(970) 247-9000 or (800) 982-6103
durangomountainresort.com

GUNNISON

Curecanti National Recreation Area and Morrow Point Boat Tour
(970) 641-2337
nps.gov/cure

LEADVILLE

Leadville, Colorado & Southern Railroad Train Tour
(719) 486-3936 or (866) 386-3936
leadville-train.com

American traditional food using organic ingredients from sustainable businesses whenever possible.

CRESTONE

Desert Sage Restaurant
12 Baca Townhouse
(719) 256-4402
Moderate
Hearty, eclectic menu of healthy food for the community, visitors, and spiritual retreats.

Lotus Cafe
175 Golden Ave.
(719) 256-4959
Inexpensive to Moderate
Breakfast, lunch, and dinner with free wireless Internet and hot beverages in a relaxed atmosphere.

CRIPPLE CREEK

Midland Depot at the Imperial Hotel
123 N. 3rd St.
imperialcasinohotel.com
Moderate

Dependable family-style Italian food in a historic hotel.

DURANGO

Carver Brewing Co.
1022 Main Ave.
(970) 259-2545
carverbrewing.com
Moderate
A popular local spot for breakfast, lunch, and dinner in a friendly brewpub atmosphere with a sunny outdoor patio.

MANITOU SPRINGS

Cave of the Winds
(719) 685-5444
caveofthewinds.com

MONTROSE

Owl Creek Pass
(970) 249-5000 or (800) 923-5515
(Chamber of Commerce)
montroseact.com

MT. CRESTED BUTTE

Crested Butte Mountain Resort
(970) 349-2222
skicb.com

OURAY

Million Dollar Highway
(970) 325-4746 or (800) 228-1876
(Chamber of Commerce)
ouraycolorado.com

PAGOSA SPRINGS

Navajo State Park
(970) 883-2208 or (970) 883-2628
(marina)
parks.state.co.us/parks/navajo

Wolf Creek Pass
(800) 252-2204 (Chamber of
Commerce)
sangres.com/features/wolfcreekpass
.htm

PUEBLO

**The Greenway and Nature & Raptor
Center of Pueblo**
(719) 549-2414
natureandraptor.org

SILVERTON

Silverton Historic District
(800) 752-4494 or (970) 387-5654
(Chamber of Commerce)
silvertoncolorado.com

Cyprus Cafe
725 E. 2nd Ave.
(970) 385-6884
cypruscafe.com
Inexpensive to Moderate
Fresh, innovative Mediterranean cuisine served for
lunch and dinner in a renovated Victorian home.

Ken & Sue's
636 Main Ave.
(970) 385-1810
kenandsues.com
Moderate
Excellent contemporary

American cuisine and good
service at a popular foodie
destination.

**Mahogany Grille at the
Strater**
699 Main Ave.
(970) 247-4433
mahoganygrille.com
Moderate to Expensive
Eclectic seasonal menu of
regional American entrees
inspired by local flavors and
ingredients.

Ore House
147 E. College Dr.
(970) 247-5705
orehouserestaurant.com
Expensive
This steak house in an Old
West atmosphere uses
seasonal, organic, and
local ingredients whenever
possible.

Serious Texas Bar-B-Q
3535 N. Main Ave.
(970) 247-2240
serioustexasbbq.com
Inexpensive to Moderate

Variety of smoked meats and sausages paired with homemade sauces and salsas.

Steamworks Brewery
801 E. 2nd Ave.
(970) 259-9200
steamworksbrewing.com
Inexpensive to Moderate
Gastropub fare includes regionally raised meats, sustainable seafood, salads, pizza, southwestern-style dishes, and vegetarian entrees.

FAIRPLAY

Asian Palate
328 E. Main St.
(719) 395-6679
theasianpalate.com
Moderate
Full sushi bar, Thai and Asian cuisine. Free wireless Internet.

Coyote Cantina
12985 Hwy. 24
(719) 395-3755
Inexpensive to Moderate
Popular spot for Mexican food and margaritas. Serving breakfast, lunch, and dinner.

Evergreen Cafe
418 N. Hwy. 24
(719) 395-8984
evergreencafebv.com
Inexpensive to Moderate
Breakfast and lunch in a historic setting, with great omelets, salads, and sandwiches, locally roasted coffee, all natural breads and meats, and many vegetarian choices.

GUNNISON

The Bean Coffeehouse & Eatery
120 N. Main St.
(970) 641-2408
thebeancoffeehouseand
eatery.com
Inexpensive
Organic and fair-trade slow-roasted coffees, specialty drinks, crepes, breakfast burritos, smoothies, salads, sandwiches, and pastries. Free wireless Internet.

Garlic Mike's
2674 N. Hwy. 135
(970) 641-2493
garlicmikes.com
Moderate to Expensive
Longtime favorite for Italian food in a friendly atmosphere.

Gunnisack Cowboy Bistro
142 N. Main St.
(970) 641-5445
Inexpensive to Moderate
Friendly cowboy bistro serving burgers, steaks, fish-and-chips, soups, sandwiches, fresh-baked desserts.

Gunnison Brewery
138 N. Main St.
(970) 641-2739
gunnisonbrewery.com
Inexpensive
Good pub food, live music some evenings.

Mario's Pizza
213 W. Tomichi Ave.
(970) 641-1374
mariosgunnison.com
Inexpensive to Moderate
Longtime local favorite

serving homemade Italian food and pizza.

Ol' Miner Steakhouse
139 N. Main St.
(970) 641-5153
Moderate to Expensive
Rustic, down-home setting and a meat-lover's dream.

The Trough
37550 US 50
(970) 641-3724
thetroughrestaurant.com
Moderate to Expensive
Steaks, prime rib, seafood, made-from-scratch side dishes, and libations.

Twisted Fork
206 N. Main St.
(970) 641-1488
twistedforkgunnison.net
Moderate
Popular, friendly, Asian-influenced American bistro with a wide range of well-prepared entrees.

LEADVILLE

City on a Hill Coffee & Espresso
508 Harrison Ave.
(970) 445-7368
cityonahillcoffee.com
Inexpensive
Good coffee, free wireless Internet.

High Mountain Pies
115 W. 4th St.
(719) 486-5555
Inexpensive
Gourmet pizzas, barbecue, and sandwiches.

Quincy's
416 Harrison Ave.
(719) 486-9765
Moderate

Affordable steaks and prime rib.

MANITOU SPRINGS

Adam's Mountain Cafe
934 Manitou Ave.
(719) 685-1430
adamsmountain.com
Inexpensive to Moderate
Largely organic offering, with many vegetarian and vegan entrees, prepared with fresh, quality ingredients.

The Briarhurst Manor
404 Manitou Ave.
(719) 685-1864 or
(877) 685- 1448
briarhurst.com
Expensive
Fine dining with classic American cuisine of steaks, lamb, game, chicken.

Coquette's Bistro and Bakery
915 Manitou Ave.
(719) 685-2420
couquettesbistroandbakery.com
Inexpensive to Moderate
Extensive selection of crepes, soups, quiches, omelets, sandwiches, and drinks.

Craftwood Inn
404 El Paso Blvd.
(719) 685-9000
craftwood.com
Expensive
Regional Colorado cuisine dinners: wild game, steaks, seafood, chicken, and vegetarian.

Sahara Cafe
954 Manitou Ave.
(719) 685-2303
thesaharacafe.com
Inexpensive to Moderate
Highly rated Middle Eastern cuisine including gyros, shawarmas, falafel, and mezze plates.

MONTROSE

Daily Bread Bakery and Cafe
346 E. Main St.
(970) 249-8444
Inexpensive
Breakfast, lunch, and home-baked goodies from a friendly staff.

Garlic Mike's Italian Cuisine
103 Rose Lane
(970) 249-4381
garlicmikes.com
Moderate
Popular, award-winning authentic Italian cuisine.

MT. CRESTED BUTTE

Avalanche Bar & Grill
15 Emmons Rd.
(970) 349-7195
avalanchebarandgrill.com
Inexpensive to Moderate
Sports bar with an extensive breakfast, lunch, après-ski, and dinner menu of main entrees, sandwiches, salads, and pizzas.

Butte 66 Roadhouse BBQ
218 Elk Ave., Ski Base Area
(970) 349-2999
Inexpensive to Moderate
Popular après-ski bar and eatery with live music and

mountain views serving freshly made barbeque.

Camp 4 Coffee
Mountaineer Square Courtyard
(also locations in Crested Butte and Crested Butte South)
(970) 349-2500
camp4coffee.com
Inexpensive
Sandwiches, burritos, pastries, and good coffee.

Django's Restaurant and Wine Bar
620 Gothic Rd., Mountaineer Square at the bus stop
(970) 349-7574
djangos.us
Inexpensive to Moderate
Extensive, seasonally changing menu of small plates inspired by the cuisines of southern Europe.

9380 Prime
Elevation Hotel
(970) 251-3030
skicb.com
Inexpensive to Expensive
Upscale but casual breakfast, lunch, après-ski dining, and popular dinner spot.

Woodstone Bar & Grille
Grand Lodge Crested Butte
(970) 349-8030
grandlodgecrestedbutte.com
Inexpensive to Expensive
All-you-can-eat breakfast buffet and hearty comfort food with an international flair for dinner.

OURAY

Backstreet Bistro
636 Main St.
(970) 325-0550
Inexpensive
Healthy alternative to fast food with full breakfast, sandwiches, soups, homemade pastries and pies.

Bon Ton Restaurant
426 Main St.
(970) 325-4951
stelmohotel.com
Moderate to Expensive
Upscale casual Italian cuisine at one of the area's finest restaurants.

Ouray Brewery
607 Main St.
(970) 325-7388
ouraybrewery.com
Inexpensive
Tasty pub fare and handcrafted beers in a friendly local setting.

PAGOSA SPRINGS

Alley House Grille
214 Pagosa St.
(970) 264-0999
alleyhousegrille.com
Moderate to Expensive
Elegant but casual atmosphere serving global/Colorado fusion cuisine in a restored cottage.

Chavalo's Taqueria
301 N. Pagosa Blvd., #B-2
(970) 731-2501
Inexpensive
Authentic Mexican food and good margaritas, a local favorite.

Farrago's Market Cafe
175 Pagosa St.
(970) 264-4600
farragomarketcafe.com
Inexpensive
Excellent selection of tasty, healthy soups, salads, pizzas, wraps, burgers, and more.

Montoya's Cafe
438 Pagosa Blvd.
(970) 264-2146
Moderate
Small-town cafe atmosphere serving Mexican and American food, breakfast burritos.

Pagosa Baking Company
238 Pagosa St.
(970) 264-9348
pagosabakingcompany.com
Inexpensive
Changing menu of sandwich and lunch specials along with fresh breads, pastries, pies, cakes, and cookies.

Pagosa Brewing Company
118 N. Pagosa Blvd.
(970) 731-2739
pagosabrewing.com
Inexpensive
Gastropub cuisine: burgers, salmon, brats, chicken, pizza, soups, salads, sandwiches, and of course, good beer.

PUEBLO

Cactus Flower Restaurant
4610 N. Elizabeth St.
(719) 545-8218
cactusflowerrestaurant.com
Moderate
Diverse Mexican cuisine prepared with fresh ingredients.

La Renaissance
217 E. Routt Ave.
(719) 543-6367
larenaissancerestaurant.com
Expensive
Casual, relaxed dining with a continental menu in an 1886 church.

Papa Jose's Union Cafe
320 S. Union Ave.
(719) 545-7476
Inexpensive
Family-owned Mexican restaurant, a local favorite, with fresh ingredients and good service.

Restaurant Fifteen Twenty One
123 N. Main St.
(719) 542-9999
restaurant1521.com
Moderate
New American cuisine with French and Vietnamese influences.

SALIDA

Salida Cafe
300 W. Sackett Ave.
(719) 539-4261
salidacafe.com
Inexpensive
Good sandwiches, soups, desserts, and coffee drinks, with music some evenings and an outdoor patio overlooking the Arkansas River.

TELLURIDE

Allreds
Top of San Sophia Gondola
(970) 728-7474
allredsrestaurant.com
Expensive
Eclectic menu of steak,

seafood, chicken, pasta, lamb, with a panoramic mountain view from the dining room.

Baked in Telluride
127 S. Fir St.
(970) 728-4775
Inexpensive
A Telluride favorite for 30 years. Breakfast, lunch, dinner, pizza, wine and beer, and numerous baked goods are available.

Honga's Lotus Petal
135 E. Colorado Ave.
(970) 728-5134
hongaslotuspetal.com
Moderate to Expensive
A Telluride institution for more than 20 years.

Pan-Asian fusion restaurant reflecting the flavors of many Asian countries.

La Marmotte
150 W. San Juan Ave.
(970) 728-6232
lamarmotte.com
Moderate to Expensive
Elegant French bistro fare with sunny patios, a quaint dining room, and a separate bar.

La Piazza Del Villaggio
117 Lost Creek Lane, Mountain Village
(970) 728-8283
lapiazzadelvillaggio ristorante.com
Expensive
Authentic Italian cuisine.

Oak
250 San Juan Ave.
(970) 728-3985
oakstelluride.com
Moderate
Southern barbecue and sides, veggie dishes, and salads.

Steaming Bean Coffee
221 W. Colorado Ave.
(970) 369-5575 or
(800) 230-2326 (bean)
thesteamingbeantelluride .com
Inexpensive
Popular local hangout with selection of coffees, breakfast, and a full bar.

DENVER & THE PLAINS →

Denver Metropolitan Area

With its former folksy label of Cow Town long retired, **Denver** is renowned as a hip, sophisticated city at the edge of the Rocky Mountains. A vibrant cultural scene, 300 days of sunshine each year, and easy access to some of the country's prettiest landscapes make the Mile High City one of the most enticing destinations in the American West.

Although the presence of the National Western Stock Show every January fills the streets with Stetson hats and cowboy boots, few would deny that Denver has become an exciting cultural center. With the nation's second-largest theatrical venue, a sizzling culinary scene, diverse music and nightlife choices, world-class museums, numerous brewpubs, seven major-league sports teams, and one of the largest bike trail systems in the country, that historical moniker of Cow Town no longer fits.

Long before the cows and the city culture arrived, Native American tribes lived here at the junction of Cherry Creek and the South Platte River. Utes, Cheyenne, Arapaho, and Cherokee hunted the plains and traveled into the mountains each

WYOMING
COLORADO

25
87
85

Fort Collins

14

Sterling

113 138 76 385

23

6

6

Greeley

287

85

34

S. Platte R.

76 6

52

34

63

Fort
Morgan

34

Yuma

59

34

79

63

385

Denver

70

36

71

36

36

86

Burlington

70

70

24

40

N

94

94

40

71

287

385

0   45 mi
0   45 km

96

96

Arkansas R.

50

50

Las
Animas

Lamar

La Junta

385

Walsenburg

25

10

350

Springfield

287

160

160

85

160

Trinidad

25

160

385

287

COLORADO
NEW MEXICO

COLORADO
OKLAHOMA

NEBRASKA

COLORADO

KANSAS

COLORADO

AUTHOR'S FAVORITES IN DENVER & THE PLAINS

Bent's Old Fort
(719) 383-5010
nps.gov/beol

Brown Palace Hotel
(800) 321-2599 or (303) 297-3111
brownpalace.com

Clyfford Still Museum
(720) 354-4880
clyffordstillmuseum.org

Confluence Park and Denver Bike Paths
South Platte River at downtown REI store
visitdenver.com/biketrails

Denver Art Museum
(720) 865-5000
denverartmuseum.org

Denver Botanic Gardens
(720) 865-3500
botanicgardens.org

Denver Performing Arts Complex
(303) 893-4100
denvercenter.org

Denver Museum of Nature & Science
(303) 370-6000
dmns.org

El Chapultepec Jazz Club
(303) 295-9126

Greenway Trail and 30-mile biking/walking path
Along the South Platte River
visitdenver.com/biketrails

Kirkland Museum of Fine & Decorative Art
(303) 832-8576
kirklandmuseum.org

Larimer Square
(303) 534-2367
larimersquare.com

Rockmount Ranch Wear
(303) 629-7777
rockmount.com

Tattered Cover Book Store
(303) 436-1070
tatteredcover.com

Washington Park
(303) 698-4930
denvergov.org/parks

summer in search of game. Trappers and explorers wandered through in the 1800s, but overall this prairie wilderness was a quiet place. In July of 1858 an event took place near the mouth of Little Dry Creek that would change the landscape and its native people forever. Gold was discovered.

From 1859 to 1861, around 100,000 gold seekers streamed into the region, lured by exaggerated tales back east of riches waiting to be found. Within 18 years Denver was the capital of the nation's 38th state, and 35,000 people lived here. Not much gold was discovered in the local streams, but in the nearby mountain towns of Central City and Black Hawk, large deposits were uncovered. Denver became a supply center, and much of the money earned in the mining camps made its way back to town. Gold brought more fortune hunters from all over

North America, but most of them did not strike it rich. Still, they flocked to the area.

By 1890 over 100,000 people called Denver home. Silver had been discovered in the previous decade, and a new era of opulence arrived. Corruption was common as city officials and police part-

trivia

Denver has 300 days of sunshine annually—more hours of sun each year than Miami Beach!

nered with underworld figures such as Soapy Smith and Lou Blonger to profit from gambling, con games, and other illegal enterprises. Miners returning from the fields found bawdy houses along Market Street catering to every budget and desire. Hustlers were waiting at gambling tables to separate the miners from their hard-earned gold. Denver's vice district during these early days was second only to those of San Francisco's Barbary Coast and New Orleans's Storyville.

According to local historian Richard Grant, "The silver barons built elaborate mansions on Capitol Hill. Gamblers, drifters and gunmen flooded the saloons and gaming halls on Larimer and Market streets. Bat Masterson tended bar here, Soapy Smith ran the West's largest gang of thieves, crooks and con artists, and anyone who was anyone in the 'Old West' paid at least a visit to Denver's mud-filled, honky-tonk streets."

Colorado moved forward into the twentieth century, and as the gold and silver petered out, ranching, farming, and manufacturing replaced mining. By 1910 the city had become the commercial and industrial center of the Rocky Mountain region, with a large cattle market and the largest sheep market in the world. By 1940, 322,000 people lived here. Denver was on its way to becoming the city it is today.

A Stroll Along the South Platte River

Early pioneers deemed the South Platte River "too thick to drink, too thin to plow." As Denver grew, the local river became a dumping ground—polluted, abused, and neglected. In 1974 a major clean-up effort began, and today it's a 30-mile greenway of parks, trails, trees, and wildlife habitat. The South Platte River Greenway Trail is a paved riverside path shared by walkers, bicyclists, birders, skaters, and joggers. Whitewater boat chutes provide thrills for kayakers and fun for spectators during spring snowmelt. Any stretch is pleasant, but some favorites are the urban section heading upriver from the confluence with Cherry Creek (by the downtown REI flagship store), and the section heading upriver from the crossing at Alameda Avenue to the trail end just north of Chatfield State Park. For more information contact Visit Denver, The Convention & Visitors Bureau; (303) 892-1505; denver.org/metro/features/bike-trails or visitdenver.com/biketrails.

TOP ANNUAL EVENTS IN DENVER & THE PLAINS

First Friday Art Walks
Santa Fe Drive Art District
First Fri of each month
artdistrictonsantafe.com

JANUARY

National Western Stock Show, Rodeo, and Horse Show
National Western Complex in Denver
early to mid-Jan
(303) 295-6124
nationalwestern.com

MARCH

Denver March Pow Wow
Denver Coliseum
(303) 934-8045
denvermarchpowwow.org

MAY

Cinco de Mayo Festival
Civic Center Park
May 5
(303) 534-8342
cincodemayodenver.com

Red Rocks Amphitheatre Summer Concerts
May through Aug
(720) 865-2494
redrocksonline.com

JUNE

Capitol Hill People's Fair
Civic Center Park
(303) 830-1651
peoplesfair.com

Cherry Blossom Festival
Sakura Square
June or July
(303) 295-1844
tsdbt.org/cherryblossom

Denver Botanic Gardens Summer Concert Series
June through Aug
(877) 435-9849
concerts.botanicgardens.org

Denver Chalk Art Festival
LoDo
early June
(303) 534-2367
denverchalkart.com

As Denver modernized, old edifices were torn down and replaced with new structures. Unfortunately, some of the classic architectural gems, the Tabor Grand Opera House and the Windsor Hotel among them, were razed to make way for modern glass-and-steel skyscrapers. But quite a few of the Victorian buildings still exist. The historic *Brown Palace Hotel* (321 17th St.; 303-297-3111 or 800-321-2599; brownpalace.com) and *The Oxford Hotel* (1600 17th St.; 303-628-5400 or 800-228-5838; theoxfordhotel.com) are alive and well. It is well worth the effort to stop in at the Brown Palace for afternoon tea or a drink in the Ship Tavern. One of the city's pleasures is to relax in the expansive, beautifully detailed atrium while sipping tea and listening to piano music.

Greeley Stampede and Rodeo
Greeley
late June through early July
(800) 982-2855
greeleystampede.org

Pridefest
Civic Center Park
(303) 733-7743
denverpridefest.org

JULY

Cherry Creek Arts Festival
Cherry Creek
early July
(303) 355-2787
cherryarts.org

Colorado Dragon Boat Festival
Lakewood
late July
(303) 953-7277
cbdf.org

AUGUST

Larimer County Fair and Rodeo
Loveland
early Aug
(970) 619-4009
larimercountyfair.org

USA Pro Cycling Challenge Race Finish
Denver Civic Center Park
usaprocyclingchallenge.com

OCTOBER

Denver Zombie Crawl
Skyline Park to 16th Street Mall
Sat closest to October 22
eyeheartbrains.com

Great American Beer Festival
Colorado Convention Center
(303) 447-0816
greatamericanbeerfestival.com

DECEMBER

New Year's Eve Downtown Fireworks
16th Street Mall
December 31
(303) 534-6161
milehighholidays.com

Zoo Lights
Denver Zoo
nightly in Dec
(303) 376-4800
denverzoo.org

History lovers will enjoy the ***Molly Brown House Museum,*** where Colorado's past is well-preserved. After she became wealthy, the "Unsinkable" Molly Brown lived her flamboyant life in this 1889 mansion of native Colorado lava stone. Following Molly's death in 1932, the building served as a rooming house. It was remodeled or divided at the whim of each successive owner. Rescued in 1971 by Historic Denver Inc., the mansion was decorated as Molly herself had done, using old photographs she had taken of her home's interior. The Molly Brown House has been restored to its former opulence. It is located at 1340 Pennsylvania St.; (303) 832-4092; mollybrown.com. Admission and a guided tour cost $8 for adults and teenagers, $6 for senior citizens 65 and older, and $4 for children 6 to 12; children 5 or younger free. Open year-round Tues through

Sat from 10 a.m. to 3:30 p.m. (last tour begins) and Sun from noon to 3:30 p.m.; closed Mon and major holidays.

Just around the corner from the Molly Brown House is the *Kirkland Museum of Fine & Decorative Art.* The museum houses an extensive collection of 20th-century decorative arts ranging from art nouveau and Bauhaus through modern and pop art. It's located at 1311 Pearl St.; (303) 832-8576; kirkland museum.org. Hours are Tues through Sun 11 a.m. to 5 p.m., and admission is $7 for adults and $6 for students, teachers, and seniors. Admission is limited to guests over 12 years old; ages 13 to 17 must be accompanied by an adult.

Colorado's *Governor's Mansion* (also known as the *Cheesman-Boettcher Mansion*), a redbrick colonial building with white stone trim, was built by one of the state's distinguished pioneer families, the Cheesmans. (Cheesman Park is named for them.) The mansion has been the executive residence of the state's governor since 1960. Furnished with luxurious art, antiques, and furniture, the house is available for limited tours. It is located at 400 E. 8th St. in Denver. For information about tours, contact the Colorado Historical Society's Office of Archaeology and Historic Preservation, 1300 Broadway, Denver 80203; (303) 866-3681; colorado.gov/governor/residence.

If you enjoy visiting historic homes, consider the *Pearce McAllister Cottage,* located at 1880 Gaylord St. Along with interior spaces that reflect upper middle-class life from 1880 through the Roaring Twenties, this 1899 home also contains the *Denver Museum of Miniatures, Dolls and Toys* with its collection of more than 10,000 objects dating from 1680 onward. Open Wed through Sat from 10 a.m. to 4 p.m. and Sun from 1 to 4 p.m. Admission costs $6 for adults, $5 for seniors, and $4 for ages 5 to 16. Call (303) 322-1053 or log on to dmmdt.org.

The *Byers-Evans House,* a mansion at 1310 Bannock St. built in 1883, has been restored to its original grandeur. Admission and a guided tour cost $6 for adults, $5 for seniors and students, and $4 for young people age 6 through 12. Children under 6 are admitted free. Hours are 10:30 a.m. to 2:30 p.m. Tues through Sat. For more information contact the Byers-Evans House at (303) 620-4933 or visit historycolorado.org.

Probably the best place in the city to learn about the area's history and prehistory is the nearby *History Colorado Center* at 1200 Broadway. The museum is open Mon through Sat 10 a.m. to 5 p.m.; Sun noon to 5 p.m. Admission is $10 for adults, $8 for seniors and students, and $6 for children 5 to 12; children under 5 free. For more information contact the History Colorado Center at (303) 477-8679 or visit historycolorado.org.

The most sumptuous of all the historic buildings in this part of Denver is the castle-like *Capitol Hill Mansion,* an impeccable, deluxe bed-and-breakfast at 1207 Pennsylvania. The mansion, a landmark building listed in the National Register of Historic Places, is not far from the Governor's Mansion and the Molly Brown House. The 1891 furniture is hand-carved oak and maple, and original Colorado landscape paintings enhance the interiors. Some rooms come with four-posters and mountain-viewing

trivia

In the 1850s, as Denver competed with other mining towns for the status of being Colorado's premier city, Denver was made up of nothing but crude cabins and one saloon—Colorado's first.

balconies. Fresh flowers, high speed Internet, cable TV, and gourmet breakfast are included with all rooms. For more information contact the Capitol Hill Mansion at (800) 839-9329; capitolhillmansion.com.

If there is one thing Denver does well (after more than 130 years of practice), it is the saloon. The first permanent structure in Denver was a saloon, and today there are sports bars, art bars, blues bars, fern bars, outdoor cafe bars,

Denver & Beer

Denver is a beer lover's bonanza. Brewing more beer than any other city in the US, Denver has a wide selection of microbreweries, brewpubs, and beer cafes. Here are a few places to begin your own beer pilgrimage:

Ale House at Amato's, 2501 16th St.; (303) 433-9734; alehousedenver.com

Breckenridge Brewery, 471 Kalamath St.; (303) 623-2739; breckenridgebrewery.com

Cheeky Monk Belgian Beer Cafe, 543 Colfax Ave.; (303) 861-0347; thecheeky monk.com

Cherry Cricket, 2641 E. 2nd Ave.; (303) 327-7666; cherrycricket.com

Falling Rock Taphouse, 1919 Blake St.; (303) 293-8338; fallingrocktaphouse.com

Flying Dog Brewery, 2401 Blake St.; (303) 292-5027; flyingdogales.com

Great Divide Brewery Tap Room, 2201 Arapahoe St; (303) 296-9460; greatdivide.com

Pint's Pub, 221 W. 13th St.; (303) 534-7543; pintspub.com

Rock Bottom Brewery, 1001 16th St., #100A; (303) 534-7616; rockbottom.com

Sandlot Brewery at Coors Field, 2145 Blake St.; (303) 298-1587

Vine Street Pub, 1700 Vine St.; (303) 388-2337; mountainsunpub.com

Wynkoop Brewing Company, 1634 18th St.; (303) 297-2700; wynkoop.com

English pubs, "Old West" saloons, rock bars, city-overlook bars, country-and-western bars, art deco bars, and even bars that don't serve alcohol. Denver, and the state in general, lead the nation in beer brewing, and the city's craft microbreweries rank among the best in the country.

In addition to an abundance of saloons, Denver has more sporting goods stores and ski shops per capita than almost any other population center in the world and a corresponding number of recreation facilities such as free outdoor tennis courts, city golf courses, and ball fields. The ***REI*** flagship store at 1416 Platte St. is paradise for outdoor enthusiasts to wander and shop as they plot their next escape into nature. The climbing wall is often crawling with kids and adults testing their skills. Grab something from the Starbucks and walk outside to Confluence Park where kayakers cavort at the junction of the South Platte River and Cherry Creek.

Denver is also a serious year-round spectator sports town with seven major-league teams. Four facilities—***Coors Field, Sports Authority Field at Mile High, Pepsi Center,*** and ***Dick's Sporting Goods Park***—offer comfortable venues for watching professional baseball, football, basketball, ice hockey, soccer, and lacrosse. Fans flock to cheer on the Rockies, Broncos, Nuggets, Avalanche, Rapids, Mammoth, and Outlaws teams as they battle their lower-altitude competitors.

All these recreational choices may mislead visitors into thinking that Denver is all ballgames and bars. But there is much more to the Mile High City than nightlife and sports. In fact, no other city between Chicago and the West Coast can match Denver's eclectic cultural landscape. A stunning addition to the arts scene is the ***Denver Art Museum's Hamilton Building.*** Designed by internationally known architect Daniel Libeskind, the playful, dreamlike geometry of the titanium-clad structure has changed the city's skyline. Constructed at a cost of more than $100 million, the new building more than doubles the museum size. Contemporary and modern, western and Native American, Asian, and European collections, as well as temporary exhibits and a spectacular rooftop sculpture garden, offer something for everyone.

trivia

Every year since 2000 the Denver Public Library has been recognized by Hennen's American Public Library Ratings as one of the top libraries in America for population centers with more than 500,000 people.

The museum is open Tues through Thurs, Sat, and Sun 10 a.m. to 5 p.m., Fri 10 a.m. to 8 p.m., and is closed Mon. Admission for Colorado residents is $10 for adults, $8 for seniors (65 and over) and students, and $3 for children 6 to 18. Children under 6 are free. Colorado

Denver for Free

Here are six Denver activities that won't cost a dime!

Colorado Sports Hall of Fame Museum
coloradosports.org

First Friday Art Walks
visitdenver.com/artdistricts

Free Days for Colorado Residents at the Denver Art Museum (first Saturday of every month)
denverartmuseum.org

Hammond's Candy Factory
hammondscandies.com

The 16th Street Mall
denver.com/16th-street-mall

US Mint Tour
usmint.gov/mint_tours

residents can enjoy the museum for free the first Saturday of each month. Admission for nonresidents is $13 for adults, $10 for seniors and students, and $5 for children. For more information contact (720) 865-5000; denverart museum.org.

The newest addition to Denver's burgeoning Cultural Arts District, the *Clyfford Still Museum* is devoted to the works of one of the most important painters of the 20th century. Representing over 90 percent of the artist's lifetime output, much of this work has been hidden from public view for 30 years but is now permanently displayed here. The museum is located at 1250 Bannock St. Open Tues through Thurs 10 a.m. to 5 p.m., Fri 10 a.m. to 8 p.m., and Sat and Sun 10 a.m. to 5 p.m. Admission is adults $10, students and seniors $6, youth 6 to 17 $3; (720) 354-4880; clyffordstillmuseum.org.

Another worthwhile stop on Denver's culture circuit is the *Museum of Contemporary Art* near Riverfront Park, which presents an eclectic mix of modern art, photography, and new media. Instead of permanent collections, the MCA rotates traveling exhibitions through its five gallery spaces, offering new art installations on a continual basis. The rooftop MCA cafe is a relaxing place for lunch with free wireless Internet and great views of downtown. Hours are noon to 9 p.m. Tues through Fri and 10 a.m. to 7 p.m. Sat and Sun. Admission is $10, $5 for students and seniors; kids under 6 are free. Located at 1485 Delgany St.; (303) 298-7554; mcadenver.org.

In addition to its high-caliber art museum, Denver is home to an impressive library suited to please the most discerning bookworm. The **Denver Public Library** at 10 W. 14th Ave. Pkwy. (720-865-1111; denverlibrary.org), with its stunning architecture and 4.8 million total holdings, happens to be one of the best—and most versatile—in the country. Come browse the stacks, use the free Internet, and see what a world-class library looks like. Denver's penchant for culture is evident across the city. Visitors can take in a play at the boldly designed **Denver Center Theatre,** part of the **Denver Performing Arts Complex** (DPAC), which is the setting for a wide variety of theater productions. DPAC, at 1245 Champa St., is home to two production companies—Denver Center Theatre Company and Denver Center Productions (DCP). Among its many roles, DCP is responsible for importing touring Broadway shows and a variety of world-class entertainment.

trivia

The Denver Center for the Performing Arts is the second-largest complex of its kind in the US, with 10 theaters seating more than 10,000 people.

Next door to DPAC is the nearly 2,700-seat **Boettcher Concert Hall,** where music lovers enjoy the offerings of the **Colorado Symphony Orchestra** and other performers. For ticket information call (303) 623-7876 or (877) 292-7979 or visit coloradosymphony.org. The season runs from September through May. Boettcher Concert Hall is located at 14th and Curtis Streets in Denver. Culturally, with its theaters, art cinemas, ballets, and classical music, the city has come of age.

Denver is a more interesting and diverse city thanks to the many ethnic groups living here. The longtime Hispanic population contributes a rich and proud heritage. With nearly a third of Denver's residents having Latino ancestry, the city offers a wide range of Hispanic culture in the form of restaurants, music, stores, and events such as the annual Cinco de Mayo celebration, the largest one in the country. Federal Boulevard north from Alameda has hundreds of businesses catering to the Hispanic market.

A sizable Vietnamese population has introduced the city to the pleasures of this delightful Asian cuisine, and the 8-block stretch of South Federal Boulevard from Alameda Boulevard to Mississippi Street has dozens of restaurants, shops, cafes, and markets, including Chinese and Thai restaurants. Japanese people have long been a part of Denver's ethnic mix, and the downtown Sakura Square with its local Buddhist temple, as well as numerous area sushi restaurants, bring a taste of Japan to the city. The Korean population is substantial, especially in the suburb of Aurora. The area around South Havana Street and

Black American West Museum & Heritage Center

Did you know that nearly one-third of America's working cowboys in the Old West were African American? The **Black American West Museum** offers a unique and much-needed look at the history of these and other African Americans and the roles they played in our nation's past. The museum is housed in the former home of Denver's first African-American doctor, Dr. Justina Ford, who delivered more than 7,000 babies during her illustrious career. Admission prices are $8 for adults, $7 for seniors, and $6 for children under 13. Open Thurs through Sat 10 a.m. to 2 p.m., Sun 1 to 4 p.m. For more information: 3091 California St., Denver 80205; (303) 482-7428; black americanwestmuseum.com.

South Peoria Street by Parker Road has dozens of excellent Korean restaurants, as well as stores and businesses.

Over the last few decades Denver has evolved from a meat and potatoes town into an exciting center for innovative and exciting cuisine. The city's culinary scene keeps expanding, with a wide range of tantalizing fare from around the globe. There's such a wide variety of eating choices that dedicated foodies could spend months exploring the many options without a single repeat.

Denver Restaurant Week in February is a 2-week celebration of culinary Denver. For 14 days, nearly 300 restaurants across the city offer a multicourse dinner for the fixed price of $52.80 (the mile-high elevation of Denver is 5,280 feet) for 2, or $26.40 for one (not including tax or gratuity). This fun event is a great way to enjoy excellent dining while sampling the many gastronomic destinations of the city. For more information go to denverrestaurantweek.com.

Some of these restaurants are familiar locations set in popular art and entertainment districts, while others are hidden off the beaten path in suburban strip malls and small neighborhoods. Hungry people can find American comfort food, Indian, Ethiopian, Nepalese, Middle Eastern, Korean, Vietnamese, Chinese, Thai, Moroccan, Greek, Armenian, Hungarian, German, Italian, Swiss, French, and of course, Mexican fare. Attempting to include the hundreds of good ones would require an entire dining guide. They are all worth exploring.

Of the many superb Asian restaurants, **Little Ollie's** in Cherry Creek (2364 E. 3rd Ave.; 303-316-8888; littleolliescherrycreek.com) consistently delivers memorable, fresh entrees. Another longtime Cherry Creek favorite is **Cherry Cricket** (2641 E. 2nd Ave.; 303-322-7666; cherrycricket.com), known for legendary burgers and a friendly neighborhood bar atmosphere.

Denver's LoDo (Lower Downtown) district brims with outstanding dining spots. *Vesta Dipping Grill* (1822 Blake St.; 303-296-1970; vestagrill.com) offers creative American cuisine with 30 signature dipping sauces. Kevin Taylor is one of the city's best-known chefs, and his *Restaurant Kevin Taylor* (91106 14th St.; 303-820-2600; ktrg.net) and *Kevin Taylor's at Opera House* (14th and Curtis Streets; 303-640-1012; ktrg.net) are culinary experiences you won't forget. *Rioja* (1431 Larimer St.; 303-820-2282) is Mediterranean-inspired but successfully ventures into a variety of unexpected ingredients and flavors. Among the best of the city's upscale Mexican restaurants is *Tamayo* (1400 Larimer St.; 720-946-1433; richardsandoval.com/Tamayo). Its rooftop patio has a great view of the mountains. *Zengo* (1610 Little Raven St.; 720-904-0965; richardsandoval .com/zengodenver) blends Latino with Asia for a wonderful fusion experience; try some of the delicious small plates meant for sharing. Many hot dog aficionados claim the best they've ever tasted came from *Biker Jim's Gourmet Dogs Cart* (16th and Arapahoe on the 16th Street Mall; 720-746-9355; bikerjimsdogs .com). The charismatic hot dog hero offers a multitude of exotic entrees: elk, antelope, buffalo, reindeer and wild boar brats, and more.

Another thriving restaurant scene is west of downtown in the Highlands neighborhood known as LoHi. *Cafe Brazil* (4408 Lowell Blvd.; 303-480-1877; cafebrazildenver.com), a neighborhood hot spot that has built a cult-like following over the years, offers all things Brazil, with bold flavors and delicious seafood. *Highland's Garden Cafe* (3927 W. 32nd Ave.; 303-458-5920; high landsgardencafe.com) serves out of two restored Victorian homes combined into a single restaurant, using seasonal, locally grown ingredients whenever possible. Housed in an old service station that's been converted into one of Denver's hottest restaurants, *Root Down* (1600 W. 33rd. Ave.; 303-993-4200; rootdowndenver.com) is another example of the city's culinary prowess. With great views of downtown and a menu that also uses locally grown and organic ingredients whenever possible, this hip neighborhood hot spot serves up creative American and global cuisine for carnivores, vegetarians, and everyone in between.

Also in LoHi, *Ale House at Amato's* (2501 16th St.; 303-433-9734; ale housedenver.com) pays tribute to the Colorado craft brewing industry with 42 beers on tap, a premium wine selection, an upscale but casual menu featuring local ingredients, and yet another panoramic view of downtown. *Linger* (2030 W. 30th Ave.; 303-993-3120; lingerdenver.com), the sister restaurant to Root Down, serves international fare, tapas, and small plates in a wonderfully eclectic dining space with, yes, more sweeping views of the city skyline. For dessert go to *Little Man Ice Cream* (2620 16th St.; 303-455-3811; littlemanicecream .com). In the summer the scene on the patio is like a town square with couples, families, and neighbors gathering under the towering steel milk can for some of the finest ice cream in town.

Over on South Federal Boulevard, among the many dozens of Vietnamese restaurants lining the street, *New Saigon* (630 S. Federal Blvd.; 303-936-4954; newsaigon.com) has been consistently good for many years. Overlook the often curt waitstaff; the food is worth the trip.

Denver's reputation as a cow town may be a thing of the past, but each January the city eagerly embraces its western heritage with the world's largest stock show. Of the numerous annual events that take place in Denver, the *National Western Stock Show, Rodeo, and Horse Show* is the biggest and longest—a yearly happening that brings rodeo, horse shows, livestock competition, and a range of entertainment showcasing the western lifestyle. Known as the Super Bowl of stock shows, the National Western was born in a circus tent in 1906, and these days the fast-charging riders, the antics of the rodeo clowns, and the pungent smells of the animals are still reminiscent of a circus. For approximately two weeks every January, it's as though old Buffalo Bill and his Wild West entertainers have returned to Denver.

More than just entertainment, the National Western remains an important stock show for ranchers. You can view more than 15,000 live, scrubbed, and brushed Herefords, Angus, Simmentals, Shorthorns, Longhorns, Arabian horses, Morgan horses, draft horses, miniature horses, ewes, and lambs, all in their neat pens. Watch shearing contests, breeding cattle auctions, and the judging of quarter horse stallions. Some 600,000 visitors flock to the arenas to buy, sell, learn, and socialize. Millions of dollars exchange hands here. This is a cowboy convention for real cowboys.

Bull riding, bareback riding, roping, steer wrestling, team roping, barrel racing, and the Mexican rodeo extravaganza are among the activities available to spectators. With more than $500,000 in prizes, rodeo competition here is among the toughest in the nation, with events taking place both afternoons and evenings. General admission tickets cost about the same as for a movie; event tickets are additional. Where else can you witness a llama auction, an Australian-style sheep-shearing contest, the world's largest bull show, and a catch-a-calf competition for teenagers, while mingling with thousands of cowboys and ranch folk? For more information call (303) 297-1166 or visit national western.com.

Got a carnivorous hankering? The *Buckhorn Exchange* is allegedly Colorado's oldest restaurant (it celebrated its centennial in 1993). It is certainly one of the most original. Moreover, it's a saloon, a magnet for celebrities and tourists, and a one-of-a-kind eatery. In addition to beef and buffalo, the Buckhorn Exchange serves elk, ostrich, yak, rattlesnake, Rocky Mountain oysters, alligator, quail, and duck. The downstairs restaurant-museum is cluttered with more than 500 taxidermy pieces, including antelope, deer, bear, wolverine, mountain goat, moose, weasel, zebra, and birds of all kinds. More than a hundred rifles, pistols, and other weapons are on display. The saloon is upstairs, complete with a giant oak bar that was shipped here by oxcart. Nearby walls are filled with 1902 photos of hunting parties; even the men's room has historic pictures of stagecoaches.

The **Buckhorn Exchange** was begun in 1893 by owner Henry H. Zietz, a cowboy and scout with Buffalo Bill; personal bodyguard of Leadville's silver millionaire Horace Tabor; and hunting guide of President Theodore Roosevelt, who arrived in his private train in front of the Buckhorn. The restaurant's official history relates that Henry Zietz "catered to cattlemen, miners, railroad builders, Indian chiefs, silver barons, roustabouts, gamblers, the great and the near-great." In December 1900 a masked gunman rode up to the restaurant, waved a .45, and demanded all money and valuables to be placed on the bar, "and be quick about it!" When the gunman rode away at a gallop, he found himself pursued by Zietz's rifle-raising customers, who "handily dispatched the miscreant to greener pastures."

After the Zietz family's death, the restaurant-museum passed into the capable hands of several historically minded Denver investors, who put large sums into restoring the building and its contents in 1978. They also raised the prices to current-day levels. The Buckhorn's redbrick building is at 1000 Osage St., 5 blocks west of Santa Fe Boulevard. Open for lunch Mon through Fri from 11 a.m. to 2 p.m.; dinner is served every night from 5:30 p.m. Mon to Thurs, 5 p.m. Fri, Sat, and Sun. For information or reservations call (303) 534-9505 or visit buckhornexchange.com.

Larimer Square is a carefully renovated, 18th-century downtown oasis with a national reputation. Along with the 16th Street Mall, it's one of the most popular destinations in Denver. In 1858, Denver's founder, General William E. Larimer, erected the city's first building here, a modest log cabin. Apparently the general had an odd sense of humor; the doors were coffin lids. As the city grew, Larimer Street became one of the most famous thoroughfares in the West. Saloons, gambling houses, and brothels catered to a steady stream of customers. It was a wild place during a boom time. The restaurants, hotels, and theaters of its heyday were renowned. Stories of what happened when the famous, infamous, and desperados of the West met made good newspaper copy. And tales of what went on behind closed doors in the neighborhood shocked a nation. Gambling and boozing were rampant.

As the years passed, Denver gradually moved uptown, and the blocks around Larimer Street became a skid row area. Thanks to the gin mills and flophouses, the handsome Victorian buildings were forgotten, although amid the grime and dirt, their architectural beauty remained. Razing was a frequent threat.

More than 100 years later, a group of Colorado businesspeople founded the Larimer Square Association for the purpose of restoring the old buildings. The excitement that once was historic Larimer Street soon returned, and today the entire lower downtown area, known as *LoDo,* is the city's hip epicenter. More than 90 restaurants, cafes, bars, coffeehouses, boutiques, businesses, and hotels fill the district, with many residing in renovated buildings well over a century old. For authentic Western wear, go to *Rockmount Ranch Wear* (1626 Wazee St.; 303-295-9126), an iconic Denver business offering Western shirts, skirts, belts, hats, and much more. Just around the corner, the *Tattered Cover* is one of the best bookstores in the country. At the northern edge of LoDo is *Coors Field*, home to the Rockies baseball team. On Market Street next to Coors Field the rooftop patio bars at *The Tavern* and *LoDo's Bar and Grill* have great views of downtown and the stadium. Skip weekend nights at both bars unless you're looking for a crowd scene. Especially on Friday and Saturday nights the district buzzes with energy as thousands of people come in search of good food, drink, and fun, but any time of the day or evening is good for strolling and discovering the charms of this historic area. A longtime favorite in this neighborhood for jazz aficionados is *El Chapultepec* (1962 Market St.; 303-295-9126), offering cheap drinks and tasty jazz several nights each week.

Larimer Square and nearby streets contain outstanding examples of early Denver Victorian architecture, complete with gaslights, handwrought leaded-glass windows, stairways, historic markers, restored cornices, and benches for relaxing and watching the world go by. In the restaurants and shops, you'll find Tiffany lamps, cherrywood bars, rosewood paneling, old wallpapers, and lead or pressed-tin ceilings. Sadly, a number of historic buildings were lost during the urban renewal development of the 1960s and 1970s, but of the ones that remain, some date back to the 1880s and 1890s. Larimer Square is now a Land-mark Preservation District, and it's listed in the National Register of Historic Places. For more information call (303) 534-2367 or visit larimersquare.com.

Among the historic district's many old buildings, *The Oxford Hotel* has been a part of Denver's colorful story since it became the city's first hotel in 1891. Today this luxury hotel is within a short walk of Coors Field, the Perform-ing Arts Complex, and the rest of LoDo. The hotel's legendary Cruise Room Martini Bar opened the day after Prohibition was repealed in 1933. Fashioned after one of the lounges on the *Queen Mary,* its art deco decor remains the same as on the day it opened, with beautifully preserved chrome and neon reflecting on wood panels. A free jukebox and an extensive menu of martinis and classic cocktails make this a popular port of call during a night out in LoDo. Find it at 1600 17th St.; (303) 628-5400; theoxfordhotel.com.

Designed by renowned architect I. M. Pei, Denver's milelong **16th Street Mall** offers the best people-watching spot in the city—a place where you can be entertained by a juggler or a bagpiper or a classic violinist, shop in large bookstores and small boutiques, join locals for happy hour at one of many watering holes, or just sit on a bench and watch Denver go by. Close to 30 restaurants, pubs, and outdoor cafes entice locals and visitors from noon onward; weekends are especially popular. Numerous fountains, 200 red oak trees, thousands of flowers, and a wide array of shopping options help make this well-lit pedestrian thoroughfare a fun place to spend several hours. Whenever you get tired of walking, hop on one of the free, ecofriendly hybrid shuttle buses that travel the length of the mall. Three pedestrian bridges at the west end of the mall connect to the Highlands neighborhood and LoHi district, which has the massive REI flagship store, excellent restaurants, hip bars, and coffee shops. For more information contact the Visit Denver, The Convention and Visitors Bureau at (800) 233-6837 or (303) 892-1505; denver.com/16th-street-mall.

From its international debut in 1892 up to the present, Denver's **Brown Palace Hotel** has lived up to its motto, "Where the World Registers." Indeed, this historic hotel is a classic. Nearly every US president since Theodore Roosevelt has spent time here. Winston Churchill, Elvis Presley, and the Beatles all slept here—though not on the same night.

"The Brown," as Denverites have nicknamed it, is a remarkable example of Victorian architecture. Upon entering the hotel lobby, your eyes are drawn upward past six tiers of wrought-iron balconies to the stained-glass cathedral ceiling. The decorative stone on the pillars is Mexican onyx. Changing displays of historical memorabilia decorate the luxurious lobby. Old guest registers, menus, and photographs take you back to relive the role the Brown Palace played in the history of Denver.

The hotel is named for its builder, Henry Cordes Brown. As Brown watched 19th-century Denver grow, he saw the need for a fine hostelry for visiting easterners who came to do business with Colorado mining companies and railroads. The builder envisioned this hotel to rise from a triangular plot of land he owned near the center of the city. Brown examined and studied the blueprints of the world's deluxe hotels before he developed his "palace."

A prominent Denver architect, Frank E. Edbrooke, designed the building in the spirit of the Italian Renaissance. Because of the geometric pattern of Brown's land, the edifice took on an unusual shape. Edbrooke gave the building a tri-frontage and then planned it so that each room faced a street. Without any interior rooms, every guest could have a view, plus morning or afternoon sunshine. The contractors constructed this soon-to-be famous landmark from Colorado red granite and warm brown Arizona sandstone.

Completed in 1892, the 10-story building had 400 rooms. Fireplaces were standard for each room, as well as bathroom taps yielding artesian water straight from the hotel's wells (as they still do today). The finest achievements in steam heating. and electricity were incorporated into the structure. The Brown was also noted as the second fireproof edifice in the country.

After four years and $1 million, Henry Brown's luxurious dream was completed. Cool water flowed from the taps; steam heat provided warmth. Ice machines kept the wine chilled and the produce fresh. Turkish baths, hairdressing parlors, billiard rooms, and a library were available for guest use. Linens, china, glassware, and silver came from the finest craftsmen. Denver society was formally introduced to the Brown Palace soon after its opening when the Tabors threw a fancy ball. In the years since, the Brown has hosted thousands of such glittering evenings.

Today the Brown Palace Hotel is listed in the National Register of Historic Places. Even in modern times it continues to provide guests with historical authenticity, Victorian charm, and good service. The original decor has been preserved, especially in the restaurants, and walking through the hotel doors feels like stepping back in time. On many Friday and Saturday nights local regulars come into the large atrium to sing along with the piano player. The Brown Palace Hotel is at 321 17th St.; (303) 297-3111 or (800) 321-2599; brown palace.com.

Since Denver's first house was built in the 1850s, the city has expanded into a variety of unique neighborhoods, each with its own flavor. These are places where locals go to relax over a meal, meet friends, and enjoy city life. There are dozens of interesting neighborhoods to explore around Denver, some sprawling for blocks, and others no more than a couple of cafes, a bar, a bookstore, and a coffee shop tucked away in a leafy backstreet. Here are a few places to begin.

The *Uptown* neighborhood just east of downtown is a mix of Victorian and Queen Anne homes with great views of the city skyline. *Restaurant Row* along 17th Avenue is lined with cafes, bistros, taco bars, coffeehouses, and a variety of popular nightclubs—almost all with outdoor patios. Try Hamburger Mary's for a bit of local color. East Colfax Avenue in the Capitol Hill neighborhood has some of the city's best music venues (Fillmore, Ogden, and Bluebird Theater), as well as numerous restaurants and the Tattered Cover Book Store. Cosmopolitan Capitol Hill is known as a gay-friendly neighborhood, and the annual PrideFest (denverpridefest.org) gay pride parade goes through here on its way to Pridefest at Civic Center Park. Cherry Creek North, running about 8

First Friday Art Walks

On the first Friday of each month, galleries and studios around town open their doors for an evening of art viewing and socializing. Art aficionados and those out for a casual night of socializing hobnob with artists, chat, flirt, and network over wine and snacks, and occasionally art is sold. It's great fun, and it's free. From 6 to 9 p.m., First Fridays center around four Denver gallery areas:

Santa Fe Drive between 5th and 10th Avenues; artdistrictonsantafe.com

Tennyson Street between 38th and 44th Avenues; tennysonst.com

Lower Downtown (LoDo) district; (303) 628-5428; lodo.org

River North (RiNo) Art District north of downtown; rivernorthart.com

blocks long by 3 blocks wide, is the upscale dining and shopping district. For three days each July Fourth weekend this is the setting for the Cherry Creek Arts Festival, celebrating the visual, culinary, and performing arts.

The *Golden Triangle Museum District* has eight of the city's museums, including the spectacular Denver Art Museum, History Colorado Center, the Clyfford Still Museum, and the Denver Public Library. The *LoHi* neighborhood borders the South Platte River, and includes Elitch Gardens Amusement Park, the Downtown Aquarium, and the Children's Museum. With numerous innovative eateries, LoHi is also one of the city's culinary destinations. The Art District on Santa Fe, just south of downtown, has more than 40 galleries, restaurants, and shops. It's the largest concentration of galleries in the city, and is one of four First Friday Art Walk sites. Five Points is one of Denver's oldest neighborhoods with blocks of Victorian homes and buildings. The main thoroughfare, Welton Street, has 75 businesses and a light-rail system, and is one of the few predominately African-American owned commercial strips in the country.

For a slice of the Vietnamese community, drive along South Federal Boulevard between Alameda and Mississippi Avenue. Dozens of restaurants and shops with signs in Vietnamese line the street. *The Far East Center* at 333 S. Federal Ave. has the highest concentration of Vietnamese stores, with an Asian market, restaurants, a bakery, and a large gift shop filled with unusual items. For more information on these and other neighborhoods see visitdenver.com/artdistricts.

Few American cities come close to matching Denver's 850 miles of biking, jogging, and walking trails. This extensive network of off-road paved and packed earth trails covers seven counties, traversing a variety of urban and rural environments. Walking or biking along these routes, you will see why Denver appears on lists of physically fit cities. These pathways are used year-round by people of all ages, shapes, and sizes. Here are some of the more popular ones.

Starting north of Denver, the **South Platte River Greenway Trail** follows the river for almost 30 miles, connecting several riverside parks on its way from Confluence Park to Chatfield Reservoir. South of Denver, the **High Line Canal Trail** follows the historic **High Line Canal**. More than 65 miles long, the canal has a wide, mostly dirt trail for much of its length. The **Cherry Creek Trail** begins at Confluence Park in Downtown Denver and follows Cherry Creek south for 15 miles to Cherry Creek Reservoir. The **Bear Creek Bike Trail** has few bears these days, but this 20-mile route from the South Platte River to the town of Morrison offers side trails connecting to Chatfield, Red Rocks, and Bear Creek Lake Parks. Stop in Morrison for ice cream and browse the antiques shops. For more information on Denver's extensive bike path system go to visitdenver.com/biketrails.

If you'd prefer to laze away an afternoon on a quiet piece of green earth instead of hiking or biking, you're in the right town. Denver has more than 4,000 acres of traditional parks and parkways ranging in size from tiny to sprawling. Considered one of the largest park systems in America, Denver's green spaces provide locals and out-of-towners a relaxing reprieve from city life. Here are some of the more well-known parks.

Civic Center Park at Colfax and Broadway lies at the heart of downtown, close to the State Capitol Building, Denver Art Museum, Denver Public Library, and the 16th Street Mall. Beautifully landscaped with expansive lawns and flower beds, and bustling with life, this is the location for events such as People's Fair, Cinco de Mayo, Taste of Colorado, and the Fourth of July celebration. Climb the steps of the Capitol to the mile-high marker for a view spanning 120 miles of Rocky Mountains on a clear day. At lunchtime when office workers flock here, this is a fun people-watching spot.

At 314 acres, **City Park** is the largest in Denver. Located a few minutes' drive east of downtown at 17th Avenue and York Street, this milelong park has flower gardens, fountains, two lakes, a historic boathouse, and lots of grass for

Explore Denver on Two Wheels

For a truly green tour of the Mile High City, explore Denver's 850 miles of off-road, paved and packed-earth bike paths through the city's bicycle sharing program, **B-cycle** (303-825-3325; bcycle.com). Red B-cycles are available at more than 50 bike stations around Denver. For a small fee, anyone can pick one up and take it sightseeing, to lunch, or on errands before returning it to any B-station.

Civic Center Eats

Every Tuesday and Thursday during the summer months through September, more than 20 local food trucks roll into the main esplanade at the Civic Center, and diners select from hundreds of gourmet lunch items between 11 a.m. and 2 p.m. From here you're within sight of the Capitol, the Denver Art Museum, and the Denver Public Library. Enjoy live music and great views while connecting with the local lunchtime scene.

picnics, soccer games, Frisbee, and snoozing under a tree. Paddleboats can be rented in summer. Every Sunday at 6 p.m. from June through early August, City Park Jazz presents free jazz concerts in the park. The park is also home to some of the city's top attractions, such as the Museum of Nature and Science and the Denver Zoo.

The **Denver Zoo** has nearly 4,000 animals representing 700 species. Natural habitats, winding paths, and large trees are spread over 80 acres, giving the zoo an open feeling. The newest exhibit, Elephant Passage, is a 10-acre area with five habitats, including the world's largest bull elephant habitat. Animals such as rhinos, tigers, and tapirs rotate through the different habitats each day. The zoo is open daily. Hours from Mar through Oct are 9 a.m. to 5 p.m., and from Nov through Feb, 10 a.m. to 4 p.m. Admission from Mar through Oct is $15 for guests 12 and older, $12 for seniors, and $10 for children 3 to 11; children 2 and younger free. Admission from Nov through Feb is $12 for adults and teenagers 12 and older, $10 for seniors, and $8 for children 3 to 11; children 2 and younger free. For more information call (303) 376-4800 or visit denverzoo.org.

trivia

The Denver Zoo got its start when an orphaned black bear named Billy Bryan was given to the mayor as a gift in 1896.

One of the city's top museums, the **Denver Museum of Nature & Science** (DMNS), is also located in City Park. DMNS includes both temporary and permanent exhibits, such as "Egyptian Mummies," "North American Wildlife," and "Botswana: Safari to Wild Africa." At the Expedition Health exhibit, take a personal, up-close journey inside your own body as you go through different activity areas while experiencing a virtual expedition up a Colorado peak. In addition, the museum is home to the Phipps IMAX Theater, a Discovery Zone with hands-on activities for children, and the Gates Planetarium. The museum is also blessed with an excellent view over City Park toward downtown and the Front Range.

DMNS is open daily from 9 a.m. to 5 p.m. except on Christmas Day. General admission is $12 for adults, $6 for children 3 to 18 and students with ID, and $8 for seniors. IMAX and Planetarium tickets are extra. For more information call (303) 370-6000 or visit dmns.org.

One of the city's most relaxing green spaces is the **Denver Botanic Gardens** (720-865-3500; botanicgardens.org). Ranked one of the nation's top botanic gardens, this 23-acre oasis just 10 minutes east of downtown has around 33,000 plants spread over 45 different gardens. The tropical conservatory houses thousands of exotic specimens from the world's equatorial regions. Go to the ecofriendly "green" roof on top of the Offshoots Cafe for sweeping panoramas of Denver and the Rocky Mountains. The summer concert series held here (concerts.botanicgardens.org) is legendary for world-class performers playing in an intimate setting. Open daily except major holidays; admission fees are adults $12.50, seniors $9.50, students and children 3 to 15 $9, and children under 3 free.

Cheesman Park, located at Franklin Street and 8th Street, attracts joggers to its crushed granite loop trail around the park. The large grassy expanses are popular with sunbathers and small groups enjoying a quiet afternoon. Families come for the large playground. A large, white-columned memorial fountain on top of the hill is a picturesque landmark and a good place to sit and contemplate those big mountains looming to the west. This is the spot to be in the evenings for one of the best sunset-over-the-Rockies spots in the city.

Just a short drive south of downtown, in a neighborhood filled with early twentieth-century brick homes, **Washington Park** is one of Denver's most popular year-round parks. Known as Wash Park by locals, these 165 acres contain 2 lakes, 54 flower beds, a 2-mile loop with separate lanes for foot and wheeled traffic, boat house, fitness center, soccer and tennis courts, and plenty of big trees. Locals love to work out here, and you can join them by renting a bike or paddleboat. If you're not inclined to take part in the activities, just find a shady spot on the grass and watch it all go past. The Old South Gaylord Street and Old South Pearl Street neighborhoods are both a short, pleasant walk from here. The park can be accessed at South Downing Street and East Louisiana Avenue.

Located 6 blocks east of Wash Park, the **Old South Gaylord Street** shopping district (southgaylordstreet.com) has more than 60 restaurants, bars, and shops blended into a mostly residential neighborhood. A few blocks southwest of Wash Park is **Old South Pearl Street** (oldsouthpearlstreet.com), another neighborhood that's been lovingly restored with old buildings converted into dozens of restaurants, wine bars, pubs, art galleries, and specialty shops. In summer Old South Pearl is host to various music and food festivals. A walk through either neighborhood on a warm summer evening is another of Denver's many pleasures.

Stretching along an 18-block, sometimes gritty run of South Broadway is *Antique Row* (antique-row.com). Beginning just south of Alameda, this eclectic collection of shops is home to one of the nation's largest concentrations of antiques dealers. Just about any kind of collectible can be found here, and sprinkled along the avenue are dozens of ethnic restaurants, used bookstores, art galleries, neighborhood taverns, pizza parlors, avant-garde clothing stores, and much more. The area comes alive at night with a smattering of clubs featuring rock, salsa, swing, and techno.

Located at Sheridan Boulevard and West 17th Avenue, *Sloan Lake Park* attracts a mixed following: retired folks, young parents pushing strollers, joggers, picnicking Vietnamese families, soccer players, bicyclists, and sunbathers. With 177 acres to spread out in, there is plenty of room for everyone. At the center of it all is enormous Sloan Lake. Quiet during the week, it comes alive on summer weekends. Each July the *Dragon Boat Festival* celebrates Asian-American culture and traditions, and dragon boats race across the lake.

Venturing just beyond the actual city limits, Red Rocks Park, Genesee Mountain Park, Chatfield State Park, and Cherry Creek State Park are all outstanding retreats. For more information about Denver's parks, contact the Denver Parks and Recreation Department's Parks Division through City Services; (720) 913-1311; denvergov.org/parks.

If you want to look down onto Denver from above, take a hike in one of the mountain parks. The Denver Mountain Parks system consists of 31 named parks and 16 unnamed areas totaling around 14,000 acres of mountains and foothills owned by the city. These parks offer a wide variety of geography and activities, and a great escape not far from the city. For more information go to mountainparks.org. Finally, before you leave the Denver metro area, delight your children (or your inner child) with a visit to the *Butterfly Pavilion and Insect Center,* located in Westminster—a short jaunt up US 36 off I-25 heading north from Denver. Replete with jungle, waterfalls, and palm trees, this 11-acre attraction is one of only a dozen or so similar institutions in the US. This "zoo" houses more than 1,200 free-flying butterflies from more than 50 species around the world. In addition, numerous other insect species, turtles, tortoises, birds, fish, and tropical plants round out the pavilion's displays.

Open daily from 9 a.m. until 5 p.m. (last entrance at 4:15 p.m.), the Butterfly Pavilion offers an escape from wintry weather with its climate-controlled, 7,200-square-foot tropical conservatory. Admission is $8.50 for adults, $6.50 for seniors and Westminster residents, and $5.50 for children 2 to 12. Children 1 and younger are free if accompanied by adults. The pavilion is located at 6252

W. 104th Ave., Westminster. For more information call (303) 469-5441 or go to butterflies.org.

The Eastern Plains

Many visitors are surprised to learn that not all of Colorado is filled with mountains, lakes, and alpine scenery. In fact, the flat eastern third of the state looks more like neighboring Kansas and Nebraska than it does the rest of Colorado. Even though it's part of this quintessentially western state, many consider this vast landscape of rolling plains more Midwest than West. Eastern Colorado is one of the most sparsely populated places in the US. The Dust Bowl period of the 1930s was hard on the region, with 2.5 million people moving out of the Plains states. Although eastern Colorado eventually saw a return to agriculture in the 1960s to 1980s, dropping agricultural prices combined with rising farming costs led to a decline in population throughout the region.

Although the eastern third of the state lacks the mountain geography of the western two-thirds, it's blessed with plenty of visually compelling landscapes. Wide open spaces stretch to the horizon, broken by an occasional grain elevator, weighing station, or windmill. The shortgrass prairie greens briefly in the spring and is home to a number of bird species. The air is cleaner here than in the cities. Small towns with feed stores, cafes, and churches are scattered across the countryside. Places like Punkin Center, Last Chance, Cope, and Otis hunker beneath the winter winds and pelting summer hail, fragments of Americana far removed from the big cities. At night main streets close down and fall silent.

Try a Yurt Vacation!

Within the *Colorado State Forest State Park,* 75 miles west of Fort Collins, the *Never Summer Nordic Yurt System* offers highly unique opportunities to cyclists.

Consider staying in a yurt here. *Yurts* are portable, round dwellings that were first used by nomadic Mongols in central Asia; they sleep six comfortably and are well situated as push-off sites for some great rides.

One such bike trip is the *Grass Creek Loop.* It's a tough 16 miles round-trip. Along the way you will pass the North Michigan Reservoir and 10,000-foot Gould Mountain.

For more information about Never Summer Nordic, Inc., go to neversummernordic .com or call (970) 723-4070. For information about Colorado State Forest State Park, log on to parks.state.co.us, then choose State Forest from the drop-down menu of parks on the left.

Although there are fewer visual thrills here compared with the rest of the state, eastern Colorado has a variety of interesting sights. Probably the most prominent landmark on the eastern plains is the **Pawnee Buttes.** Part of the 200,000-acre Pawnee National Grassland, these twin buttes can be seen from many miles away.

A gravel road leads up to the Buttes trailhead. From there, a 1.5-mile path takes you on foot or by mountain bike to the first butte, the western one. The eastern butte lies a quarter-mile east. From a plateau the trail drops to the prairie floor, crossing open pastureland before dropping again into a deep ravine. Cream-colored chalk cliffs form the promontories. This is shortgrass prairie, not much higher than tundra. The steady winds keep plant growth low to the ground. Prickly pear cactus, blue gramma grass, sagebrush, and buffalo grass grow no higher than 6 inches. This constant wind, combined with poor farming practices, created the ecological Dust Bowl disaster of the 1930s, when drifts of wind-driven topsoil piled up like snow over fences, closing roads and killing crops. The **Pawnee National Grassland** and the **Comanche National Grassland** in southeastern Colorado were created when the federal government withdrew the land from agricultural use and consolidated the parcels into protected terrain.

In his book *Centennial,* author James A. Michener renamed these landmarks the fictitious "Rattlesnake Buttes." The book is based on life in the area during pioneer days. About the buttes Michener wrote, "They were extraordinary, these two sentinels of the plains. Visible for miles in each direction, they guarded a bleak and sad empire."

Lack of water and trees do not stop the many prairie species of birds from flourishing in this country. Lark buntings—the Colorado state bird, with its distinctive white wing patches against a black body—thrive here. So do horned larks, meadowlarks, kestrels, larkspurs, mountain plovers, common nighthawks, and long-billed curlews—some of the 200 species recorded here. A 36-mile self-guided birding tour is a great ride over the prairie in a car or on a mountain bike. Cattle share this area with pronghorn; across the prairie there are occasional windmill-powered water tanks for stock. For information contact Pawnee National Grassland, 660 O St., Greeley 80631; (970) 346-5000; fs.fed.us/r2/arnf/about/organization/png/index.shtml.

trivia

Horace Greeley's original concept for his namesake town was a utopian agricultural colony modeled after the Oneida, New York, experimental settlement.

The city of **Greeley** (named after Horace Greeley, the newspaper publisher) is 49 miles northeast of Denver, surrounded by agricultural farmlands.

The town is infamous for its fragrant feedlots, and the fields beyond the town limits grow sugar beet, barley, and other crops. The twelfth most populous city in the state, it is home to the *University of Northern Colorado* (UNC). The late James Michener was one of the UNC's famous alumni and later a teacher there. He was inspired to write his bestselling novel *Centennial* through his familiarity and on-location research in Greeley and surroundings.

Much of the local sightseeing relates to Greeley's past. At the *Centennial Village,* you can visit dozens of historic exhibits, including a sod house, a homesteader's wagon house, and a one-room rural school. In addition, Centennial Village has graceful Victorian homes. In all, some 45 structures on 8 acres take the visitor through the history of the High Plains, spanning the years 1860 to 1930. Open May through Sept Tues through Sat, 10 a.m. to 4 p.m. Admission is $5 for adults 18 to 59, $3 for 60 and older, and $2 for children 3 to 17; children 2 and under are free. On Sat add $1 to each rate. For more information call (970) 350-9220 or visit centennialvillagemuseum.com.

For another historic look at the area, visit the *Meeker Home Museum,* formerly the home of Nathan Meeker. Nathan Meeker was the founder of Greeley, and the agricultural editor of Horace Greeley's *New York Tribune.* This graceful, 2-story adobe home built in 1870 contains many of his furnishings and the plow that turned the first sod in the Union Colony. Learn about his untimely death in the White River Massacre, and how his family struggled to survive without him. Located at 1324 9th Ave., it's listed in the National Register of Historic Places. Open the first Sat of each month 10 a.m. to 4 p.m. from May through Sept; $3 for adults, $2 for seniors, $1 for children 3 to 17, and free for children 2 and under. For more information contact (970) 350-9220; greeleymuseums.com.

To the west, nestled against the foothills, *Fort Collins* may well be the most sophisticated community in northern Colorado. With 130,000 inhabitants, it is the fifth most populous city in the state. Colorado State University is here, and as with many larger college towns, the city has no shortage of good

Western Summertime Celebrations

The *Greeley Stampede* is held from the last week of June to the first week of July, with nine rodeos, parades, and fireworks, as well as events on all downtown plazas. The rodeos are at Island Grove Park, 14th Avenue and "A" Street. For more information call (970) 356-7787 or visit greeleystampede.org. The *Weld County Fair* takes place in late July at the same location, with horse shows and livestock displays, plus various contests. For more information call (970) 356-4000 or go to weldcountyfair.com.

restaurants and cafes, bars, bookstores, and shops catering to 20-somethings. The city shows up on those annual "Best Small Towns To Live In" lists, and a stroll through the pedestrian Old Town Square and neighborhoods to the south and west will soon show you why. Large shade trees, historic preservation of homes and buildings, outdoor sculptures, fountains, shops, and art galleries give visitors and residents alike plenty of reasons to linger.

In a state famous for its wealth of microbreweries, Fort Collins shines. Two of the best-known, *New Belgium Brewing Company* and *Odell Brewing Company,* offer inside looks at how these finely crafted brews are created. Each is a must for beer lovers. New Belgium is at 500 Linden St.; (970) 221-0524; newbelgium.com. Free tours are given Tues through Sat. Tours often fill up in advance; go online or call ahead to reserve a tour time. Odell is at 800 E. Lincoln Ave.; (970) 498-9070; odells.com. Free tours are given Mon through Sat at 1, 2, and 3 p.m. on a first-come, first-served basis. Arrive at least 30 minutes before a tour to sign up for a space.

To see how beer is brewed on a large scale, take a free tour at the *Anheuser-Busch Brewery* at 2351 Busch Dr.; (970) 490-4691; budweisertours.com.

For beer aficionados, the *Colorado Brewers' Festival* in Fort Collins is the place to be during the last week of June. Nearly 60 Colorado beers and 35 Colorado breweries will be ready for visitors. The event takes place in the historic downtown area, with food and live music from great Colorado bands. For more information call (970) 484-6500 or visit downtownfortcollins.com.

The Fort Collins region is known for its nearby fly-fishing possibilities. Among others, you might head up the scenic *Poudre Canyon* and the Cache la Poudre River, which is consistently recognized as having some of the finest trout fishing in the state. For more information contact Canyon Lakes Ranger District, Arapaho & Roosevelt National Forests, 2150 Centre Ave., Building E, Fort Collins; (970) 295-6700; fs.fed.us/r2/arnf.

River Adventures in Northern Colorado

A *Wanderlust Adventure* in Fort Collins will give you the opportunity to see and feel the *Poudre River* firsthand. Since 1982, more than 135,000 people have enjoyed trips run by this Fort Collins–based outfitter. From 3-hour trips for the whole family to daylong and multiday paddling affairs, their tours are guaranteed to give anyone a workout. Wanderlust has a trip to fit everyone (minimum age of 7 for easiest trip). Trips run from May through Aug and range in price from $49 to $105 per person. For more information contact A Wanderlust Adventure; (800) 745-7238; awanderlust adventure.com.

Thin Air, Fast Bikes & High Terrain

Colorado is home to the USA Pro Cycling Challenge, the most demanding bike race ever held on American soil. Every August, after seven days of riding through some of the most picturesque terrain in the world, professional riders sprint into Denver's Civic Center Park on the final stage for an epic finish and a day of parties for spectators. Visit usaprocyclingchallenge.com for info.

For camping and boating, try **Horsetooth Reservoir** west of town. Open year-round, Horsetooth has 1,900 acres of water, which attracts summer crowds with camping, hiking, boating, biking, climbing, or just relaxing with a picnic lunch. There's little shade here and it can get hot in summer, so come prepared for the sun. To reach Horsetooth Reservoir, drive west on CR 38E (Harmony Road) from its intersection with Taft Hill Road in Fort Collins. Park permits are available from stations throughout the park; cost is $7 per vehicle. For more information contact Larimer County Parks and Open Lands, 200 W. Oaks St., Fort Collins; (970) 498-7000; co.larimer.co.us/naturalresources/horsetooth.htm.

There are many single-track and paved trail biking options in and around Fort Collins. Pick up a free map of the city's bikeway system, illustrating the 56 miles of local bike trails, lanes, and routes. Maps are available at most Fort Collins bicycle shops, or download it online at fcgov.com/bicycling/bike-maps.php.

Close to Fort Collins, **Lory State Park** offers great hiking as well as single tracks for more advanced bike riders. This former ranch is now a 2,400-acre park with 26 miles of trails that tempt bikers with challenging mountain biking almost year-round; snow is frequent in winter, but abundant sunshine keeps the trails relatively clear.

Just beyond the park entrance at the Timber Recreation Area is the **Timber Trail.** This single-track, 3.7-mile route is moderately technical, climbing steeply through grass and shrublands to a pine forest. From south Fort Collins, take Harmony Road/CR 38E west. Turn right onto 23N. Proceed north to the T-intersection. Turn left at the stop sign onto 42C. Go north to Lodgepole Drive and turn left. Go 1.6 miles to the park entrance. The park is open daily; hours vary according to the season. Cost is $7 per vehicle.

Horsetooth Mountain Park at the southwest side of Horsetooth Reservoir has a variety of jeep roads and single-track trails that are popular with local mountain bikers.

Just south of Fort Collins is **Loveland.** It's only about half the size of Fort Collins, yet it has carved a national name for itself. Loveland calls itself "Colorado's Sweetheart City." Each year hundreds of thousands of sacks of

Valentines are packaged inside larger envelopes and re-mailed here. Town volunteers hand-stamp them with a Valentine's verse and send them on to the lucky recipient, postmarked Loveland. Cupid has worked here since 1947, making sure that Valentine's cards have that extra touch on the outside of the envelope. Around 200,000 Valentines are sent out annually.

Loveland is a pretty city with a small-town atmosphere. With a historic downtown, antiques shops, 27 public parks, and year-round events and entertainment, it's worth stopping in "Cupid's Hometown." For more information contact the Loveland Chamber of Commerce at (970) 667-6311; loveland.org.

One of Colorado's quirkiest attractions is located a few minutes east of Limon on the eastern plains. The **World's Wonder View Tower** is home to a grand assortment of pickled freak animal displays, kitschy artifacts, antiques, and interesting junk. Known locally as the Genoa Tower, it was supposedly confirmed in 1934 as the highest point between Denver and New York City. From a distance the place looks bustling, but on closer inspection those people are really pieces of wood wrapped in fabric, and the cars are rusting hulks that stopped running decades ago. Inside, room after room of treasures and eccentricities await perusal. Climb 87 steps to the top of the tower for views of the Rockies and surrounding plains. Open daily from Mar through Sept or by appointment Oct through Apr; for more information call (719) 763-2309.

The eastern plains of Colorado saw much travel and bloodshed in the early days of this country. Indians, trappers, traders, settlers, Mexicans, and the Spanish used what was called the Santa Fe Trail, which followed the Arkansas River for many miles. After cutting across the southeast corner of what is now Colorado, the trail reached the area around present-day **La Junta,** then turned south over Raton Pass into New Mexico.

A Walk on the Wild Side

Set on 720 acres of rural, rolling grasslands 50 miles east of Boulder at Keenesburg, *The Wild Animal Sanctuary* is home to more than 290 lions, tigers, wolves, leopards, bears, mountain lions, and other large carnivores living freely in large social groupings. The animals have been rescued from abusive or illegal situations and are kept in large, humane habitats and given expert care and exceptional diets. Observation decks and walkways provide numerous opportunities to view and photograph the animals as they roam through 20 large-acreage habitats. Open every day except major holidays and during bad weather. For more information call (303) 536-0118 or visit wildanimalsanctuary.org.

Arkansas Valley Fair

Billed as the oldest continuous fair in Colorado, the Arkansas Valley Fair in Rocky Ford is a 5-day celebration each August featuring parades, music, entertainment, horse races, livestock shows, and the best cantaloupes in the world. Find out more at (719) 254-7723; arkvalleyfair.com.

Bent, St. Vrain & Company, a frontier trading and retailing business, built and owned **Bent's Old Fort** near what is now La Junta. Beginning in 1833, for the next 16 years it was the only major permanent white settlement on the Santa Fe Trail between Missouri and the Mexican settlements to the south. The fort was a trading destination for Mexicans, Indians, adventurers, and trappers, and a place to repair wagons, get supplies, livestock, food, and water, and rest awhile after a long and dangerous journey. The famous scout Kit Carson was a hunter for the fort from 1831 to 1842.

The fort provided goods for several groups. Mexico obtained quality manufactured items from the US. Native Americans got cookware, metal, rifles, and other goods. Trappers acquired supplies, a market for their furs, and the company of other people following lonely months of hunting. Bent, St. Vrain & Company traded with all these folks and among themselves. Furs from the trappers and buffalo robes from the Arapaho and Southern Cheyenne made their way back east, where they were sold at a handsome profit.

In the mid-1800s, Bent's Old Fort was caught between resentful Indians and the whites who were moving in on them. The Indian wars began and trade faded away. Charles Bent was killed in a revolt in Taos, New Mexico, while serving as governor of the state, and St. Vrain left to do business farther south. Cholera spread through the Indian tribes.

The fort was destroyed under mysterious circumstances in 1949. Most historians believe that after William Bent tried unsuccessfully to sell the fort to the US Army, he mined it with explosives and gunpowder and blew it up. What was left of the fort was abandoned and fell into ruins.

Original sketches, paintings and diaries, and archaeological excavations were used to rebuild the fort in 1976. Designated by the National Park Service as a National Historic Site, Bent's Old Fort has been constructed as close as possible to its original design, using authentic materials and tools. Today, the adobe structure remains a monument to past and present-day craftspeople whose skill and patience built and rebuilt it again.

Just outside La Junta, Bent's Old Fort stands much as it did more than 160 years ago. To preserve the authentic atmosphere of this trade center, visitor parking is a quarter-mile from the building. The paved walk toward the fort, with its backdrop of cottonwood trees by the Arkansas River, is a stroll into history. In deference to realism, there are no concessions for food, drink, or curios.

Uniformed park employees are often on hand to answer questions. But to get into the spirit of the place, join one of the $3-per-person ($2 for children 6 to 12) guided tours conducted by an individual dressed in period clothes. These "interpreters" stay in character, thanks to the authentic costumes. The tours, which run from June 1 to September 1, are fun and informative, giving visitors a feel for life around the fort in the 1880s.

Scheduled special events take place throughout the year, such as Wagons Ho! Trail Transportation through Time, the Fur Trade Encampment, and Hispanic Heritage Day. For more information contact Bent's Old Fort, National Historic Site, 35110 Hwy. 194 East, La Junta 81050; (719) 383-5010; nps.gov/beol. Open every day except Thanksgiving, Christmas, and New Year's Day. Open June 1 through August 31 from 8 a.m. to 5:30 p.m.; September 1 through May 31 from 9 a.m. to 4 p.m. From US 50 in La Junta take Hwy. 109 north 1 mile to Highway 194. Go east for 6 miles to the fort.

For a trip even further back into history—150 million years further back—visit ***Picket Wire Canyonlands*** in ***Comanche National Grassland,*** about 25 miles south of La Junta. Picket Wire opened to the public in 1991. The attractions? The clear footprints of dinosaurs on a solidified limestone shelf just a few feet over the Purgatory River, as well as Native American rock art and pioneer ruins. In a quarter-mile stretch there are more than 1,300 dinosaur footprints in four different layers of rock, forming North America's largest dinosaur track site. Though the area is considered extremely fragile, mountain biking and hiking are allowed in Picket Wire. From a parking area near a cattle pen, an 8-mile ranch road takes bikers and hikers across a high mesa, then drops suddenly into the canyon. Alongside the trail, the relics of abandoned adobe houses, a church, a graveyard, and ranch buildings hold up against the dry climate.

On your way along the dusty trail you may catch glimpses of the current inhabitants: coyote, badgers, antelope, quail, kestrels, orioles. Stay out of the

Melon Capital of the World

Located 11 miles northwest of La Junta, tiny ***Rocky Ford*** is famous around the state for honeydew, watermelon, and especially cantaloupe. Each August harvesting begins, and numerous roadside stands offer some of the best melons in the county.

Comanche National Grassland

After the Dust Bowl catastrophe of the 1930s, the federal government set up programs to protect tracts of land from further ruinous farming and grazing practices. Comanche National Grassland was created in 1960 from one of those protected areas, and today more than 460,000 acres of prairie grassland and canyon remain much as they were centuries ago. The area was used by ancient American Indians and remnants of their time here remain, including rock art thousands of years old as well as the remains of rock shelters and tepee rings. More than 320 species of birds have been recorded here, and several canyons—Picket Wire, Vogel, Carrizo, Picture, and Cottonwood—offer hiking, biking, prehistoric rock art, and in the case of Picket Wire, dinosaur tracks. For more information go to the ranger office at 1420 E. 3rd St., La Junta 81050; (719) 384-2181.

tall grass, which is ideal snake habitat. The dinosaur tracks are marked by small signs pointing the way. Right next to the river, you come to a shelf of limestone that looks like someone mucked around in it while it was wet. On further examination you will discover that these muddlings are dinosaur tracks. Two different types of dinosaur left these track. The immense *Apatosaurus* left big holes like you'd expect from an elephant, only much larger. The meat-eating *Allosaurus* left distinctive three-toed, wicked-looking footprints. Many scientists consider this site to be a national treasure.

Petroglyphs are scattered around the rock canyon walls. These etchings aren't identified by signs; you have to find them on your own. This rock art is anywhere from 375 to 4,500 years old. These are precious ancient artifacts, and they should not be touched; leave them so others can enjoy them. If time is important, do this trip for the dinosaur tracks alone.

This region of the state gets very hot in summer. Fill your tank with gas before driving out to the area. Take plenty of water and a hat while hiking. To prevent rattlesnake encounters, watch where you put your hands and feet. Solo travel is generally not recommended; if you go alone, let someone know where you are going and arrange to check in when you return. The distance to the dinosaur tracks one way is 5.3 miles. Although there are no commercial campgrounds here, primitive camping is permitted anywhere in Comanche National Grassland except in Picketwire Canyon. Contact the Comanche National Grassland, 1420 E. 3rd St., La Junta 81050; (719) 384-2181; santafetrailscenicand historicbyway.org/pwdino.html.

Places to Stay in Denver & the Plains

DENVER

Brown Palace Hotel
321 17th St.
(303) 297-3111 or
(800) 321-2599
brownpalace.com
Expensive
Historic elegance at the edge of downtown.

Capitol Hill Mansion Bed & Breakfast
1207 Pennsylvania St.
(303) 839-5221 or
(800) 839-9329
capitolhillmansion.com
Moderate
Turn-of-the-20th-century opulence in the Capitol Hill neighborhood; family and gay friendly.

Castle Marne Bed & Breakfast
1572 Race St.
(303) 331-0621
castlemarne.com
Moderate
Historic mansion furnished with period antiques.

Curtis Hotel
1405 Curtis St.
(303) 571-0300 or
(800) 525-6651
thecurtis.com
Expensive
Fun, pop-culture boutique hotel in the heart of downtown.

Denver Marriott City Center
1701 California St.
(303) 297-1300 or
(800) 228-9290
marriott.com
Moderate to Expensive
Sophistication and good service with a convenient LoDo location.

Four Seasons Hotel Denver
1111 14th St.
(303) 389-3000
fourseasons.com/denver
Expensive
Renowned Four Seasons hospitality, amenities, and spa in the heart of the theater district.

Hotel Monaco
1717 Champa St. at 17th
(303) 296-1717 or
(800) 990-1303
monaco-denver.com
Expensive
Modern luxury in a historic building within walking distance to many downtown attractions.

Hotel Teatro
1100 14th St.
(303) 228-1100 or
(888) 727-1200
hotelteatro.com
Expensive
Luxurious downtown boutique hotel with 2 fine-dining restaurants.

Hyatt Regency Denver at Colorado Convention Center
650 15th St.
(303) 436-1234 or
(800) 492-8804
denverregency.hyatt.com
Expensive

AAA four-diamond, good downtown location, with stunning views of Denver and mountains from the Peaks Lounge.

Inn at Cherry Creek
233 Clayton St.
(303) 377-8577
innatcherrycreek.com
Moderate to Expensive
Friendly, homey 35 rooms, located in the upscale Cherry Creek North neighborhood.

Magnolia Hotel
818 17th St.
(303) 607-9000 or
(888) 915-1110
magnoliahoteldenver.com
Moderate
Old World charm with modern style in a historic downtown building.

Oxford Hotel
1600 17th St.
(303) 628-5400 or
(800) 228-5838
theoxfordhotel.com
Expensive
Richly furnished historic boutique hotel in the heart of LoDo.

Queen Anne Bed & Breakfast
2147-51 Tremont Place
(303) 296-6666
queenannebnb.com
Moderate to Expensive
Full gourmet breakfast is offered in this quiet location in a Victorian mansion minutes from downtown.

FOR MORE INFORMATION

DENVER

Visit Denver, The Convention & Visitors Bureau
1555 California St., Ste. 300, 80202
(303) 892-1505 or (800) 233-6837
visitdenver.com

FORT COLLINS

Visit Fort Collins
19 Old Town Square, Ste. 137, 80524
(800) 274-3678 or (970) 232-3840
visitftcollins.com

GREELEY

Greeley Convention & Visitors Bureau
902 7th Ave., 80631
(970) 352-3566 or (800) 449-3866
greeleycvb.com

LOVELAND

Loveland Chamber of Commerce
5400 Stone Creek Circle, Ste. 200, 80538
(970) 667-6311
loveland.org

Residence Inn Denver City Center
1725 Champa St.
(303) 296-3444 or
(800) 593-2809
marriott.com
Expensive
Complimentary breakfast, rooftop hot tub, close to 16th Street Mall.

Warwick Denver Hotel
1776 Grant St.
(303) 861-2000
warwickdenver.com
Moderate
Casually chic within a short stroll to downtown attractions.

FORT COLLINS

Armstrong Hotel
259 S. College Ave.
(970) 484-3883 or
(866) 384-3883
thearmstronghotel.com
Moderate
Landmark historic hotel with complimentary cruiser

bikes in the heart of Old Town Fort Collins.

Best Western University Inn
914 S. College Ave.
(970) 484-2984 or
(888) 484-2984
bwui.com
Moderate
Centrally located in Old Town across from the university and close to New Belgium Brewing.

Colorado Cattle Company & Guest Ranch
70008 WCR 132, New Raymer
(970) 437-5345
coloradocattlecompany .com
Expensive
All-inclusive, adults-only working cattle ranch experience combined with comfortable accommodations.

Edwards House Bed & Breakfast
402 W. Mountain Ave.
(970) 493-9191 or
(800) 281-9190
edwardshouse.com
Moderate
Elegant, romantic accommodations a few blocks from Old Town.

Hilton Fort Collins
425 W. Prospect Rd.
(970) 482-2626
hiltonfortcollins.com
Moderate
Standard Hilton quality, conveniently located near college campus. Charge for wireless Internet.

Sheldon House Bed & Breakfast
616 W. Mulberry St.
(970) 221-1917 or
(877) 221-1918
bbonline.com/co/sheldon house
Moderate
Cozy turn-of-the-20th-century B&B with a friendly innkeeper.

GREELEY

Country Inn and Suite by Carlson
2501 W. 29th St.
(970) 330-3404 or
(888) 210-1746
countryinns.com
Moderate
Hot breakfast and wireless Internet included with all rooms.

Fairfield Inn Greeley
2401 W. 29th St.
(970) 339-5030
marriott.com
Moderate
Newly renovated, clean hotel with friendly staff.

Sod Buster Bed-and-Breakfast Inn
1221 9th Ave.
(970) 392-1221 or
(866) 501-8667
thesodbusterinn.com
Moderate
Ten distinctly decorated rooms come with delicious gourmet breakfasts and free wireless Internet.

LA JUNTA

Hampton Inn La Junta
27900 Hwy. 50
(719) 384-4444
Moderate
Clean and modern with friendly staff, hot breakfast included.

Midtown Motel
215 E. 3rd St.
(719) 384-7741
midtownlajunta.com
Inexpensive
Clean and affordable, with complimentary wireless Internet.

LOVELAND

Best Western Crossroads Inn & Conference Center
5542 E. US 34
(970) 667-7810
bwloveland.com
Moderate
Conveniently located near I-25, with a dinner restaurant and lounge, complimentary breakfast, free Internet access, pet-friendly.

Budget Host Exit 254 Inn
2716 SE Frontage Rd.
(970) 667-5202
budgethost.com
Inexpensive
Free Internet, small pets accepted, coin laundry facilities, heated pool.

Candlewood Suites
6046 E. Crossroad Blvd.
(970) 667-5444
ichotelsgroup.com
Inexpensive to Moderate
On-site fitness center, high speed Internet, pets allowed.

Places to Eat in Denver & the Plains

DENVER

Buckhorn Exchange
1000 Osage St.
(303) 534-9505
buckhorn.com
Expensive
Wide range of carnivore entrees including steak,

game, and waterfowl in a colorful, historic setting.

Cafe Brazil
4408 Lowell Blvd.
(303) 480-1877
cafebrazildenver.com
Moderate
Authentic South American cuisine from land and sea.

Cholon Bistro
1555 Blake St., Ste. 101
(303) 353-5223
cholon.com
Moderate to Expensive
Asian traditional and fusion with lunch, dinner, and small bites menu.

Elway's
2500 E. 1st Ave., Unit 101
(303) 399-5353
1881 Curtis St.
(303) 312-3107
elways.com
Moderate to Expensive
Steaks, raw seafood bar, and much more in an elegant setting.

Highland's Garden Cafe
3927 W. 32nd St.
(303) 458-5920
highlandsgardencafe.com
Expensive
Contemporary American cuisine on a daily menu based on seasonal ingredients, with patio and garden dining options.

Il Posto
2011 E. 17th St.
(303) 394-0100
ilpostodenver.com
Moderate to Expensive
Northern Italian dishes, with organic produce and meats when possible, in a hip cosmopolitan space.

Little India
330 E. 6th Ave.; 1533 Champa
(303) 871-9777 or 629-5777
littleindiadenver.com
Moderate
One of the city's best for Indian, excellent lunch buffet.

Little Ollie's
2364 E. 3rd Ave.
(303) 316-8888 or
(720) 941-5009
littleolliescherrycreek.com
Moderate
Long one of Denver's favorites for Chinese, with fresh ingredients and a well-executed menu.

Lucile's Creole Cafe
275 S. Logan St.
(303) 282-6258
luciles.com
Inexpensive to Moderate
Classic Creole-inspired breakfast and lunch in a fun Cajun setting.

Mezcal Restaurant
3230 E. Colfax Ave.
(303) 322-5219
mezcalcolorado.com
Inexpensive to Moderate
Authentic Mexican taqueria/cantina, with home-style regional cuisine and excellent margaritas in a warmly decorated setting.

Mizuna
225 E. 7th Ave.
(303) 832-4778
mizunadenver.com
Expensive
Highly rated, seasonal menu from a creative kitchen offering some of the city's most innovative cuisine.

My Brother's Bar
2376 15th St.
(303) 455-9991
Inexpensive
Classic burger place and Denver institution with a long history and a lively back patio local scene.

New Saigon Restaurant
630 S. Federal Blvd.
(303) 936-4954
newsaigon.com
Moderate
Consistently voted the best Vietnamese restaurant in town.

Panzano Restaurant
909 17th St.
(303) 296-3525
panzano-denver.com
Expensive
Consistent, exceptional northern Italian cuisine.

Restaurant Kevin Taylor
1106 14th St.
(303) 820-2600
restaurantkevintaylor.com
Expensive
Creative and delicious contemporary fusion of French, American southwest, and Asian rim influences.

Rioja
1433 Larimer St.
(303) 820-2282
riojadenver.com
Moderate to Expensive
Creative Mediterranean-inspired menu with local and seasonal ingredients when possible.

Root Down
1600 W. 33rd Ave.
(303) 993-4200
rootdowndenver.com
Moderate to Expensive
Organic, natural, and local ingredients whenever possible, a top foodie destination with a hip ambience.

Steuben's
523 E. 17th Ave.
(303) 830-1001
steubens.com
Moderate
Classic American regional cuisine and comfort food.

Strings Restaurant
1700 Humboldt St.
(303) 831-7310
stringsrestaurant.com
Expensive
Hip, popular, and bustling, this venue offers new American cuisine with creative noodle dishes and fresh seafood.

Tamayo
1400 Larimer St.
(720) 946-1433
richardsandoval.com/tamayo
Moderate to Expensive
Contemporary twists on traditional Mexican cuisine and a great patio dining scene.

Vesta Dipping Grill
1822 Blake St.
(303) 296-1970
vestagrill.com
Expensive
Longtime Denver favorite with seasonal entrees; choose from an extensive variety of dipping sauces.

OTHER ATTRACTIONS WORTH SEEING IN DENVER & THE PLAINS

DENVER

Art District on Santa Fe
828 Santa Fe Dr.
(303) 292-3455
artdistrictonsantafe.com

Elitch Gardens Theme & Water Park
2000 Elitch Circle
(303) 595-4386
elitchgardens.com

History Colorado Center
1200 Broadway
(303) 447-8679
historycolorado.org

Lower Downtown (LoDo) Historic District
1616 17th St.
(303) 628-5428
lodo.org

Museum of Contemporary Art
1485 Delgany
(303) 298-7554
mcadenver.org

16th Street Mall
16th and California Streets
(303) 534-6161

US Mint
320 W. Colfax Ave.
(303) 405-4761
usmint.gov/mint_tours/

Wings Over the Rockies Air & Space Museum
7711 E. Academy Blvd.
(303) 360-5360
wingsmuseum.org

EADS

Sand County Massacre National Historic Site
Approx. 23 miles east of Eads
(719) 438-5916 or (719) 729-3003
nps.gov/sand

FORT COLLINS

Lincoln Center
(970) 221-6735
lctix.com

GENOA

World's Wonder View Tower
30121 Frontage Rd.
(719) 763-2309

GREELEY

Fort Vasquez
(970) 785-2832
historycolorado.org/museums/
fort-vasquez-museum

LA JUNTA

Bent's Old Fort National Historic Site
35110 CO 194 E
(719) 383-5010
nps.gov/beol/index.htm

Comanche National Grassland
South of La Junta; ranger office at 1420 E. 3rd St.
(719) 384-2181

ROCKY FORD

Arkansas Valley Fair
Rocky Ford
(719) 254-7723
arkvalleyfair.com

Wynkoop Brewing Company
1634 18th St.
(303) 297-2700
wynkoop.com
Inexpensive to Moderate
Colorado's first brewpub offers a hearty menu of pub food to accompany its highly acclaimed beers.

Zengo
1610 Little Raven St.
River Front Park
(720) 904-0965
modernmexican.com
Moderate to Expensive
An exquisite blend of Latin and Asian fusion flavors and styles along with an extensive specialty cocktail menu.

FORT COLLINS

Beau Jo's Colorado Style Pizza
100 N. College Ave.
(970) 498-8898
beaujos.com
Inexpensive to Moderate
Legendary pizza and an extensive menu make this one of Colorado's best pizza joints.

Canino's Italian Restaurant
613 S. College Ave.
(970) 493-7205
caninositalianrestaurant
.com
Inexpensive to Moderate
Family-owned Italian restaurant serving from an extensive menu in a homey setting in a historic building.

Coopersmith's Pub and Brewing Company
5 Old Town Sq.
(970) 498-0483
coopersmithspub.com
Inexpensive to Moderate
Innovative pub menu and good beer in a fun setting.

Pablo's Pizza
2720 Council Tree Ave.
(970) 682-2189
pablospizza.com
Moderate
Creative, award-winning pizza, warm panini sandwiches, and homemade soups.

Rio Grande Mexican Restaurant
143 W. Mountain Ave.
(970) 224-5428
riograndemexican.com
Moderate
This Colorado chain serves fresh and filling Mexican food and legendary margaritas.

GREELEY

Coyote's Southwestern Grill
5250 W. 9th St.
(970) 336-1725
Moderate
Locally owned, authentic southwestern and Mexican cuisine with a twist.

Fat Albert's Food & Drink
1717 23rd Ave.
(970) 356-1999
fat-alberts.com
Inexpensive to Moderate
Nice selection of sandwiches, dinners, salads, and desserts.

Rio Grande Mexican Restaurant
825 9th St.
(970) 304-9292
riograndemexican.com
Moderate
This Colorado chain serves fresh and filling Mexican food and legendary margaritas.

LOVELAND

Black Steer
436 N. Lincoln Ave.
(970) 667-6679
blacksteerrestaurant.com
Moderate to Expensive
Consistently voted best place for steak in Loveland; menu includes homemade soups, seafood, salads, and pastas.

Peaks Restaurant
405 E. 5th St.
(970) 663-7288
thepeakscafe.com
Inexpensive
Comfort food for breakfast and lunch only in historic downtown Loveland.

Sofia's Bistro
1120 N. Lincoln
(970) 669-2229
sofiasbistro.com
Moderate
Upscale yet casual breakfast, lunch, and dinner with a menu ranging from American to international cuisine.

Index

INSIDERS' GUIDE®

The acclaimed travel series that has sold more than 2 million copies!

Discover: Your Travel Destination.
Your Home. Your Home-to-Be.

Albuquerque

Anchorage &
   Southcentral
   Alaska

Atlanta

Austin

Baltimore

Baton Rouge

Boulder & Rocky Mountain
   National Park

Branson & the Ozark
   Mountains

California's Wine Country

Cape Cod & the Islands

Charleston

Charlotte

Chicago

Cincinnati

Civil War Sites in
   the Eastern Theater

Civil War Sites in the South

Colorado's Mountains

Dallas & Fort Worth

Denver

El Paso

Florida Keys & Key West

Gettysburg

Glacier National Park

Great Smoky Mountains

Greater Fort Lauderdale

Greater Tampa Bay Area

Hampton Roads

Houston

Hudson River Valley

Indianapolis

Jacksonville

Kansas City

Long Island

Louisville

Madison

Maine Coast

Memphis

Myrtle Beach &
   the Grand Strand

Nashville

New Orleans

New York City

North Carolina's
   Mountains

North Carolina's
   Outer Banks

North Carolina's
   Piedmont Triad

Oklahoma City

Orange County, CA

Oregon Coast

Palm Beach County

Palm Springs

Philadelphia &
   Pennsylvania Dutch
   Country

Phoenix

Portland, Maine

Portland, Oregon

Raleigh, Durham &
   Chapel Hill

Richmond, VA

Reno and Lake Tahoe

St. Louis

San Antonio

Santa Fe

Savannah & Hilton Head

Seattle

Shreveport

South Dakota's
   Black Hills Badlands

Southwest Florida

Tucson

Tulsa

Twin Cities

Washington, D.C.

Williamsburg & Virginia's
   Historic Triangle

Yellowstone
   & Grand Teton

Yosemite

**To order call 800-243-0495
or visit www.Insiders.com**

Already "Been There, Done That"?
Then Get Off the Beaten Path!

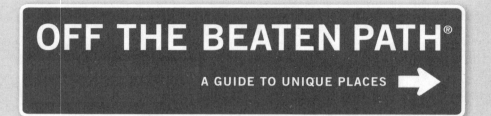

OFF THE BEATEN PATH®

A GUIDE TO UNIQUE PLACES →

"For the traveler who enjoys the special, the unusual, and the unexpected."—*The Traveler* newsletter

Alabama	Kansas	Nevada	Quebec
Alaska	Kentucky	New Hampshire	Rhode Island
Arizona	Louisiana	New Jersey	South Carolina
Arkansas	Maine	New Mexico	Southern California
British Columbia	Maritime Provinces	Metro New York	Tennessee
Colorado	Maryland & Delaware	Upstate New York	Texas
Connecticut		North Carolina	Utah
Dakotas	Massachusetts	Northern California	Vermont
Florida	Michigan	Ohio	Virginia
Georgia	Minnesota	Oklahoma	Washington, D.C.
Hawaii	Mississippi	Oregon	West Virginia
Idaho	Missouri	Pennsylvania	Wisconsin
Indiana	Montana	Philadelphia	Wyoming
Iowa	Nebraska	Puerto Rico	

To order call 800-243-0495
or visit www.GlobePequot.com